DISSENT

Dissent: A Radical History of the Clitheroe Parliamentary Constituency

ROGER SMALLEY

First published in 2018 by Scotforth Books

British Library Cataloguing-in-Publication data
A catalogue record for this book is available from the British Library

ISBN 978-1-909817-37-1

Printed and bound by Jellyfish Solutions

Contents

Acknowledgements

The standard histories of Clitheroe, meticulously researched and elegantly written by Langshaw, Ainsworth, Self Weeks and others, primarily examine legal and constitutional issues relating to the town's governance. This study is indebted to them insofar as they deal with dissent, however their focus is on those who exercised political power, not those who challenged it, and so other sources have also been used. Many of these are held in collections referenced in the chapter endnotes and the bibliography. I am grateful especially to the staffs of Clitheroe and Nelson public libraries, the Working Class Movement Library in Salford, the Lancashire Archives in Preston, the Towneley Hall museum, and Independent Labour Publications for preserving and making available these sources, and to John Smith and Jack Aston for providing other material that has been incorporated into the text.

Abbreviations

BCP	British Citizen Party
BSP	British Socialist Party
CRDC	Clitheroe Rural District Council
FOR	Fellowship of Reconciliation
FAU	Friends Ambulance Unit
FWVRC	Friends War Victims Relief Committee
ILP	Independent Labour Party
LRC	Labour Representation Committee
NCA	National Charter Association
NCC	Non-Combatant Corps
NCF	No Conscription Fellowship
NUWSS	National Union of Women's Suffrage Societies
PUDC	Padiham Urban District Council
SDF	Social Democratic Federation
TUC	Trades Union Congress
UDC	Union of Democratic Control
WSPU	Women's Social and Political Union
£. s. d.	The monetary system in use during the period covered by this study: 12 pence (d) = one shilling (s), 20 shillings = one pound (£).
cwt	hundredweight: a measure of weight approximately equal to 50 kilograms. 20 cwts = one ton.

List Of Illustrations

Introduction

Clitheroe has been represented in the House of Commons since 1558. For almost 300 years its two MPs were elected by a handful of voters, but over time legislation widened the franchise, extended the constituency, and halved its parliamentary entitlement. Nevertheless an electoral unit designated 'Clitheroe' existed until 1983 and its history has been frequently chronicled. The purpose of this study is to examine an aspect of that history which has been overlooked – the role played in it by dissent, that is to say by those who resisted the political establishment in some way.

Elizabeth I granted Clitheroe representation in the expectation that its MPs would support her policies, but the constituency regularly disappointed the queen and her successors in government, for it often rejected conformity in favour of change. Such instances occurred most frequently in connection with the growing demand for the voice of the working class to be heard by the country's lawmakers, and so the emphasis in the following pages is on the period between the 1880s and the 1930s when new organisations challenged the traditional holders of power and sometimes wrested it from them.

*

Despite its moving boundaries, the centre of the constituency was always the town of Clitheroe. The lords of its castle ruled the area in pre-parliamentary times. Its first free burgesses built a Moot Hall in which to discuss local matters in the medieval period. Victorian municipal government was conducted in a newly built Council chamber, and from its steps successful parliamentary candidates were proclaimed. Even when the industrial revolution transformed the economy of the area from agriculture to manufacturing, it was Clitheroe, the smallest and most northerly of the towns within Lancashire's cotton belt, not its larger rivals, that remained the political heart of the constituency.

The Clitheroe division underwent three major adjustments. The first, in 1832, brought in neighbouring villages such as Chatburn, Pendleton and Whalley. The second, in 1885, added the rapidly growing mill towns to the east. In 1918, when the new constituency of Nelson and Colne was created, many of these were transferred to it and replaced by communities to the west, including Hurst Green and Chipping. When the Clitheroe constituency was abolished in 1983 its various parts were subsumed by adjacent or new divisions – Burnley, Pendle, Hyndburn and Ribble Valley. Thus vanished an institution which for over 400 years had affected the lives of the inhabitants of this corner of the north west, traditionally considered conservative, but in fact full of dissidents. Some like Selena Cooper and David Shackleton became nationally important and their place in history is assured. Others have been forgotten, yet their achievements were immense. Ethel Carnie and T. D. Benson made political contributions well beyond the Clitheroe constituency, and Louisa Higson and William Seedall, amongst many others, committed themselves to improving the lives of the working class within it. Their efforts are recorded here.

Figure 1 – The Clitheroe Region

Source: adapted from M. Brigg (ed.), *A Lancashire Weaver's Journal 1856–1864, 1872–1875* (The Record Society of Lancashire and Cheshire, vol. CXXII, 1982).

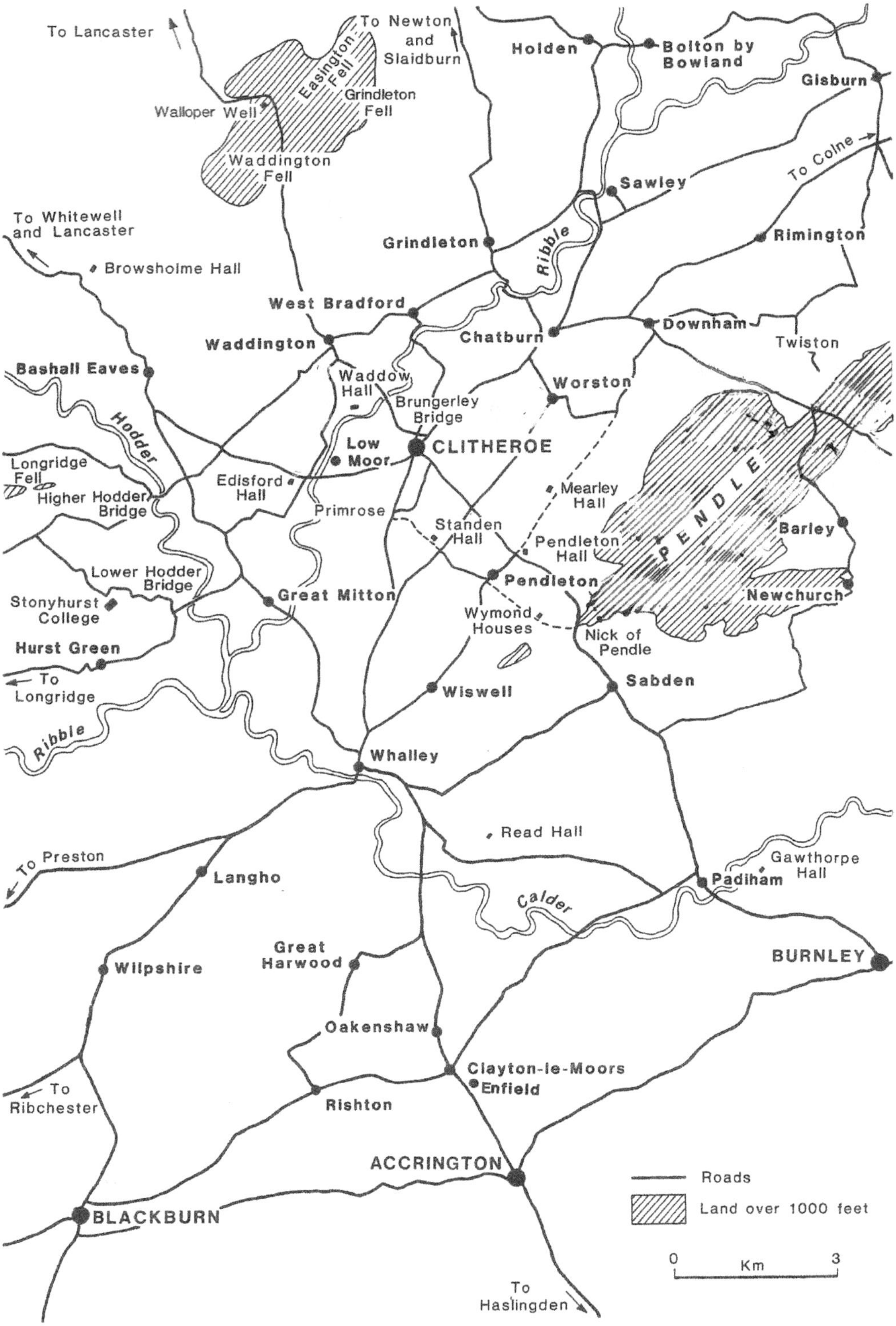
To Lancaster
To Newton and Slaidburn
Easington Fell
Grindleton Fell
Walloper Well
Waddington Fell
Holden
Bolton by Bowland
Gisburn
To Colne
Sawley
To Whitewell and Lancaster
Browsholme Hall
Grindleton
Ribble
Rimington
West Bradford
Waddington
Chatburn
Downham
Twiston
Bashall Eaves
Waddow Hall
Brungerley Bridge
Worston
Hodder
Low Moor
CLITHEROE
Longridge Fell
Edisford Hall
Mearley Hall
Higher Hodder Bridge
Primrose
PENDLE
Standen Hall
Barley
Pendleton Hall
Lower Hodder Bridge
Pendleton
Stonyhurst College
Great Mitton
Newchurch
Wymond Houses
Nick of Pendle
Hurst Green
To Longridge
Sabden
Wiswell
Ribble
Whalley
Read Hall
To Preston
Gawthorpe Hall
Langho
Padiham
Calder
Great Harwood
BURNLEY
Wilpshire
Oakenshaw
Clayton-le-Moors
Enfield
To Ribchester
Rishton
ACCRINGTON
Roads
Land over 1000 feet
0 Km 3
BLACKBURN
To Haslingden

Chapter 1
The Origins Of Dissent

Archaeological evidence indicates prehistoric and Roman settlement in the Clitheroe area, and later it became a target for Viking, Mercian and Northumbrian expansion, however the town developed only after the Norman Conquest when Roger of Poitou became its first Lord.[1] He fulfilled his administrative responsibilities in the usual Norman way by building a castle in a prominent position from which he could control his territory for the new regime. Roger's successors, the de Lacys, gradually strengthened the earth and wood original so that by the end of the twelfth century the stone keep that still stands had been completed. The town that grew up around the castle was served by the church of St. Mary Magdalene from the early-twelfth century, two fairs a year from 1205, a weekly market from 1292, and a borough court from 1296.[2]

With the failure of the de Lacy line in the fourteenth century Clitheroe passed to the earls, later dukes, of Lancaster. The first of these was Thomas Earl of Lancaster, a grandson of Henry III and cousin of the reigning monarch Edward II. He led that faction which opposed the influence of Gaveston, the royal favourite, and arranged his murder in 1312. Indeed after the collapse of Edward II's prestige following the Scottish victory at Bannockburn in 1314, Thomas became *de facto* ruler of the country. His own bad government provoked a reaction in favour of Edward which in Clitheroe took the form of the Rising of 1315, when Sir Adam Banaster seized the castle and commandeered its store of weapons. The incident played little part in the overthrow of Earl Thomas, who was defeated by a resurgent court party at Boroughbridge in 1322 and subsequently executed, but it is the first documented example of political dissent in the town's history.[3]

*

Representative government in England dates from the mid-thirteenth century. At that time it took the form of selection by sheriffs of knights, initially four per county, and their powers were consultative only. In 1265 this arrangement was modified when Simon de Montfort, in the name of Henry III, directed sheriffs to appoint two knights from each shire and two burgesses from each town within their jurisdictions. A further modification was introduced in 1295 when Edward I summoned two knights from each shire, two citizens from each city, and two burgesses from each borough to the so-called 'Model Parliament'.[4] Ten men represented Lancashire in that assembly, two knights for the county and, in the absence of cities, two burgesses each for the boroughs of Lancaster, Preston, Wigan and Liverpool. However the entitlement was frequently forgone because local taxes to defray the expenses incurred were resented, and between 1359 and 1547 no Lancashire borough sent members to parliament, the county being represented solely by two knights of the shire.[5]

Clitheroe was added to Lancashire's borough list in 1558 as one of 145 new parliamentary constituencies created by Elizabeth I. It has been argued that much of the increase in the size of the House of Commons in her reign resulted from pressure by politically ambitious local elites for representation, and there is evidence that this was the case in some areas, but not in Clitheroe, for it lay within the Duchy of Lancaster which had been a royal possession since 1399 and the queen directly controlled borough rents and tolls on fairs, markets and corn mills. Clitheroe therefore became a political pawn, its members of parliament expected to give loyal support to Elizabeth's legislative programme in order to counterbalance the growing strength of independently-minded shire knights.[6]

In the sixteenth century the franchise was limited and varied from one constituency to another. Clitheroe was a burgage tenure borough, that is to say the right to vote was attached to a property. Little is known of the process by which Clitheroe's first MPs were elected, but it is doubtful that many contests took place, for few of the gentry who qualified to fill the role would have been able to afford the expense of residence near Westminster, or be prepared to undertake the formidable journey between Lancashire and London regularly. Their identity, however, is known. (See Appendix II, p. 177.) A common pattern in Elizabethan two member constituencies was for few representatives to have local connections and that is true of Clitheroe, for although Richard and Thomas Greenacres of Worston were among its earliest members, only four of the eighteen elected for the borough to Elizabethan parliaments had such links.[7]

During the 1640s Clitheroe's two MPs led the revolution against the crown in the constituency. Both Ralph Assheton and Richard Shuttleworth raised troops for Parliament which helped to defeat the invading Scots at the Battle of Preston in 1648, and Assheton rose to the rank of Commander-in-Chief in Lancashire. Cromwell commended his regiment for its bravery but Parliament withheld its pay, and when ordered to demobilise some elements from it seized Clitheroe castle in protest. Disputes about pay and other grievances were ongoing throughout the conflict and had often been brutally supressed, but the Clitheroe rebels were dealt with leniently by comparison. They disbanded when arrears of £1,444 were paid, although the castle was slighted and the borough was deprived of representation in the Cromwellian parliaments of the 1650s.[8]

The first post-civil war election to be held in Clitheroe was therefore after the restoration of the monarchy in 1660, when one of the borough's seats was coveted by both William White and William Hulton.[9] White's victory was contested, and on appeal a House of Commons committee ruled that Hulton, who had received fewer votes, was nevertheless elected because White's support came from 'the freemen at large' rather than 'the free burgesses' who were the only legally enfranchised group. The same circumstances caused Ambrose Pudsey to be awarded the seat over his rival Sir Ralph Assheton in 1662, and John Weddle to unseat Fitton Gerard in 1694.[10] Clearly the interpretation of what constituted a voter was at the root of these controversies. Burgesses who owned property in the borough qualified whether they lived in it or not, but the right of freemen to vote depended on their landlords. It was the property that carried the vote, so if the landlord used it to qualify as an elector his tenant could not, but if the landlord had other property that gave him the qualification then the tenant could. Such an arrangement earned Clitheroe the reputation of being a 'pocket borough', for it encouraged wealthy individuals to acquire vote-bearing properties which they could then let to political sympathisers with the expectation of influencing election outcomes.

In the eighteenth century the Listers and the Asshetons frequently exploited this situation. The two families were intermarried, and from 1716 they agreed to buy up vote-bearing burgages jointly in an attempt to rig Clitheroe elections. This compact enabled the Listers and the Asshetons to share the constituency's two seats for half a century, but in 1780 Thomas Lister secretly purchased more burgages, so that by the time of the poll 30 votes were controlled by Lister, 19 by Assheton, and 53 were jointly controlled. Out of the total electorate only 11 votes could be considered independent, insufficient to prevent not only Lister's return with 33 votes but that of his nominee John Parker with 30. The incumbent MP Assheton polled only 17 and was therefore unseated despite his attempts to persuade parliament to invalidate the result. This sort of practice made a nonsense of the voter roll, and contemporary commentators on the situation pointed out that although Clitheroe nominally had 90 electors, in reality it had only two.[11]

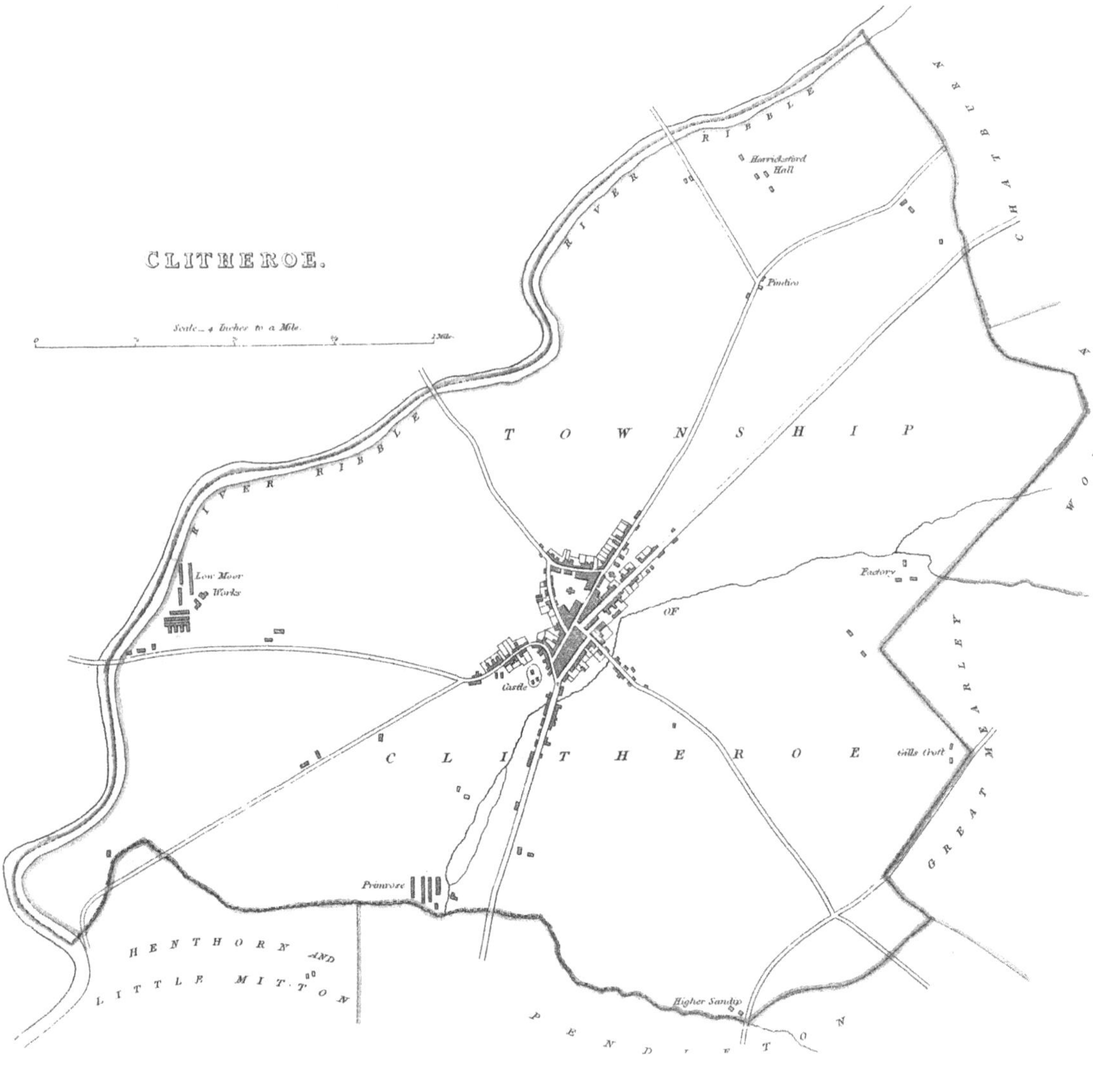

Figure 2 – The Boundaries of the Clitheroe Constituency 1558–1832

Source: Clitheroe public library local studies collection. P12.

The 1780 Clitheroe election is an example of the sort of corrupt practice that disgraced Georgian politics, and even after Lister lost interest in the constituency it remained available to the highest bidder. In 1804 that was John Cust, Earl Brownlow, who bought a group of properties with voting rights known as the Ribblesdale burgages.[12] He paid £40,000 for them, more than twice their market value, and by doing so secured the election of his representatives. It was not until 1832 that this sort of abuse was eradicated,

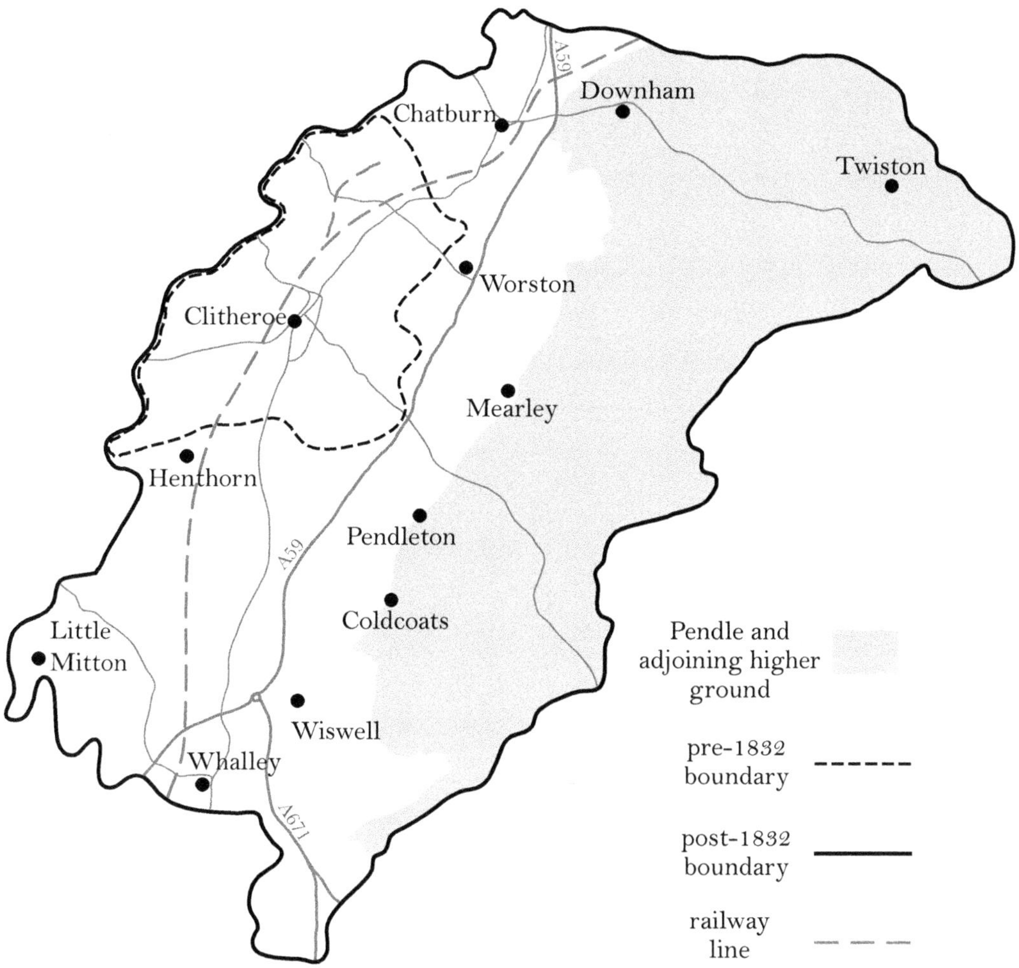

Figure 3 – The Boundaries of the Clitheroe Constituency 1832–1885. Communities within the constituency

Source: The Report of the Boundary Commissioners for England and Wales 1868 – Clitheroe. Clitheroe public library local studies collection. P29/491461240.

for the Great Reform Act of that year transferred the right to vote from property to people, giving the qualification in borough constituencies like Clitheroe to male householders and those who paid at least £10 a year in rent. The Act also redistributed parliamentary seats and some pocket boroughs lost their members, but Clitheroe was one of 30 towns with fewer than 4,000 inhabitants to keep its representation, although it was reduced from two to one.[13]

Clitheroe's electorate was increased to 306 by the Great Reform Act, and the boundaries of the constituency were redrawn to embrace the surrounding area as well as the borough. This brought in new voters, 24 from Downham for example, 8 from Mitton, Henthorn and Coldcoates, 21 from Pendleton, 33 from Whalley and 23 from Wiswell.[14] (See Figures 2 and 3.) The electorate was thus more than tripled, and although this was still less than 10 per cent of the constituency's population the traditional influence of the great local families had been curbed and an era of a new sort of politics inaugurated.

*

The adjustments to its boundaries that were made in 1832 are linked to Clitheroe's transformation from a market and administrative centre to a textile town during the industrial revolution. The first mill, at Low Moor, opened in the late-eighteenth century, and by 1900 there were 14, most of them weaving businesses. They attracted migrants from areas of economic decline who were looking for work, and as a result Clitheroe's population rose from 1,368 in 1801 to 11,780 in 1871. Most of them could not vote, but they nevertheless made an impact on elections. In 1832 it took a violent form. The candidates were the Liberal John Fort of Read Hall, a local mill owner, and John Irving, a calico printer who had opposed the Reform Act and stood in the Conservative interest. Irving's nomination was resented by many in the borough because they considered him to be an ultra-Tory reactionary. The Clitheroe malcontents were supported by a reputed 10,000 like-minded protestors from neighbouring towns who prevented Irving from addressing voters from an upper window of the Swan Inn. The candidate was shouted down and pelted with stones, and his entourage was harried as it withdrew towards Whalley. By then the Riot Act had been read, and a military detachment from Burnley attacked the crowd. Contemporary accounts vary, but perhaps eight or ten bystanders were seriously injured. Five more were arrested and charged with disturbing the peace, although in due course they were acquitted. One newspaper likened the incident to Peterloo, the infamous Yeomany charge on those attending a political meeting in Manchester in 1819.

In 1832 about 1,000 operatives worked at Low Moor mill, over 800 of whom were women. The owners failed to prevent them from joining the throng in Clitheroe on the day of the disturbance, but urged them to be orderly. Jeremiah Garnett expressed outrage at the behaviour of the soldiers, for he believed his workers were peaceable bystanders and several of them were hurt, but when he confronted Irving with his complaint he was accused of having incited the mob to riot.[15]

The events surrounding Irving's candidacy prompted questions in the House of Commons, and local sentiment against him remained so strong that he cancelled plans to visit Clitheroe again, nevertheless on election day he polled a respectable 124 against Fort's 157. The secret ballot was not introduced until 1872, so the way the qualified electors voted is known. (See Figure 4.) The list shows that most landowners, gentlemen (esquires) and professionals (clergymen and surgeons for example) voted for Irving. His campaign had also been backed by Lord Brownlow, and before 1832 this would have ensured his success, so Fort's victory can be attributed to the liberalisation of the franchise. But, more significantly, it indicates that if workers were denied the vote they would seek their objectives through alternative methods, though those that were used in Clitheroe elections of the 1840s and 50s gained the constituency a name for bribery and corruption.

Ill health forced the retirement of John Fort prior to the 1841 election, and Matthew Wilson of Eshton Hall near Skipton was invited to replace him as the Liberal candidate. The Conservatives' choice was Edward Cardwell who was influential within the party and a close friend of its leader Sir Robert Peel. The Chartists also hoped to contest the seat on a programme of universal manhood suffrage and further political reform, but their representative was unable to afford the required £25 deposit and could not be nominated.

Arrangements for voting followed a well established pattern. On 1 July bands paraded around the town mingling with the crowd, many of whom wore partisan colours, Liberal orange and blue or Tory dark blue and red.[16] The candidates spoke at the hustings in Market Place, and a straw poll taken of those present (who included both the qualified and the ineligible) was won by Wilson. The election proper took place the following day, borough voters using the polling station in the Town Hall, voters from the out-townships a building in Castle Street. The count showed a narrow victory for Wilson who polled 175 votes to Cardwell's 170, however the Conservatives claimed that up to a dozen of their supporters had been 'bottled', that is to say prevented from getting to the poll by opposition agents, and petitioned parliament to reverse the result. The ensuing enquiry found that some Cardwell voters had indeed been kidnapped, and others bribed, and when the scrutiny of the list of electors was completed Cardwell had a majority of one. Wilson, who had sat as Clitheroe's MP during the intervening eight months, stood down in order to avoid further legal expenses and was replaced by Cardwell in the House of Commons.[17]

CLITHEROE ELECTION.

Poll Book of the Election of the Borough of Clitheroe, held on the 11th December, 1832, alphabetically arranged, and numbered according to the order in which the Electors gave their Votes,—being the first Election for the Reformed Parliament.

No.	Elector	Vote
1	Aspinall John, Esq., Standen-hall,	Fort.
	Abbott Rev. Philip, Clitheroe, Returning Officer.	
282	Allen Rev. J. T., Well-hall,	Irving.
	Assheton William, Esq. Downham, absent from sickness	
	Ainsworth Caleb, Barrow,	Neuter.
231	Arkwright William, Clitheroe,	Irving.
74	Arkwright John, Innkeeper, do.	do.
230	Altham Thomas, jun., Druggist, do.	do
161	Altham Thomas, sen., Farmer, Low Moor,	do.
84	Altham George, Farmer, Twiston,	Fort.
210	Anderson William, Joiner, Clitheroe,	Irving.
164	Alston James, Innkeeper, do.	Fort.
165	Atkinson Wm., Saddler, do.	do.
23	Aspinall Thomas, Farmer, Mitton,	do.
	Bell John, Esq., Clitheroe,	Neuter.
	Brocklehurst Wm., Esq., Returning Officer.	
	Brooks William, Esq., Whalley,	Neuter.
167	Bowman Thomas, Druggist, Clitheroe,	Fort.
208	Baldwin Leonard, Ironmonger, do.	Irving.
195	Baldwin Richard, Surgeon, do.	do.
166	Bailey William, Grocer, do.	Fort.
168	Bulcock Ben., Cotton manufacturer, do.	do.
177	Braithwaite George, Miller, Henthorn,	do.
176	Battersby Leonard, Barber, Clitheroe,	do.
211	Bell John, Glazier, do.	Irving.
169	Briggs George, Clogger, do.	Fort.
25	Boothman James, Farmer, Henthorn,	do.
178	Boothman John, Blacksmith, Low Moor	do.
136	Burnett Robert, Gardener, Clitheroe,	Irving.
185	Burnett William, do. do.	do.
	Baxter Robert, Innkeeper,	Neuter.
179	Barrett James, Labourer, Low Moor,	Fort.
180	Battersby John, do. do.	do.
233	Briggs John, Farmer, Chatburn,	Irving.
63	Barton Francis, do. do.	do.
162	Barton George, Cooper, do.	do.
8	Briggs Thomas, Innkeeper, do.	Fort.
10	Brown John Holdsworth, do. do.	do.
9	Briggs Richard, Farmer, do.	do.
101	Barton John, do. Downham,	Irving.
56	Boothman Jonathan, do. do.	Fort.
60	Bulcock James, do. do.	do.
50	Bulcock Richard, do. do.	do.
57	Broxup Thomas, do. do.	do.
19	Braithwaite Wm., do. Mitton,	Irving.
218	Briggs Thomas, do. Cold Coates,	do.
85	Bulcock John, do. Twiston,	Fort.
92	Bulcock James, do. do.	do.
	Bulcock Thomas, do. do.	Neuter.
99	Baldwin James, do. do.	Irving.
27	Bulcock Robert, do. do.	do.
198	Bramley Lawrence, do. Whalley,	do.
159	Bramley Thomas, Innkeeper, do.	do.
18	Bulcock William, Farmer, Brookhouses,	do.
43	Bulcock James do. Wiswell,	do.
138	Bulcock Richard, do. do.	do.
45	Bulcock William, do. do.	do.
28	Brewer John, do. do.	do.
62	Badger James, Innkeeper, Worston,	do.
3	Clayton Thomas, Esq., Carr Hall,	do.
15	Cottam Adam, Esq., Whalley,	do.
6	Carr Thomas, Esq., Clitheroe Castle,	do.
181	Clithero William, Printer, Clitheroe,	Fort.
274	Cockshott Walter, Ironmonger, do.	do.
261	Cook William, Shopkeeper, Low Moor,	do.
61	Campbell Thomas, Farmer, Downham,	do.
68	Chatburn Henry, do. do.	do.
199	Collinge Giles, do. Pendleton Hall,	Irving.
	Clegg Thomas, Carter, Whalley,	Neuter.
146	Coulthurst William, Farmer, Wiswell,	Irving.
16	Clegg John, do. do.	do.
42	Clegg Thomas, do. Barrow,	do.
196	Clegg Robert, do. Wiswell,	do.
114	Catlow John, Calico Printer, Barrow,	do.
143	Craven Matthew, do. Wiswell,	Fort.
33	Clegg James, do. Hall Foot,	Irving.
11	Dugdale John, Shopkeeper, Chatburn,	Fort.
31	Dixon Robert, Alley's Fold, Clitheroe,	Irving.
115	Darnbrough Richard, Grocer, do.	do.
201	Dewhurst Wm. B., Watch Maker, do.	Fort.
55	Dawson Robert, Beer Retailer, do.	Irving.
275	Dawson John, Farmer, Bawdlands,	Fort.
247	Dawson James, Grocer, do. Clitheroe,	do.
112	Dawson John, York-street, do.	Irving.
258	Dean James, Up-Brooks Factory, do.	Fort.
262	Driver Robert, Labourer, Low Moor,	do.
217	Dean Richard, Grocer, Lower Gate, Clitheroe,	do.
202	Dean Robert, Surgeon, Clitheroe,	do.
66	Dugdale, Richard, Innkeeper, Mitton,	Irving.
93	Duerden Thomas, Shoemaker, Sabden,	Fort.
116	Duerden Francis, Farmer, do.	do.
117	Duerden Thomas, do. Twiston,	do.
173	Dewhurst Paul, Grocer, Whalley,	Irving.
135	Drake William, Miller, do.	do.
102	Dean Thomas, Farmer, Nether Town,	do.
12	Embley Christopher, Farmer, Chatburn	Fort.
222	Earnshaw Thomas, Innkeeper, Pimlico	Irving.
	Edge William, Grocer, Clitheroe	too late.
160	Embley Henry, Duck-street, do.	Irving.
263	Embley William, Carrier, do.	Fort.
251	Earnshaw John, Farmer, do.	do.
254	Embley Stephen, Pawnbroker, do.	do.
252	Earnshaw Mark, Surgeon, do.	do.
214	Elliott John, Cutler do.	Fort.
77	Eastham James, Joiner, do.	Irving.
69	Embley John, Farmer, Downham	Fort.
119	Embley John, do. Lower Standen	do.
120	Entwistle Enoch, Innkeeper, Sabden	do.
118	Ellis John, Farmer, Pendleton	do.
111	Eatough Adam, Grange, Whalley	Irving.
137	Eatough John, Nether Town, do.	do.
175	Fielding John, Hatter, Well gate, Clitheroe	do.
7	Garnett Jeremiah, Esq., Roefield, do.	Fort.
249	Garstang James, Surgeon, Clitheroe,	Irving.
174	Green William, Farmer, Cheapside, Chatburn	do.
172	Green John, do. Ridden Hey, Clitheroe	do.
239	Greenhalgh Thomas, Printer do.	Fort.
220	Garforth John, Innkeeper do.	Irving.
264	Garnett Thomas, Cotton Spinner do.	Fort.
70	Greenwood Matthew, Miller, Downham	do.
	Granger Hugh, Innkeeper, Whalley	Neuter.
171	Green John, Farmer and Land Agent, do.	Irving.
158	Green James, Farmer, Whalley Abbey	do.
163	Holgate John, Farmer, Lane Side, Chatburn	do.
13	Hitchen William, Farmer, do.	Fort.
35	Hall William, do. do.	do.
205	Hothersall Richard, Innkeeper, Bellman	do.
209	Hoyle Giles, Farmer, Horrocksford	Irving.
30	Herd James, Carter, Clitheroe,	do.
215	Hibbert William, Bookkeeper, Primrose do.	Fort.
227	Haworth John, Grocer do.	do.
	Hide Thomas, Gentleman do.	Neuter.
221	Harris John, Farmer do.	Irving.
280	Hayhurst John, Wheelwright do.	Fort.
32	Hopwood John, Farmer, Duck-street do.	Irving.
203	Haworth John, Brewer, do.	Fort.
200	Horsfall, Wm., Esq., Shaw Cottage do.	do.
213	Hornby James, Joiner do.	do.
98	Harrison John, Saddler do.	Irving.
113	Haworth Thomas, Toilor do.	do.
204	Hodgson John, Manager, Primrose do.	Fort.
235	Holden Richard, Grocer, Long Row do.	do.
240	Hodgkinson Arthur, Shoemaker do.	do.
219	Harrison John, Farmer, Brungerley	Irving.
126	Hargreaves James, do. Low Moor	do.
75	Harris Roger, Plasterer, York-street, Clitheroe	do.
279	Hartley William, Solicitor, do. do.	Fort.
232	Hall Henry, do. Duck-street do.	Irving.
71	Harrison Richard, Farmer, Downham	Fort.
	Hargreaves Henry, do. do.	Neuter.
265	Hartley Christopher, do. do.	Fort.
46	Hanson John, do. Lane Side, Mearley	do.
52	Hayhurst William, do. Bank End, Mitton	Irving.
121	Holden George, do. Pendleton,	Fort.
120	Hitchon Robert, do. Lower Standen	do.

No.	Name, occupation and residence	Vote
134	Heyworth John, Blacksmith, Whalley	Irving.
86	Hartley Bernard, Farmer, Nether Town	do.
87	Hartley Richard, do. Shaw Houses Whalley	do.
2	Hardy Richard, Surgeon, do.	Fort.
17	Hargreaves George, Farmer, Wiswell	Irving.
152	Hayhurst Thomas, do. do.	Fort.
144	Hargreaves James, do. do.	do.
153	Hindle Roger, do. do. Moor	do.
51	Hargreaves Henry, do. Worsaw-hill, Worston	do.
53	Hayes Joseph, do. do.	Irving.
54	Hayes John, do. do.	do.
216	Kay Richard, Butcher, Clitheroe	Fort.
89	Kenyon Thomas, Farmer, Nether Town, Whalley	Irving:
91	Lister James, Grocer, Clitheroe,	do.
238	Lofthouse John, Tailor, do.	Fort.
29	Laycock David, Carrier, Lower Gate, do.	Irving.
253	Lawton James, Flat's Row, do.	Fort.
236	Loynd, John, Labourer, Low Moor do.	do.
90	Lofthouse, James, Sands, Whalley	Irving.
110	Lord William, Blacksmith, do.	do.
65	Lobley John, Joiner, Toll Bar, do.	do.
	Lonsdale John, Farmer, Augrem Green, Worston	Neuter.
277	Marsden Lawrence, Brooks, Clitheroe	Fort.
188	Myers Henry, Roper, Well Gate, do.	do.
237	Mercer James, Grocer, Castle-st., do.	do.
224	Mercer Edmund, Cotton Manufacturer, do.	do.
72	Mercer William, Farmer, Downham,	do.
124	Midgley John, do. Knoll Top, Mearley,	Irving.
129	Mercer Edward, Farmer, Pendleton,	Fort.
	Myers Thomas, Grocer, Whalley,	Neuter.
88	Martin John, Nether Town, do.	Irving.
	Myers John, Farmer, Wiswell Shaw	Absent.
14	Noble Rev. Richard, Vicarage, Whalley,	Irving.
207	Nowell John, Joiner, Lower Gate, Clitheroe	do.
250	Oddie, Wm. L., Esq., Solicitor, do.	do.
34	Parkinson Richard, Farmer, Chatburn	Fort.
194	Pilling Henry, Farmer, near Pimlico	Irving.
123	Procter Thomas, Innkeeper, Causeway House	do.
148	Penny John, Tailor, Church Brow, Clitheroe	do.
256	Petty Joseph, do. Market-Place, do.	Fort.
259	Pryor Thomas, Engraver, Little Moor, do.	do.
248	Parkinson George, Farmer, Parson Lane do.	do.
245	Place Richard, do. do.	do.
190	Parkinson James, Grocer, Low Moor do.	do.
197	Preston Thomas, Farmer, Little Mearley	Irving.
78	Parkinson Thomas, do. Whymond Houses, Pendleton	do.
130	Peel Thomas, Farmer, Pendleton	Fort.
131	Peel John, do. do.	do.
132	Peel James, do. do.	do.
139	Preston George, Schoolmaster, Whalley	Irving.
145	Peel William, Farmer, Wiswell,	Fort.
267	Robinson Henry, Grocer, Church Brow	do.
184	Read John, Blacksmith, Lower Gate,	Irving.
266	Roberts Henry, Designer, Parson Lane	Fort.
182	Robinson John, Mr. Assheton's Steward, Downham	Irving.
80	Robinson William, New Close, do.	Fort.
58	Robinson Thomas, Farmer, do.	do.
73	Robinson William, do, Hook Cliffe do.	do.
	Riley Richard, Bobbin Turner, Whalley	
40	Ramsbottom, William, Farmer, Wiswell	Irving.
4	Starkie Le Gendre Nicholas, Esq., Huntroyde	do.
36	Shaw William, Farmer, Chatburn,	Fort.
225	Smalley Richard, Innkeeper, Clitheroe,	do.
149	Smithies Thomas, Shoemaker, Well Gate do.	Irving.
206	Standen Matthew, Innkeeper, Castle-st. do.	do.
191	Stewart John, Draper, do. do.	Fort.
183	Squires Thomas, Butcher, Parson Lane do.	Irving.
271	Smithies Bichard, Farmer, High Moor do.	Fort.
269	Seed John, do. Goosebutts do.	do.
193	Satterthwaite William, Joiner, York-st. do.	do.
228	Sutcliffe James, Farmer, Higher Standen	do.
246	Swales Hannibal, Labourer, Low Moor,	do.
26	Sparrow Stephen, Esq., Castle-street, Clitheroe	do.
76	Summersgill Joseph, Lodging-house, Salford, do.	Irving.
226	Sutcliffe Robert, Grocer, do. do.	Fort.
186	Shaw Thomas, Farmer, Hook Cliff, Downham	Irving.
21	Silverwood William, Farmer, Mitton,	Fort.
122	Schofield Ellis, do. Pendleton	Irving.
20	Southworth Henry, do. Standen Hey	Fort.
133	Smith John, do. Limes House, Pendleton	do.
140	Smith William, Wheelwright, Sabden,	do.
151	Slinger Robert, Farmer, Pendleton,	Irving.
141	Schofield John, do. do.	Fort.
94	Smith John, do. Coolham, Twiston	do.
187	Silverwood Francis, Innkeeper, Whalley	Irving.
212	Speak James, Farmer, Wiswell,	Fort.
154	Sutcliffe Isaac, do. Wiswell Moor	do.
242	Taylor, John, Esq., Moreton Hall	Irving.
243	Thomson James, Esq., Primrose,	Fort.
276	Thompson John, Hatter, Clitheroe	do.
125	Thompson James, Shoemaker, do.	Irving.
278	Trappes Robert, Esq., Solicitor, Clitheroe	Fort.
127	Townson Henry, Rag Dealer, Well Gate	Irving.
255	Taylor Robert, Clogger, Clitheroe,	Fort.
81	Tattersall Christopher, Farmer, Hey House, Downham	do.
95	Taylor Thomas, do. Hill Top, Twiston	do.
96	Taylor John, sen., Manufacturer, Twiston Mill	do.
97	Taylor Robert, do. do.	do.
	Taylor John, jun., do. do.	absent.
104	Taylor Thomas, do. do.	Fort.
156	Topper Stephen, Portfield, Whalley,	do.
	Tomlinson Thurston, jun., do.	absent.
41	Tomlinson Thurston, sen. Lower Clerk Hill	Irving.
	Tomlinson Thomas, Farmer, Wiswell Hall	absent.
260	Vickers Joseph, Labourer, Low Moor	Fort.
176	Whalley Rev. J M., Clerk Hill	Irving.
5	Whalley Robert, Esq. do.	do.
257	Whitaker Charles, Esq., Symmonstone	do.
37	Whittaker George, Kemp Stone, Chatburn	Fort.
38	Wilson James, Farmer do.	do.
39	Wignall James do. do.	do.
64	Whittam John do. do.	Irving.
268	Watson Henry, Currier, Clitheroe	Fort.
273	West William, Inkeeper do.	do.
	Welch Edmund, Tailor do.	Neuter.
67	Wilkinson James, Innkeeper Dock Hill do.	Irving.
	Whalley Henry, Postmaster do.	No vote.
192	Wallace John, Draper do.	Fort.
270	Walker Benjamin, Clothier do.	Irving.
189	Whittaker Ralph, Spinner do.	Fort.
272	Whitaker Thomas, Spirit Merchant do.	do.
147	Whittaker George, Moon's Lane Top do.	Irving.
244	Watson John, Painter do.	Fort.
234	Wilkinson John, Solicitor do.	Irving.
	Walmsley George, Butcher do.	No vote.
223	Wearing James, Carter, Salford do.	Irving.
229	Whitehead Thomas, Innkeeper, Downham	do.
150	Whalley Richard, Farmer, Lane Head, do.	do.
82	Wilkinson John, do. do.	Fort.
	Wilkinson James, do. do.	Neuter.
103	Whitaker John, do. Mearley Hall	Irving.
47	Wilkinson James, do. Fields, Mearley	Fort.
24	Whitaker William, do. Henthorn	do.
22	Whipp John, do. Mitton Hall	do.
79	Whitaker John, do. Wilkin Heys, Pendleton,	Irving:
142	Whitaker William, do. Well Springs do.	Fort.
105	Watson James, do. Brown Low, Twiston	do.
106	Whipp William, do. Fearnside House, do.	do.
107	Whipp Robert, do. Lower Higson's do.	do.
108	Whipp Thomas, do. Red Syke, do.	do.
109	Wilkinson William, do. Wilkinson's do.	do.
157	West James, Painter, Whalley	do.
	Wilson Thomas, Innkeeper, do.	Neuter.
241	Whitle Robert, Esq. do.	Irving.
44	Whittam John, Farmer, Nether Town	do.
100	Walton James, do. Wiswell Eaves	do.
155	Whitaker John, do. Wiswell Moor	Fort.
50	Wilson Richard, do. Barker Field, Worston	do.
49	Wilson William, do. do.	do.
48	Wilson John, do. do.	do.
83	Yates James, do. Downham	do.

STATE OF THE POLL.

For John Fort, Esq.	157
For John Irving, Esq.	124
Majority for Mr. Fort	33

Figure 4 – The 1832 electorate

Source: Clitheroe public library local studies collection. P12.

Cardwell did not stand in the next election, in 1847, preferring to retire after the defeat of Sir Robert Peel in 1846 over the issue of the Corn Law,[18] and, perhaps surprisingly after the controversy surrounding the 1841 contest, Matthew Wilson was returned unopposed. His attempt at re-election in 1852, however, was again marred by scandal. On that occasion Wilson's Tory opponent was John Aspinall of Standen Hall. The candidates were able to give their speeches from the hustings on 6 July, when Wilson easily won the straw poll, but both sides had paid men from Padiham and Burnley to intimidate their opponents, and many Tory supporters were forcibly prevented from gaining access to Market Place. Two local boxers tried to influence the result, the Tory champion 'Dick Unlicked' taking on and defeating a radical stonemason over 13 bareknuckle rounds. The fight was viewed not as entertainment or a sporting challenge, but as a serious attempt to sway the decision of the voters.[19]

Satirical placards, handbills, and blatant bribery also played their part in agitating the crowd. By 2.30 p.m. on polling day, 7 July, the situation was so badly out of hand that Aspinall refused to present any more pledged Tories to the returning officer, and his solicitor served the mayor with a legal form of objection about the way the election was being conducted. It is not surprising therefore that Wilson polled 221 to Aspinall's 188. The result was queried the following February, and a Select Committee of the House of Commons heard evidence from 43 witnesses which revealed that bribes of up to £100 had been paid to electors to vote for Wilson. He was, consequently, unseated, but not replaced by Aspinall because further depositions showed that much Tory malpractice had also occurred. Instead the election was 'declared void for bribery and treating' and a by-election ordered.[20]

The admonishment of the House of Commons had no effect, for the re-run was equally flawed. It saw a return to the tactic of 'bottling', on this occasion of potential Tory voters who were held and made drunk at Hareden, a Liberal house at the entrance to the Trough of Bowland. On polling day, 28 May 1853, they were smuggled into Clitheroe via the quiet road from Waddington and presented at the polling station before they sobered up. All voted for the Liberal candidate Richard Fort, but their apostacy failed to affect the outcome, for after the count Aspinall still had a majority of seven. On petition an investigating committee again discovered widespread bribery and intimidation, the result was once more annulled and a second by-election was called.[21]

It took place on 23 August 1853, this time between candidates untarnished by corruption, and was won by the Conservative Le Gendre Starkie of Ashton Hall, who polled 216 votes against the 205 cast for his

Liberal opponent Jonathan Peel of Accrington. At last the astonishing sequence of invalidated elections had come to an end. In a period of 12 years three elections had been subjected to parliamentary scrutiny and the outcome overturned for a variety of offences, an appalling record even by the standards of an age when electoral fraud was commonplace.

*

Between 1853 and 1872 Clitheroe held five more elections, all in the era of public voting when illegal practices could be expected in a constituency where it had become endemic. However four of them were won by unchallenged candidates and no trouble ensued. The judgement of John O'Neil, a Low Moor weaver writing of the 1857 election, was that 'the whole proceedings did not last above an hour and terminated peaceably. Mr Hopwood was returned without opposition'.[22] The only contested election during this period was that of December 1868. It was the last to be held before the introduction of the secret ballot and the first in which a wider electorate could participate, for a new parliamentary reform act in 1867 had extended the franchise to include not only householders who paid rates, but also lodgers who paid £10 a year in rent. A Royal Commission evaluated constituency boundaries at the same time, but in the case of Clitheroe decided against changing them. The report did, though, find that only 54 out of 1,977 male occupiers paid under £10 in annual rent, so the 1867 Act enfranchised many of the constituency's working class, including John O'Neil and other Garnett employees.[23]

The sitting MP was the Conservative Ralph Assheton of Downham Hall, who had been returned unopposed on the death of Richard Fort, his Liberal predecessor, in the July 1868 by-election. But when a General Election was called for December of that year he faced a Liberal challenge from the Surrey barrister Charles Roundell. This campaign too was memorable as much for its violence as its politics. It has been claimed that workers at Wellfold Foundry made a hundred knuckle dusters for use in the Conservative cause, and several battles in which they were used took place in the town – outside the 'Stop and Rest' beerhouse, near the Co-operative store in Moor Lane, on Whalley Road, in Castle Street – and over 100 policeman had to be drafted into Clitheroe to prevent further bloodshed. Nevertheless both candidates produced manifestos which were debated at frequent meetings throughout the constituency and on the hustings.[24] (See Figure 5.) The matters raised included the price of bread, the expansion of educational provision, the introduction of the secret ballot, and the need for a less expensive foreign policy, but the main divisive issue was Ireland. On this Assheton equivocated, failing to comment on Gladstone's plan to compensate tenants who improved their lands, and showing only luke-warm interest in the contemporary controversy about the privileged position of the protestant church in Ireland. Roundell, by contrast, supported a fairer deal for Irish tenants, better representation for Ireland in parliament, the opening of Trinity College Dublin to catholics, and the disestablishment of the Irish protestant church which, he claimed, oppressed the mainly catholic population with tithes and enjoyed privileges which were out of all proportion to the number of its adherents. (See Figures 6 and 7.)

Roundell's policies found favour with the newly enfranchised voters of Nonconformist Low Moor, but he lost the election, polling 693 votes against Assheton's 760. The victor played on his local connections, for the Asshetons were an ancient family much revered in the area. It proved a winning tactic and helped him to retain the seat for the next 12 years. The Liberals suspected that threats of dismissal had been made to potential Roundell voters during the 1868 election,[25] but such concerns were soon addressed, for in 1872 the Ballot Act was passed providing for secret voting to replace nomination on a public platform.

Figure 5 – The Clitheroe hustings

Source: S. Clarke, *Clitheroe in its Old Coaching and Railway Days* (Advertiser and Times, Clitheroe, 1929) opposite p. 65 in 'Railway Days'.

This is the only known photograph of hustings in the town. It shows the structure erected for the July 1868 by-election. Many of the platform party have been identified as Conservatives, undoubtedly because the Liberal candidate withdrew shortly before polling.

TO THE

ELECTORS OF THE BOROUGH

OF CLITHEROE.

GENTLEMEN,

Having been informed that the representation of our ancient Borough in the House of Commons has already been a matter of anxious discussion amongst you, and as I have already received promises of support from many influential persons, I hasten to declare my intention of soliciting the honour of your suffrages at the next Election.

It is uncertain when a vacancy may occur, and it is impossible now to discuss in detail the subjects that may then be before the Country.

Should you honour me with your confidence as your Representative in Parliament, I would give a general support to the Conservative Party, believing, as I do, that the principles on which they act, are those most conducive to the happiness and prosperity of all classes of Her Majesty's subjects: at the same time I would feel myself at liberty to vote for what I might believe to be a good measure from whichever side of the House it might come.

Whilst I think that to ensure peace we ought to be prepared for war, I consider the policy pursued at the present time by the Secretary of State for Foreign Affairs deserving of all praise and I should be glad to see that policy result in a reduction of Armaments, and a consequent reduction of expenditure.

Although an attached Member of the Church of England, I have always been and still am in favour of freedom of opinion on religious matters, and whilst I view with great jealousy the present attack on the supremacy of the Protestant faith in Ireland, I would endeavour to give a calm and dispassionate consideration to any scheme which may be proposed to rectify the anomalies at present existing in that country.

The Educational question has occupied, and doubtless will continue to engage, the attention of Parliament, and any well-considered measure on this subject would have my support.

I need not remind you that my interests are intimately connected with your own, and that, should you return me as your Member, private interest and public duty would alike prompt me to make every exertion to promote the welfare of all classes amongst you.

I beg to remain, Gentlemen,

Your obedient Servant,

RALPH ASSHETON.

DOWNHAM HALL,
27th March, 1868.

Figure 6 – Ralph Assheton's Address to those qualified to vote in the General Election of 1868

Source: Clitheroe public library local studies collection. P12.

TO THE

ELECTORS & NEWLY-ENFRANCHISED ELECTORS

OF THE BOROUGH OF CLITHEROE.

GENTLEMEN,

At a crisis of supreme importance in the history of the nation, I solicit the honour of becoming your Representative in the new Parliament.

The Reform Act of 1867 has inaugurated a new order of things. Old party combinations, old traditions of government, have passed away. A new motive power, new principles, have been called into action. The Imperial Government must henceforth be essentially national.

I accept the change with the heartiest satisfaction. I have that confidence in the ultimate moderation and good sense of my fellow-countrymen, that I regard the wide extension of the franchise as an unmixed good:—as refounding our institutions upon a sound and broad popular basis: as tending to unity at home, and to security and respect abroad.

The questions of absorbing public interest are the Irish question, and the Education question.

The bane of Ireland is ascendancy—the ascendancy of a privileged, anti-national Church: the ascendancy of an absentee, unsympathetic proprietary.

As a measure of justice, in the interest of the Church at home, in the interest of Religion itself, in the paramount interest of the Empire, of which Ireland is the present weakness and the potential strength, I advocate the disestablishment and equitable disendowment of the Irish State Church.

But the Irish Church is already doomed. I hail the recent vote of the House of Commons as a harbinger of better times: as a keynote of reconciliation: as a prerogative message of peace and goodwill from the English to the Irish people.

The question of the tenure of land in Ireland is beset with difficulties. With deference to great authorities, I venture to think that heroic remedies are not called for; but that the solution of the problem is to be sought in the securing by law to the Tenant the value of his permanent improvements: in the removal of artificial restrictions upon free commerce in land: and, above all, in the bestowal upon the Irish people of a real representation in the Imperial Parliament.

I regard the Ministerial proposal to grant a Charter to a Roman Catholic University as an insidious offer, of the most abnormal and retrograde nature. It is an attempt to set off privilege against privilege: to intrench, at any cost, the citadel of existing sectarian exclusiveness. In common with the friends of liberal education at our own Universities, I shall rather give my strenuous support to those who seek to nationalize the existing University of Dublin, and to throw open the honours and emoluments of Trinity College, freely and impartially, to all classes and denominations alike of Her Majesty's Irish subjects.

In Education, generally, I uphold the golden rule of perfect religious equality. Building upon the sure foundation of respect for conscience, respect for learning, and the recognition of the claims of equal citizenship, I regard our Elementary Schools, our Endowed Grammar Schools, and our Universities, as a manifold heritage, dedicated from ancient times to national uses: as graduated parts of one great national system: to be severally reconstituted, governed, and administered, in accordance with living needs, and large national objects.

I advocate therefore security being taken for the provision throughout the country of Primary Schools, sufficient in number, efficient in quality: the enforced application of School Endowments to purposes of public educational utility: the opening and extending to the nation the benefits of our Colleges and national Universities.

By thus impressing upon our noble Educational Endowments a truly national character, by opening an avenue to ability, and enabling the flower of our youth, without respect of birth, or class, or creed, to obtain the highest education which our Schools and Universities can give, we shall not only prevent shameful waste, but also bind together the forces of English society.

I wish to see the Foreign Policy of the country conducted upon the basis of respectful, self-respecting courtesy towards foreign Governments: and of friendship—cordial, fraternal friendship towards the people of the United States.

I am in favour of the Ballot, as the necessary complement of the recent extension of the franchise.

In all other domestic questions, I believe myself to be in accord with the matured principles of the party of progress.

While professing my supreme allegiance to the Liberal cause, I look upon Mr. Gladstone as my political leader, as the hope of the nation, the true friend of the people: as the Statesman of largest heart and widest sympathies, who, standing upon the ancient ways, will best know how to moderate between the old and the new, between the glorious but outworn traditions of the past, and the national hopes and aspirations of the future.

I am, Gentlemen,

Your obedient Servant,

CHARLES SAVILE ROUNDELL.

GLEDSTONE,
8th April, 1868.

J. FIELDING, PRINTER, CASTLE-ST., CLITHEROE.

Figure 7 – Charles Roundell's Address to Clitheroe's expanded electorate, 1868
Gledstone was Roundell's country residence near Skipton.

Source: Clitheroe public library local studies collection. P12.

The secret ballot did much to check the abuses of the past, although indirect bribery through candidates' subscriptions to local institutions still continued. However no irregularities were reported at subsequent Clitheroe elections. That of 1874 resulted in another victory for Ralph Assheton, who defeated his Liberal challenger Ebenezer Kay by 896 votes to 804, but at the General Election of 1880 Assheton lost to Richard Fort, the 24 year old son of the former member, by 200 votes out of the 2,000 cast, the largest majority in the constituency's history thus far.[26]

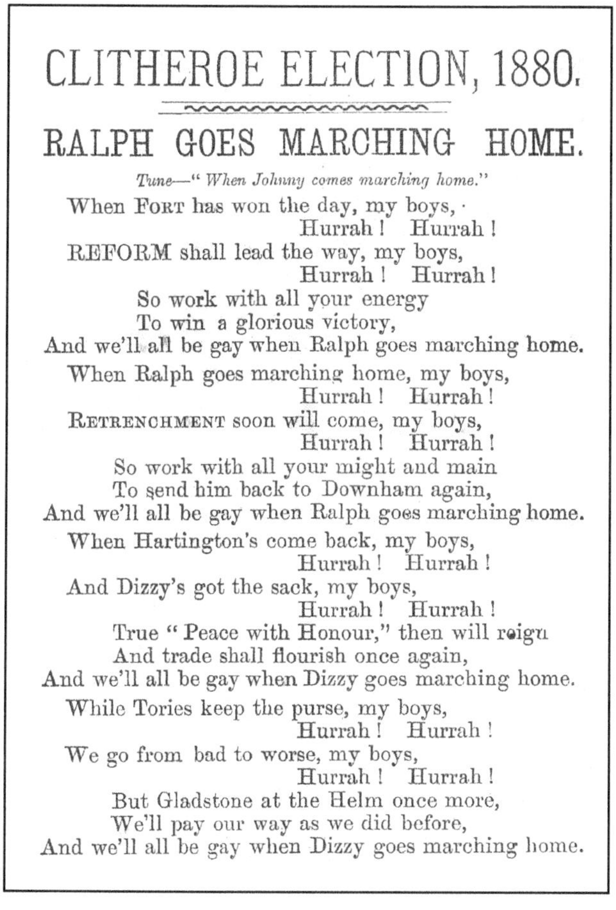

CLITHEROE ELECTION, 1880.

RALPH GOES MARCHING HOME.

Tune—" When Johnny comes marching home."

When FORT has won the day, my boys,
Hurrah! Hurrah!
REFORM shall lead the way, my boys,
Hurrah! Hurrah!
So work with all your energy
To win a glorious victory,
And we'll all be gay when Ralph goes marching home.

When Ralph goes marching home, my boys,
Hurrah! Hurrah!
RETRENCHMENT soon will come, my boys,
Hurrah! Hurrah!
So work with all your might and main
To send him back to Downham again,
And we'll all be gay when Ralph goes marching home.

When Hartington's come back, my boys,
Hurrah! Hurrah!
And Dizzy's got the sack, my boys,
Hurrah! Hurrah!
True " Peace with Honour," then will reign
And trade shall flourish once again,
And we'll all be gay when Dizzy goes marching home.

While Tories keep the purse, my boys,
Hurrah! Hurrah!
We go from bad to worse, my boys,
Hurrah! Hurrah!
But Gladstone at the Helm once more,
We'll pay our way as we did before,
And we'll all be gay when Dizzy goes marching home.

Figure 8 – One of the campaign songs used by Clitheroe Liberals during the General Election of 1880

Source: Clitheroe public library local studies collection. P1.

Nationally the Liberals won 352 seats to the Conservatives' 237. Hartington was Queen Victoria's preference to replace Disraeli ('Dizzy' in the song) as prime minister, but she was persuaded to accept Gladstone despite her dislike of both his domestic reform agenda and his belief in 'retrenchment' and 'Peace with Honour', i.e. withdrawal from imperial adventures.

On both occasions the absence of disturbances of any kind was remarked upon with relief, for at last it seemed that it was the issues, rather than any other factor, that determined the outcome of elections.[27] In 1880, certainly, they outweighed Assheton's previous advantage of deference to his family irrespective of his political opinions, for the electorate decisively rejected his support for the continued use of flogging as a punishment in the army, his opposition to the extension of the franchise in the counties, his belief that prospective town councillors should be chosen only from amongst property owners, and his refusal to condone an extension to polling hours to give working-class voters a better chance of being able to cast their ballots. These were policies that led to Assheton being accused of 'holding views that would have been considered barbarous in the twelfth century'.[28] It was Fort's ability to mobilise working-class support against such policies that led to his victory in 1880. Liberal election songs were widely distributed and enthusiastically taken up (see Figure 8), a fleet of carriages was made available to convey qualified working men to the polling stations, and the protection provided by the secret ballot enabled many of them to ignore the urgings of their employers to vote Conservative. William Smith, the chief Conservative agent, complained in vain that the secret ballot had caused voters to renege on pre-election promises that should have given his candidate a majority of a hundred.[29]

Smith's reaction to defeat vindicated the new system, for it brought greater integrity into election procedures, but workers who were entitled to vote still had a choice only of political parties created to further the interests of the middle and upper classes.

Notes and References

1 There is also place name evidence of Clitheroe's origins, for example the Celtic clyd dwr means 'a crag by water', and the Danish how means 'a hill'.

2 A. Langshaw, *Clitheroe's Thousand Years* (Borough Printing Company, Clitheroe, no date) pp. 1-3, 131-132.

3 W. Farrer and J. Brownbill (eds.) *The Victoria History of the Counties of England, Lancashire, vol. 6* (Dawson, Folkestone, 1992) pp. 360-361. D. Best, *A Short History of Clitheroe in Lancashire* (Carnegie, Preston, 1988) p. 20.

4 From 1254 each diocese was directed to submit an estimate of the aid it could grant the king, supplementing the advisory role previously allowed spiritual magnates, but the lower clergy were not otherwise represented. It has been argued that until 1373 this formula for the composition of the House of Commons was provisional and frequently transgressed. See C. Bryant, *Parliament : The Biography, vol. 1* (Doubleday, London, 2014) pp. 43-59.

5 W. Pink and A. Beavan, *The Parliamentary Representation of Lancashire (County and Borough) 1258-1885* (Henry Gray, London, 1889) pp. 6-7.

6 J. Tanner, *Tudor Constitutional Documents A.D. 1485-1603* (CUP, Cambridge, 1951) p. 515. Henry VIII's first House of Commons had 298 members, 224 of whom represented boroughs. Elizabeth's first had 398, 300 of whom, including Clitheroe's two, were borough members. See J. Neale, *The Elizabethan House of Commons* (Jonathan Cape, London, 1950) pp. 141-142, 224.

7 A. L. Rowse, *The England of Elizabeth* (Macmillan, London, 1950) p. 306. H. Forrest, 'Notes on Clitheroe elections up to c. 1860' (Clitheroe public library local studies collection, file P12).

8 C. Ainsworth, 'Clitheroe : The Parliamentary History of a Rotten Borough' (Clitheroe public library local studies collection, file P12) p. 20. E. Broxap, *The Great Civil War in Lancashire 1642-51* (MUP, Manchester, 1973) pp. 167 and 174. Three branches of the Assheton family were involved in the Civil War – Ralph Assheton of Whalley was the Parliamentary Commander-in-Chief in Lancashire. Ralph Assheton of Downham, another parliamentarian, was deputy lieutenant of the county. A third Ralph, of Middleton, was a royalist.

9 General George Monk, who had engineered the restoration of Charles II, was given the title Duke of Albermarle and the lands of the Honour of Clitheroe as his reward. See W. Farrer and J. Brownbill *op.cit.*, p. 361.

10 W. Pink and A. Beavan, *op.cit.*, pp. 246-247.

11 T. Oldfield, *The Representative History of Great Britain and Ireland* (Baldwin, Cradock and Joy, London, 1816) Vol. 4, p. 112.

12 H. Forrest, *op. cit.* The Ribblesdale burgages were valued at £18,000. Brownlow bought them for £40,000 from the Lister family. The three great local families that dominated pre- Reform Act politics in Clitheroe were the Asshetons (Barons Curzon from 1794, Viscounts Curzon from 1802); the Listers (Thomas Lister who broke the family compact in 1780 was the first Baron Ribblesdale); and the Custs (John Cust who bought the Ribblesdale burgages in 1804 was Earl Brownlow).

13 W. Pink and A. Beavan, *op.cit.*, p. 9.

14 H. Forrest, *op.cit.*

15 James Thomson of Primrose and Jeremiah Garnett of Roefield, *Narrative of Occurrances at Clitheroe on Tuesday 31 July 1832* (J, Burrell, Blackburn, 1832) in 'Clitheroe Miscellaneous', Lancashire Archives LE02CLICLI. *Leeds Patriot and Yorkshire Advertiser*, 11 August 1832, p. 4; *London Evening Standard*, 4 October 1832, p. 3.

16 Party colours at this time were not settled, and could change from one election to the next and from one part of the country to another. In 1868, for example, Clitheroe Liberals sported pink and green, Tories red, white and blue. See S. Clarke, *Clitheroe in its Old Coaching and Railway Days* (Advertiser and Times, Clitheroe, 1929) 'Coaching Days' p. 43, 'Railway Days', p. 65.

17 S Clarke, 'Coaching Days', *op.cit.*, pp. 43-44; H. Forrest, *op.cit.*

18 The Corn Law was introduced in 1815 to protect the landed interest against foreign competition. It was a cherished Tory policy, but it kept the price of bread artificially high and by 1846 Peel felt unable to support its continuance, thus splitting the Conservative Party and causing his resignation. Cardwell went on to have a successful career within the Liberal Party as President of the Board of Trade (1852-55), Chief Secretary for Ireland (1858-61), Chancellor of the Duchy of Lancaster (1861-64), Colonial Secretary (1864-66), and Secretary for War (1866-74). He is best remembered as the reorganiser of the British Army during the last of these appointments.

19 S Clarke, 'Railway Days', *op.cit.*, pp. 62-63; H. Forrest, *op.cit.*

20 W. Pink and A. Beavan, *op.cit.*, p. 271. See also S. Clarke, 'Railway Days', *op.cit.*, pp. 65-67.

21 *Ibid.*

22 J. O'Neil, *A Lancashire Weaver's Journal 1856-1864, 1872-1875*, M. Brigg, ed., (Record Society of Lancashire and Cheshire, vol. CXXII, 1982) p. 36.

23 Report of the Boundary Commissioners for England and Wales 1868 – Clitheroe, p. 83. Clitheroe public library local studies collection, P29/491461240.

24 S Clarke, 'Railway Days', *op.cit.*, pp. 70-74. The 1868 Election was the last at which hustings were used in Clitheroe. The photograph (Figure 5) shows what

they were like, although it is of the hustings erected in Market Place for the uncontested July 1868 by-election necessitated by the death of Richard Fort, the sitting MP who had been returned unopposed at the General Election of 1865.

25 Unattributed press cutting, Clitheroe public library local studies collection, file P15.

26 Fort polled 1,078 to Assheton's 882. His victory made him the youngest member of the new House of Commons.

27 See Clitheroe public library local studies collection, file P21, and J. O'Neil, *op.cit.*, p. 169.

28 Clitheroe public library local studies collection, file P21.

29 *Ibid.*

Chapter 2

The Impact Of Industrialisation

Richard Fort's success in 1880 made him the last MP to represent the borough of Clitheroe as it was then defined. The Redistribution of Seats Act of 1885 greatly enlarged the constituency, adding to it Sabden, Padiham, Read, Cliviger, Burnley without the borough, Briercliffe, Brierfield, Barrowford, Nelson, Colne, Newchurch-in-Pendle, Trawden and Foulridge. (See Figure 9.) This changed the nature of the constituency out of all recognition. It was no longer an ancient borough with an agricultural hinterland, albeit with an industrial infrastructure that had been superimposed during the earlier nineteenth century, for the additions were overwhelmingly new textile communities with predominantly working-class populations.[1] This was significant because redistribution was part of a Parliamentary Reform Act which also extended the ballot to those adult males who had previously been denied the right to vote by the £10 lodger qualification. Nationally an extra 2,000,000 were thus enfranchised, and the new Clitheroe division now had 12,698 registered voters out of a total population of 60,273. Of these only 1,596 lived in the old borough, a number exceeded by Colne with 2,207 and Nelson with 2,410.[2]

There was much opposition to these changes. Clitheroe was jealous of its independent status, fearful that its future parliamentary representatives would not be local men, and the absorbed mill towns complained that the lack of rail links with Clitheroe would make it difficult to communicate with the administrative centre of the constituency.[3] Nelson and Colne had a point, for local geography required a circuitous railway journey via Blackburn in order to circumnavigate Pendle Hill, but Clitheroe's concerns were not entirely realised at subsequent elections. In 1885, for example, the candidates were Sir Ughtred Kay-Shuttleworth of Gawthorpe Hall in Padiham (see Figure 10), and J.O.S. Thursby, a Burnley mill owner. Both therefore considered themselves local, and they opened their campaigns in Clitheroe, Sir Ughtred using the Liberal Club in Wellgate as his headquarters, Thursby the Conservative Club in Castle Street.

Sir Ughtred spoke in favour of continuing the Liberals' long-standing commitment to Free Trade, and stressed the presence in the constituency

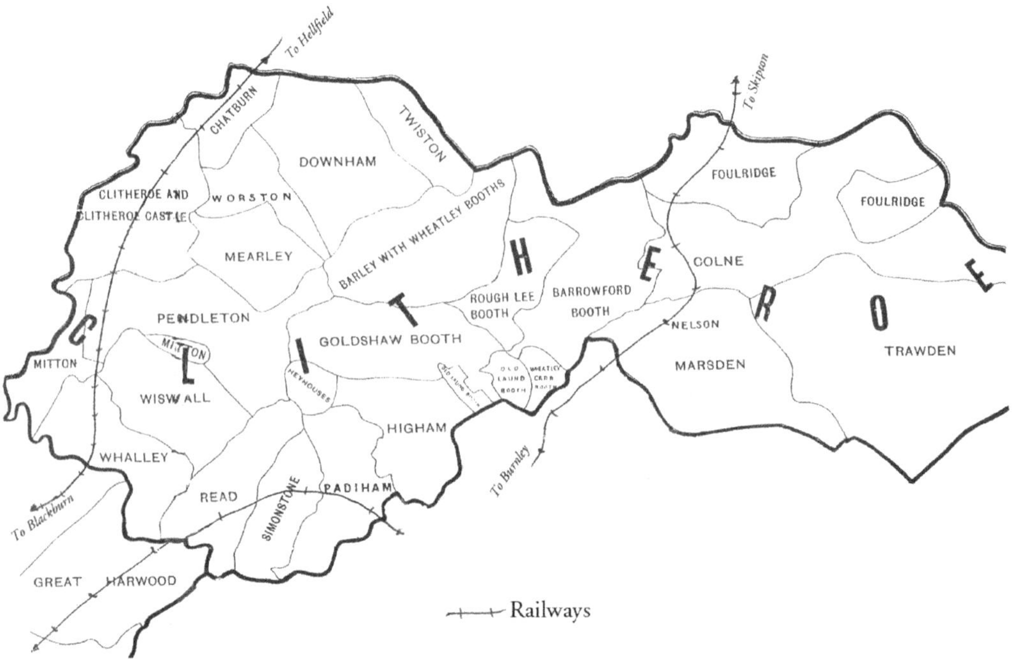

Figure 9 – The Boundaries of the Clitheroe Constituency 1885–1918

Source: Clitheroe public library local studies collection,
file P1, from PG's scrap book.

of Sabden, the industrial village where the great Free Trade advocate Richard Cobden had built a cotton mill. He also supported Home Rule for Ireland, free elementary education, limited opening hours for public houses, equality of opportunity in the armed forces, and equality of standing for churches of all denominations as venues for weddings. He had little to say about foreign policy, however, aware that the Liberal Party's attempts to disengage from aggressive imperialism was unpopular because it was blamed for the plight of General Gordon and his forces then besieged in Khartoum. Thursby exploited this issue for all it was worth, and called for better religious education in schools, the expansion of foreign markets, and reduced taxation.[4]

By now the calming effect of the secret ballot on voting behaviour was well established, although memories of Clitheroe's stormy past were recent enough for one commentator to remark on how quietly the General Election of 1885 passed off.[5] Circumstances favoured the Liberals, for

Figure 10 – Sir Ughtred Kay-Shuttleworth, Liberal Member of Parliament for Clitheroe from 1885 to 1902

Source: S. Clarke, *Clitheroe in its Old Coaching and Railway Days* (Advertiser and Times, Clitheroe, 1929) opposite p. 81 in 'Railway Days'.

the substantial Roman Catholic vote which had inclined to the Conservatives hitherto, had been alienated by recent attacks on that religion by Clitheroe's Anglican clergy. Temperance voters were also solidly for the Liberal candidate because of his stance against public houses opening on Sundays, and the textile unions campaigned hard for Sir Ughtred. His victory was impressive, for the Liberal majority of 2,359 was larger than in any other north Lancashire seat which returned a Liberal. Indeed 1885 was considered a high water mark for Clitheroe Liberals, and Sir Ughtred sustained it over the next 17 years and through four more elections until his move to the House of Lords in 1902. This was a period when Conservative governments were usually in power, and Liberals tended to think of Clitheroe as a bastion of dissent. However the local Liberal heyday as champions of the oppressed coincided with the emergence of new political parties which aimed at separate representation of the working class in parliament, and the changing nature of the constituency would make it one of their earliest testing grounds.

*

John Parker opened the area's first cotton mill in 1791 beside the river Ribble at Low Moor. It was taken over by Jeremiah Garnett and Timothy Horsfall in 1799, and in 1858 Jeremiah's nephew, Thomas, bought Horsfall out and established the company of Thomas Garnett and Sons. The sons were William, who was 32, and James, aged 29. Together they managed the mill as partners, but James also kept a diary and it is a key source for

Figure 11 – James Garnett, junior partner in the business of Low Moor mill and chronicler of its fortunes from 1858 to 1900

Source: *Photographic Material on Garnett Family of Clitheroe* (Clitheroe public library local studies collection, G3 GAR).

understanding how the business was run in the later nineteenth century.[6] (See Figure 11.)

The brothers took over the business at a propitious time, for the textile industry was booming. In 1850, for example, the value of cloth exports had been £25,000,000, but by 1872 this figure would rise to £80,000,000, and ten years later Lancashire exported 82 per cent of all cotton goods produced.[7] The Garnetts shared in this prosperity disproportionately because of the family's enterprise and innovation. Low Moor mill was the only one in the area to have both spinning and weaving capacity, and the necessary investment to ensure good profits. Before the installation in the 1820s of extra water wheels, new power looms, and a gas works, average output was 14,000 lbs. of yarn and 2,500 pieces of cloth per week, but the new machinery increased production to 35,000 lbs. and 4,500 pieces by 1860 (See Figure 12). The work force also grew, and an adjacent village built to provide the necessary housing.[8]

Success was achieved despite significant operating difficulties. The first of several fires broke out in 1852, when only prompt action by operatives prevented a major conflagration, and in 1891 another was similarly contained.[9] An ongoing problem was the quality of raw cotton imported from Surat in north west India, for the fibre was tough and short, it deteriorated from exposure in transit, and bales were stuffed with grass to make up the negotiated weight of the orders. This conundrum was overcome when United States sea island cotton became available from the 1840s, a variety that was cleaner and had soft, long fibres that were easier to work, but supplies were interrupted during the American Civil War (1861–65) by the Union blockade of Confederate ports. The strategy was implemented so effectively that Southern privateers could carry only three per cent of the needs of Lancashire manufacturers, and by the end of 1861 stocks in hand had become seriously depleted.[10]

By November of that year 49 Lancashire mills had closed and 119 were on half time. Weaving districts were particularly badly hit. Blackburn, for example, was a town of full employment in 1861 and 22 new mills were under construction, but a year later 36,000 of its 120,000 inhabitants had become dependent on poor relief.[11] In Clitheroe 1,051 out of 2,739 textile workers were receiving relief in 1862, a rate that made it the worst affected mill town in the county.[12]

Business acumen enabled the Garnetts to cope with the cotton famine better than most. James' diary entry for 5 February 1861 recorded that 'although not so good as last year by a long way, the balance is pretty satisfactory'; on 23 April 1862 he claimed 'the balance has proved equal to our expectations'; and on 25 February 1863 he considered that profits were 'satisfactory considering the little we have run this year'. Indeed between October 1863 and August 1864 a new turbine to replace one of the water wheels was installed at a cost of £435, and the brothers speculated in other ventures. Some, such as the proposed Ribblesdale Railway and the Whitewell Lead Mining Company failed, but those in local banking, insurance and steel production increased their income and helped them to ride out the emergency comfortably.[13]

Figure 12 – Low Moor mill

Source: O. Ashmore, *Low Moor, Clitheroe : A Nineteenth Century Factory Community* (H. Rawson, Manchester, 1966) between pp. 144–45.

However speculation was accompanied by hard-headed realism. When cotton was in short supply the Garnetts would sell it on rather than make it into yarn or cloth if it was more cost effective to do so. The diary shows that on 3 February 1862 the firm sold 250 bales at 13*d* a pound in preference to using it in the mill, and as the price of American sea island rose, inferior cotton from India, Egypt and Peru was used instead. Such methods gained the approval of some commentators and caused them to congratulate the Garnetts on their ability to keep most of their hands working regularly,[14] nevertheless there were periods between 1861 and 1865 when Low Moor mill was closed or running short time, and workers had no option but to seek charity. The Clitheroe Relief Committee raised £2,525, of which £100 was contributed by the Garnetts. The family also gave four hundredweight of coal to each Low Moor household and started a sewing school to help the female unemployed make an alternative income.[15]

But there are indications that James Garnett begrudged supporting the poor. His diary states that he thought the rates he paid should have been enough to cover his responsibilities in this respect, and that idleness would be the inevitable consequence of charity. It could be argued, therefore, that he used relief contributions primarily as a means of control. That is to say he was essentially a paternalist who deployed contemporary capitalist techniques to ensure a docile and deferential workforce.

*

The roots of paternalism lie in the way society was organised in the Medieval period, when lords received duties from their vassals and in return gave them protection. The principle of mutual obligation was reinforced by the church, for canon law required that alms be given to the needy faithful and that parish priests act as paternalist examples for their secular counterparts to follow. This system was so successful that it has been claimed the poor were better cared for in the thirteenth century than in the nineteenth.[16]

Tudor law formalised earlier practice by imposing a property tax to fund poor relief, but now it was restricted to those considered 'deserving', and the 'undeserving' were treated by local magistrates as vagrants in need not of help but discipline. State responsibility for the poor was further modified in the seventeenth century when scientific progress led to a new view of the universe in which the chain of being, a metaphor for paternalism, was replaced by acceptance of personal autonomy and the transfer of welfare responsibilities to the individual. In the eighteenth century the growth of capitalism caused another shift in relations between employers and workers, making them the subject of market forces rather than paternal concerns. These developments led Edmund Burke to complain in 1756 that 'pity, benevolence and friendship are almost unknown in high places'.[17] Yet paternalism underwent a revival in the nineteenth century. Parliamentary commissions revealed that widespread abuse of labour had been a result of the industrial revolution, and writers like Thomas Carlyle (*Chartism*, 1839) and Benjamin Disraeli (*Sybil: or The Two Nations*, 1845) raised awareness of inequality and suffering. It was characterised as 'the condition of England' question and pre-occupied the governments of the day.

The nature of the paternalism that emerged from these concerns was complex, but in Lancashire it took two main forms. The first was typified by Edmund Ashworth who established the New Eagley mill on the Irwell near Manchester in the 1830s. It was commodious and well ventilated, as were the houses of his workers, which had lavatories and up to six rooms. An infant school gave two hours education a day to children between the ages of nine and thirteen, and Sunday and evening schools provided for their elders. As a consequence 98 per cent of Ashworth's employees could read and 45 per cent could write in the 1850s. Church attendance was required, although the denomination was not prescribed, sobriety and cleanliness were encouraged, evergreens were planted to enhance the environment of the mill, and work was rewarded or penalised according to its quality.[18]

Ashworth showed that the factory system need not be a brutalising force, for New Eagley's improved living and working conditions resulted in a more profitable business, but a different sort of paternalism is typified by the Hornby family of Blackburn. Hygienic weaving sheds, decent housing, education and temperance formed no part of this model. Worker deference was achieved, rather, by the promotion of blood sports, football, cricket and treating. Treats were given to mark royal weddings or when Hornby family members got married, dinners and dances were organised to celebrate the success of British imperialism, and railway excursions paid for by the firm became regular events from the 1850s. All that was required in exchange were the votes of enfranchised employees for a Hornby or his Tory nominee. This formula was remarkably successful even after the 1872 Ballot Act, and Blackburn became notorious as a Conservative working-class constituency throughout the later nineteenth century.[19]

Aspects of both these models can be seen in the paternalism of the Garnetts at Low Moor. In the early nineteenth century the mill had used pauper children supplied by orphanages and workhouses. The 1809 Health and Morals of Apprentices Act obliged employers to provide such children with some education, a requirement the Garnetts fulfilled by marching them the three miles there and back, in special uniforms, to Sunday School at St.

Mary's church in Clitheroe.[20] The village amenities added later were entirely due to Garnett generosity. They built the school in St. Anne's Square, gave £1,000 towards the cost of building St. Paul's Anglican church, and provided the land on which the United Methodist chapel in Nelson Street was erected. The first Mechanics Institute and Reading Room opened in High Street in 1853, and the second in St. Paul's Street in 1903 as a result of Garnett family initiatives. They installed a water supply for the village in 1856, converted the back-to-backs they had originally built into more spacious terrace houses, and planted pear trees next to every front door.[21] (See Figure 13.) James Garnett's diary also shows that in 1863 he paid his own doctor £5 to vaccinate all his tenants during a smallpox outbreak. It further shows that although a pub was not allowed in the village, a football team was formed and was good enough to reach the second round of the FA Cup in 1883.

Figure 13 – Workers' housing at Low Moor in the 1890s, with pear trees provided by the Garnett family

Source: M. Brigg (ed.), *A Lancashire Weaver's Journal 1856–1864, 1872–1875* (The Record Society of Lancashire and Cheshire, vol. CXXII, 1982) between pp. 39–40. Reproduced from a photograph owned by Mrs B. Buckley.

CENTENARY OF

LOW MOOR MILLS,

APRIL 14TH, 1899.

On Friday next the time will be
To celebrate our Jubilee;
We'll march round th'tip and up front street,
Until at Joe Holt's we shall meet.

From there to Church on Friday go
At half past Ten, as all do know,
And there give thanks to God who's given
Beef and plum pudding all from Heaven.

Last Jubilee in 49
Dolly Barrett took a part,
Along with Mr. Jerry
They led the ball so smart

Old Betty Potty, Molly Loggin—
Nanney Pickup too—
Along with Jimmy Landlord—
They played the bottle through.

Stone chimney's gone since then,
The old water wheel as well;
Soa now we can do without them
They've really been to sell.

Ne'er mind about these changes,
We'll have a jolly time;
We'll dance to tommy talkers
And listen to their rhyme.

Old bacon then shall fairly shine,
We'll plank our pig at bottom;
We'll stick to baceon aye for aye
Until we're weaving cotton.

The mill stands firm to day,
With men at helm to sway;
They'll make it swim right up to th'brim
For aye, for aye, for aye!

Since Sammey Twatchman used to work
Among the narrow cloth,
We've added Throstles that can sing—
And send the threads right through the ring,
And girls that work there, laugh and sing
Hurrah hurrah.

Success and prosperity to our mill,
Good feeling twixt master and men,
While ever there's grass that grows in the yard
No doubt we shall hear the pay-hen.

There's Jack Seedall with his lurry and hosses.
There's no doubt he swaggers a good bit;
And weel he might with the mare that traces,
For she's a regular good tit.

We've Souling Bill and Cunningham,
Painters and paviers too,
They think they're men of pomp
But we'll show 'em what to do.

Mr. William, Mr. James, and the family,
We wish them health and success
And pray that the heavenly blessing
May each of them all possess.

Then three cheers for good old Bacon—
The crest that none shames to hear;
Three cheers for all families of Bacon
We wish we'd flitch in each chair.

Now we've come to th'end of our tether
And we know that we all shall agree
That if we can have but fine weather
We shall certainly have a good spree

We finish now with a right good wish
That all who get their dinner,
At the Jubilee may have a spree
And never goa noa thinner.

J. Robinson, Printer, Clitheroe.

Figure 14 – The 1899 tribute presented by Low Moor workers to their employers

Source: J. Mitcalf (ed.), *The Heritage of Low Moor Mill* (Jenny Press, Clitheroe, 2017) p. 8.

Treating at Low Moor mill followed the Hornby pattern, most spectacularly to celebrate the centenary of its founding. Over a thousand dignitaries, employees and their families were invited to a banquet for which 800 lbs. of beef and 700 lbs. of fish took pride of place on a lavish menu. The workers responded by presenting their employers with an illuminated address praising them for their benefactions, and a song. (See Figure 14.) The composition is unpolished, but it shows something of the nature of Low Moor paternalism and the apparent deference of the operatives – thankfulness for employment (verse eight), admiration for technological innovation (verse nine), calling down blessings on the family (verse thirteen).

So it would seem that Garnett paternalism was exemplary, and supremely effective in creating harmonious relations between employer and employee. William and James, we are told, were benefactors of the highest order, running their business efficiently but ethically, always having in mind the welfare of their workers. There is much truth in this impression, but it is based mainly on James' diary and sympathetic press reports, and these are not impartial sources.[22] Fortunately a more balanced view of nineteenth century Low Moor can be formed, for James Garnett was not its only chronicler.

*

John O'Neil moved to Lancashire in 1855. He was a self-educated political activist, and had been involved in reform campaigns in Carlisle before wage reductions for weavers there forced him to seek work elsewhere. After a brief spell in Bentham, and following the death of his wife, he moved to Low Moor and remained a Garnett employee until his death in 1876. His daughter Jane also worked at Low Moor and other mills in Clitheroe, and until her marriage in 1862 she and her father lived at 15 St. Anne's Square as Garnett tenants. (See Figure 15.) John O'Neil kept a diary, the surviving parts of which cover the years 1856 to 1864 and 1872 to 1875. It offers a corrective to James Garnett's view of life and work in the village, for it is often critical of the factory system and the way Low Moor mill was managed.

O'Neil was a good weaver, and his ability to handle three looms rather than the usual two gave him an income higher than that of many Garnett employees. The 1847 Factory Act had limited working hours for those under seventeen, but male adults had no such protection and a 60 hour week was commonplace. John O'Neil accepted long hours because they gave him a wage he could live on, sometimes as much as *22s 6d*, enough to cover every

Figure 15 – St. Anne's Square, Low Moor

Source: O. Ashmore, *Low Moor, Clitheroe : A Nineteenth Century Factory Community* (H. Rawson, Manchester, 1960) between pp. 44–45.

Number 15 was the home of John and Jane O'Neil from 1855 to 1876.

day needs and an occasional investment, such as the £5 share he took in the proposed Clitheroe Commercial and Cotton Spinning Company in 1860.[23] At the end of 1856 he wrote:

> 'I am in rather better circumstances than I was at the beginning [of the year] and Jane is also a good deal better. She has plenty of good clothes, more than she had in her life before, and if nothing happens I will have a new suit this next summer'.[24]

The qualification 'if nothing happens' is telling, for it draws attention to the frequent fluctuations in textile workers' incomes caused by market forces. In January 1862, for example, O'Neil's wages fell by a third because the Surat was 'such rubbish…we cannot do half the work we used to', and during the winter of 1863–64 he could earn only a shilling a day on the few occasions the mill was running.[25] The Clitheroe Relief Committee gave him three shillings as well, but it made a weekly total which, John claimed, 'barely kept me alive'. He often visited his brother in Preston on Sundays, but now, he admitted, 'I am too poor to go anywhere, so I must stay at home'.[26] He began to run out of clothes and bedding and saw no way of obtaining more, for, he claimed, the Garnetts broke their promise to provide better quality cotton and they did not remit their tenants' rent as many north Lancashire masters did during hard times. In August 1864 O'Neil grumbled 'it is shameful the work we have at present. I had only 6*s* this last week with very hard work, and there was some had less than me'.[27]

Like so many textile workers John O'Neil remained philosophical about his predicament during the American Civil War, and was able to find the moral strength to endure the privations it caused because he supported the Union's opposition to slavery. James Garnett, by contrast, favoured the Confederacy, hoping General Lee's successes would lead to a Southern victory and a quick resumption of cotton supplies.[28] Perhaps this calculation earned O'Neil's contempt, although his diary does not mention it, however he certainly resented being directed to vote for William Garnett's preferred candidate in the Clitheroe municipal elections of 1858 and 1859. William later became a pillar of the local Conservative establishment, acting as a

Figure 16 – William Garnett

Source: Clitheroe public library local studies collection. G2.

Senior partner at Low Moor mill, councillor, alderman, mayor, JP and Freeman of the Borough of Clitheroe.

JP, serving 30 years as councillor and alderman and three times as mayor, a public service record for which he was made a Freeman of the Borough in 1905, (see Figure 16), but in the 1850s he was a Liberal. O'Neil too was a Liberal and was prepared to vote as he was bid. What he objected to was his employer's assumption that he could interfere with the political convictions of his tenants and deprive them of pay for the time they were away from their looms fulfilling his wishes.[29]

As far as John O'Neil was concerned the Garnetts' brand of paternalism amounted to social and political control, an unwarranted intrusion on his freedom of thought and action. He acknowledged their benefactions, but he nevertheless considered that the Garnetts exploited their workers. He believed they deliberately limited relief during the cotton famine years because they preferred to use the money for capital investment. One consequence of this was petty economies such as charging starving villagers ½*d* for soup, another was the average wage reductions of 1*s* 9*d* a week, a cut of 12½ per cent, which were introduced in 1865 even though trading conditions had by then improved. The Garnetts also opposed emigration schemes aimed at giving their employees the chance of a better future in the colonies because this might create a labour shortage at Low Moor.[30]

Other workers, whose views went unrecorded, would have shared John O'Neil's reservations about the motives of their employers. The resulting resentment was a major factor behind the industrial unrest of the nineteenth century.

Notes and References

1 Colne, for example, had a population of over 36,000 in 1881 according to the census returns for that year.

2 Qualified voters in the principal communities that made up the post 1885 constituency were distributed as follows:

Barrowford	696	Nelson	2,410	Habergam	132
Briercliffe	285	Cliviger	375	Newchurch-in-Pendle	305
Brierfield	761	Chatburn	210	Padiham	1,461
Burnley without	423	Clitheroe	1,596	Read	291
Colne	2,207	Foulridge	171	Sabden	203

See *Manchester Evening News*, 21 October 1885, p.6.

3 *Preston Guardian*, 20 December 1884; 10 January 1885 (both unpaginated).

4 Unattributed press cuttings from the scrapbook of 'PG'. Clitheroe public library local studies collection, file P1.

5 S. Clarke, 'Railway Days', *op.cit.*, pp. 76-77. Clitheroe's polling stations were in Church Street, Moor Lane and the Wesleyan School.

6 O. Ashmore, 'The Diary of James Garnett of Low Moor, Clitheroe, 1858-65. Part 1, Years of Prosperity 1856-60; Part 2, The American Civil War and the Cotton Famine 1861-65', in *Transactions of the Historic Society of Lancashire and Cheshire*, 121 (1969) pp. 77-98 and 122 (1970) pp. 105-173. O. Ashmore, 'Low Moor, Clitheroe : A Nineteenth Century Factory Community', in *Transactions of the Lancashire and Cheshire Antiquarian Society*, (73-74, 1964-65) pp. 124-152.

7 J. Walton, *Lancashire : A Social History 1558–1939* (MUP, Manchester, 1987) p. 198.

8 O. Ashmore, Part 2, *op.cit.*, pp. 128-130.

9 *Preston Chronicle*, 16 October 1852, p. 6; *Lancashire Evening Post*, 7 August 1891, p. 6.

10 B. Ellinger, 'The Cotton Famine 1860-1864', *Economic History* (3,9,1934) p. 152.

11 N. Longmate, *The Hungry Mills* (Temple Smith, London, 1972) p. 152.

12 J. O'Neil, *op.cit.*, pp. xxix–xxx.

13 O. Ashmore, Part 2, *op.cit.*, p. 129.

14 J. Watts, *The Facts of the Cotton Famine* (Simpkin, Marshall, London, 1866) p. 233.

15 *Ibid.*, pp. 233 and 252.

16 B. Tierney, *The Medieval Poor Law* (University of California Press, 1959) p. 109.

17 D. Roberts, *Paternalism in Early Victorian England* (Croom Helm, London, 1979) p. 19.

18 *Ibid.*, p. 176.

19 D. Beattie, *A History of Blackburn* (Carnegie, Lancaster, 2007) p. 224. J. Walton, *op.cit.*, p. 38.

20 S. Clarke, 'Railway Days', *op.cit.*, p. 38.

21 O. Ashmore, 'Low Moor Clitheroe, A Nineteenth Century Factory Community', *op.cit.*, pp. 149-151. The two Low Moor Mechanics Institutes of 1853 and 1873 were replaced by the present Reading Room and Club in 1903. See also M. Brigg, 'Life in East Lancashire, 1856-60', the transcript of a lecture given 19 September 1968, pp. 100, 104, 132-133, Clitheroe public library local studies collection, M132.

22 See for example *Preston Guardian*, 21 April 1849 on the firm's 50th anniversary celebrations, and *Burnley Express*, 3 September 1887 which profiles James Garnett in a long article entitled 'The Ancient Borough of Clitheroe and its Mayor'. The *Express* was owned by J.O.S. Thursby, the unsuccessful Conservative candidate for the Clitheroe division in the election of 1885, who was a Garnett family friend.

23 J. O'Neil, *op.cit.*, p. 108.

24 *Ibid.*, p. 30.

25 *Ibid.*, pp. 131-132.

26 *Ibid.*, p. 139.

27 *Ibid.*, p. 142.

28 *Ibid.*, p. 134. O. Ashmore, Part 2, *op.cit.*, p. 115.

29 J. O'Neil, *op,cit.*, pp. 72 and 90.

30 O. Ashmore, Part 2, *op.cit.*, pp. 116, 118, 120 and 125, and R. Hall, 'A poor cotton weyver : poverty and the cotton famine in Clitheroe'. (*Social History*, 28, 2, 2003) pp. 237 and 242.

Chapter 3

The Social And Economic Response

Despite the parliamentary reform acts of 1832, 1867 and 1884, many in the working class were denied redress at the ballot box throughout the nineteenth century. They naturally sought alternatives, and some amelioration was provided by trade unions and self help organisations, but before their formation the tradition of violent dissent remained common. Starving handloom weavers took part in food riots in Clitheroe in 1808,[1] and in the aftermath of the Luddite disturbances of 1811 and 1812 Low Moor mill became a target for machine breakers. The incident took place in 1826 soon after power looms had been installed in the factory, and it has been presented as a battle between loyal Garnett employees and vandal off-comers.[2] Some of the saboteurs were indeed from places as far distant as the Colne Valley, but others were more local and their action was dictated by desperation, for mechanisation had caused the collapse of handloom weavers' wages. Their plight moved farmers to offer them oatcakes and buttermilk as they marched towards Clitheroe, and according to Thomas Duckworth who was a participant in the attack, the yeomanry cavalry deployed from Manchester shared their rations with them. But the soldiers had brought artillery, and in the face of overwhelming odds the insurgents withdrew.[3]

Worker resentment about poor pay and conditions could be set aside during the good times, but they soon surfaced during the bad, especially, after the formation of trade union branches from the 1850s. Weavers' Associations were established in Blackburn in 1854, Padiham in 1856, Great Harwood, Church and Accrington in 1858, and Clitheroe in 1859.[4] John and Jane O'Neil joined the Clitheroe Power Loom Weavers' Union in February 1859, and John became its president in April 1860 after a strike at his place of work. The *Preston Guardian* attributed it to the sacking of one of the hands for misconduct, but O'Neil's diary suggests it resulted from complaints about dust from the warps which the Garnetts refused to do anything about. Help was sought from the East Lancashire Power Loom Weavers' Friendly Association, whose representative advised the strikers to demand a pay rise of five per cent as well as rectification of the dust problem. The hope was that this would bring Clitheroe mills in line with the Blackburn Standard List, a union devised wage scale which incorporated the notion of 'local disadvantages', that is to say the different expenses faced by mill owners depending, for example, on the price of building materials or the cost of transport to the Leeds/ Liverpool canal. In the case of Low Moor local disadvantages were calculated to be five per cent, but the union still considered that Garnett workers were underpaid.[5]

This was a prosperous period for cotton manufacturers, and the Garnetts were able, if with reluctance, to offer a five per cent increase, but by then a wider dispute involving textile workers in much of north Lancashire had begun, and many Clitheroe operatives supported it. The focus of dissent was Colne, where masters continued to refuse their employees Blackburn List wages, and the consequence was a strike which lasted almost a year. Clitheroe weavers contributed between £25 and £28 a week from June 1860 to March 1861 to help the Colne strikers, and other union branches gave much more, but it made no difference to the outcome for the strike failed. The masters' victory was due not only to their ability to weather the loss of production better than their employees, but because they brought in blacklegs from Coventry to keep their mills going. They outmanoeuvred the unions whose officials were accused of incompetence and fraud for the way they handled the dispute.[6]

The industrial unrest in north Lancashire in the late 1850s and early 1860s, and the emergence of a unionised work force, prompted the mill owners to combine in response. In May 1859 William Garnett and Robert Dewhurst, owner of the Salford Bridge mill, met a deputation from the Burnley Associated Masters at the Swan Hotel in Clitheroe and they agreed to offer mutual support if further trouble occurred. It was a shaky pledge however, for when it was tested by the strike of 1860–61 the Clitheroe masters failed to aid their Colne counterparts.[7] One reason for this was another serious dispute in Clitheroe.

By 1861 there were 20 textile mills in mid-Ribblesdale, eleven of them in Clitheroe itself, four of which – Waterloo, Albion, Shaw Bridge New, and Victoria – had started production during the previous three years,[8] but in February 1861 the masters told the operatives that if they would not accept a 10 per cent reduction in wages the mills would close. This ultimatum was precipitated by changing trading circumstances, for a long period of prosperity for cotton manufacturers had been brought to an abrupt end by the outbreak of civil war in the United States. Mass meetings took place in and around the town, some attended by up to 2,000 workers, to hear union representatives urge them to resist. A frequent speaker was John O'Neil. His main argument was that Clitheroe masters were not justified in claiming hardship through increased costs caused by 'local disadvantages' because in

Clitheroe water rates and building materials were cheaper than elsewhere, and more than compensated for the extra cost of gas and carriage.[9]

The threatened lockout deteriorated into a bitter dispute. A bank loan and contributions from neighbouring branches enabled strikers to be given 1*s* 6*d* on three occasions during March 1861, and the masters were accused of paying agents to disrupt union meetings. At the end of the month five of the leading Clitheroe employers proposed the creation of a panel of arbitration made up of three nominees from each side and the Reverend Fielding, vicar of St. Mary's, who was to act as a neutral umpire. The panel recommended a 2½ per cent wage cut, judging that local disadvantages cost the masters 1½ per cent and the workers one per cent. The masters were outraged that their claims had not been taken more seriously, and the operatives complained that their partial wage restoration was inadequate, nevertheless the compromise was accepted and production resumed, though fitfully because of the continuing difficulty of obtaining raw materials.[10] The Garnetts believed that arbitration had treated them unfairly and dismissed John Wood, one of their weavers, who was considered to be the union official responsible for the strike.[11]

The unrest of the early 1860s was accompanied by a growing politicisation amongst Clitheroe operatives. A surviving handbill issued at the time of the 1865 General Election shows that Low Moor workers were at the forefront of efforts to gain a better deal from their employers through promoting a candidate sympathetic to reform. (See Figure 17.) But lacking the right to vote the authors also threatened to boycott the businesses of 'enemies of the people', the term they used for Tory or anti-reform shopkeepers. Richard Fort won the election, although there is no way of knowing how great a part the campaign of the Low Moor workers played in it, nor what role individuals such as John Wood or John O'Neil had in the composition of the handbill.

*

When more normal circumstances were re-established Clitheroe trade unionists continued to grumble, about the quality of the cotton for example, or the length of the working week, but there were no more major strikes until 1878. It has been argued that late Victorian England was an increasingly orderly and law abiding society, and statistics do indeed show a sharp decline in crimes of violence and public disorder during this period.[12] Events in north Lancashire in 1878 contradict the trend, however. In that year the prospect of 10 per cent wage cuts was again raised by the

FORT
FOR EVER!!

At a numerously attended Meeting of the Householders of LOW MOOR, the following Resolutions were unanimously agreed upon by the Operatives, who have witnessed with the deepest feelings of indignation and contempt, the exertions making in the BOROUGH OF CLITHEROE, by certain individuals who have on all occasions shewn themselves to be enemies to the Rights of the People, and strenuous advocates for the perpetuity of the old scandalous Tory Faction: which corrupt and abominable system, if continued, will unavoidably reduce the great bulk of the community, to POVERTY, STARVATION, and WANT; and not being privileged with a power to Vote according to the £10 franchise, they have come to these Resolutions in order to meet the above existing evil.

1.—That as a New and Reformed Parliament is intended to uproot and destroy this system, we are determined to do every thing in our power that the law permits, to frustrate any attempt that shall be made to send to a Reformed Parliament, an enemy to the broad principles of Reform.

2.—That we, the Operatives of LOW MOOR, in order to carry into effect the last resolution—do now unite—as with one heart and soul, in a fixed and most resolute determination, to abstain from spending our money with such Corn Dealers, Grocers, Butchers, Innkeepers, Publicans, Druggists, Drapers, Ironmongers, Shoemakers, Tailors, &c. &c.—and all others as shall be found aiding, or any way supporting, a Candidate of the principles or character, specified in the last resolution.

3.—That we further resolve, individually and collectively, to use all the influence we possess, with our respective Friends and Neighbours, &c., to carry this our determination into effect.

4.—That we further resolve, that the names of all those Shopkeepers, of whatever sort or description; and all our Opponents who shall prove themselves the **ENEMIES** of the **PEOPLE**, by promising or giving their Votes to a Tory Candidate, shall be printed at the expense of the Low Moor Committee of Reformers, on large Placards, similar to those containing the names of persons in Arrears to the Church Rates, &c., and headed "**PERSONS IN ARREARS TO REFORM**," and posted on the Walls of the Town.

H. WHALLEY, PRINTER, CLITHEROE.

Figure 17 – The part played in the 1865 General Election by voteless Low Moor mill workers

Source: Clitheroe public library local studies collection.

masters because of an acute trade depression, and by mid-April 100,000 cotton factory workers were on strike. This time the masters would neither compromise nor accept arbitration, and in Blackburn their intransigence led to an attack on the home of Raynsford Jackson, the leader of the employers. His house at Wilpshire was burned to the ground and many were injured in the associated rioting.[13] No one was killed, but shots were fired in Oswaldtwistle and Great Harwood, the Starkie Arms was attacked in Padiham, and in Burnley a warehouse at Kay's mill was looted.

Trouble began in Clitheroe on 17 May when windows were smashed at Salford Bridge mill and Little Moor House, Robert Dewhurst's residence. This caused the authorities to swear in 53 special constables and request military assistance. It arrived from Leeds in the form of a detachment of the 17th Lancers. They were billeted in the Swan and Royal Hotel in Castle Street, from where they dispersed a crowd which had ignored the Riot Act and stoned the Town Clerk when he read it. (See Figure 18.) But although the cavalry quelled the disturbance they could not end the strike. During the following three weeks several attempts at compromise were made but none succeeded, and by mid June the unions called the strike off on the employers' terms. The failure was blamed not on the union negotiators, who had consistently urged their members to protest peacefully, but on the perpetrators of the violence, for it had served only to stiffen the masters' resolve.[14]

The unions were taken by surprise in 1878. Much of the disorder in Clitheroe was spontaneous, suggesting an unplanned release of resentment after more than a decade of industrial peace. Consequently union reserves were low, and as the rioting became widespread mutual support was difficult to organise and a strike pay fund hard to collect and distribute. However defeat did not weaken the workers' belief that their view of the cotton industry's problems was correct. They thought overproduction was the cause of the depression, not foreign competition as the masters maintained. For the operatives, then, the solution was a temporary reduction in output through short-time working. In these circumstances the employees would have accepted wage cuts because the result, they were sure, would be a return to prosperity, full-time working, and a restoration of wage levels.

*

Within a decade some of the masters had recognised the merit of their workers' argument and applied it. In September 1888, for example, the

READING THE RIOT ACT.

SOLDIERS CLEARING THE STREETS (1878).

Figure 18 – Contemporary woodcuts illustrating the violence that accompanied the 1878 strike against 10 per cent wage cuts in Clitheroe

Source: S. Clarke, *Clitheroe in its Old Coaching and Railway Days* (Advertiser and Times, Clitheroe, 1929), 'Railway Days', pp. 83 and 85.

Whipp brothers, who owned both the Commercial and Victoria mills, and the Garnetts at Low Moor, 'intimated their intention of continuing for the present to run four days a week' in direct response to a proposal to that effect which had been put to them by the Clitheroe Weavers' Association.[15] But this change of heart was not universal, and discontent remained strong amongst Clitheroe's cotton operatives.

The weavers at John Southworth's Brooks mill stopped work in February 1885 'alleging that they were being underpaid by 1*s* 4*d* per cut on certain sorts'.[16] The weft spinners at Victoria mill came out on strike in September 1888 accusing the Whipps of providing 'bad work and low wages'.[17] In August 1887 250 weavers struck at Salford Bridge mill claiming they were being cheated of a penny a piece. The argument in this case was over a technicality, the amount of gold thread used in a specialised process, but union representatives urged continued resistance against such 'sharp practices' which they considered were tantamount to 'criminal offences' by 'dishonest capitalists'.[18] An ugly situation that could have led to violence was defused by Mr Cossidenas, the employer, who agreed to pay his workers according to the Blackburn List and remove Robert Cook, the manager's son, whose arrogance had sparked the dispute.

A year later Grindleton weavers walked out for more than ten weeks. The village mill had only recently been acquired by Whittaker, Sons, and Aspin, for whom the operatives agreed to work for 10 per cent below the Blackburn List. The strike began when the weavers realised they were being paid less than the negotiated rate, which they had only accepted because of Grindleton's local disadvantages. The masters justified the extra cuts on the grounds that their costs were higher than they had expected. Grindleton's greater distance from coal supplies in Accrington incurred a charge of 3*s* a ton more in cartage than delivery to Clitheroe, for example, and yarn deliveries to Grindleton were 2*s* 3*d* more than to Chatburn. The Whittakers also claimed that loom rents would cost them £224 13*s* over the seven years of their lease, and water power £56. A *Clitheroe Times* investigation concluded that although these disadvantages were partly offset by the cheaper cost of living in Grindleton, the strikers should nevertheless drop their demands until the following March when orders inherited from the previous owners would have been fulfilled.

Whittaker, Sons, and Aspin welcomed the newspaper's analysis. They threatened to sell their yarn rather than use it to give their employees work unless the strike was called off, and the Grindleton weavers were obliged to return on these terms. The union had been unable to intervene because of other disputes in Clitheroe itself, Low Moor, Holmes mill and Brewery mill all juggling lay offs with short time working in the hope of keeping some production going during a trade depression.[19]

In March 1891 Brooks mill weavers were again on strike, this time demanding that Southworth pay them Blackburn List wage rates, and by August they had been joined by weavers at Jubilee mill, which was also owned by Southworth. Throughout the 25 weeks of the dispute the Clitheroe Weavers' Association supported the strikers with payments from a fund to which contributions had also been made by other north Lancashire branches. On this occasion union solidarity was successful in forcing Southworth to concede the Blackburn List and to pay his employees the shortfall which had caused them to stop work back in March. However 40 strikers found their looms had been allocated to blacklegs in the interim, and some of them never regained their places.[20]

But perhaps the most serious stoppage since 1878 occurred in 1897 when 2,000 Clitheroe weavers from all of the towns 14 mills (see Figure 19) went on strike. The dispute was again caused by the threat of five per

Figure 19 – Details of textile mills in Clitheroe in the late 1890s

Source: S. Clarke, *Clitheroe in its Old Coaching and Railway Days* (Advertiser and Times, Clitheroe, 1929), 'Railway Days', p. 288.

LIST OF MILLS IN CLITHEROE.

Name of Mill.	Style or Firm.	Name of Manager.	Class of Goods Woven.	No. of Looms.	No. of Spindles.
Salford Bridge Mill	Holgate Bros. Ld. (Burnley)	Mr. Norman Redman	Plain and Fancies	368	none
,, ,,	Edmundson, Trafford & Co. (Nelson and Clitheroe)	Mr. John Trafford	Plains and Fancies	310	none
,, ,,	Roberts & Co. (Burnley)	Mr. T. Thistlethwaite	Prints & Flannelettes	305	none
Waterloo Mill	Duckworth & Edleston	Mr. Thos. Metcalfe	Fancies	436	none
Jubilee Mill	John Southworth & Sons	Mr. Hy. Lester	Fine Plains & Fancies	1190	none
Brooks Mill	John Southworth & Sons	Mr. James Holden	Fine Plains & Fancies	739	none
Albion Mill	Percy Thwaites & Co.	Mr. James Sagar	Plains and Fancies	327	none
Claremont Mill (formerly Brewery)	Claremont Manufactg. Co	Mr. E. Bradley	Plains	413	none
Shaw Bridge Mill	Gaddum, Rusden & Co., Ld.	Mr. W. Mellor	Fancies	500	none
Foulsykes Mill	Foulsykes Manufactg. Co.	Mr. Hy. Fleetwood	Plain (a few fancies)	522	none
Victoria Mill	Whipp Bros.	Mr. J. S. Aspden	Cotton Spinning		15,336
Commercial Mill	John Mercer	ditto	Plain and Fancies	575	30,000
Low Moor Mills	Thos. Garnett and Sons	Mr. John Ormerod	Plain	1157	58,550

Holmes Mill (late Mercer and Hodgson's) is partially dismantled and idle.

Primrose Mill (late Mercer and Hodgson) is totally dismantled and now the property of Messrs. Whipp, Bros.

cent wage cuts to protect the masters against local disadvantages, and it was settled only when, after 16 weeks, the operatives agreed to accept their employers' offer to reduce the cut to 2½ per cent. This was a major event which preoccupied the town for months and was commemorated there annually for some years.[21]

*

Direct action through strikes had become the standard response of Clitheroe workers to employers who sought to keep wages down, but it was a hit and miss strategy with uncertain outcomes. During the nineteenth century therefore other ways of improving the condition of the working class were tried, part of a proliferating pattern of dissent that looked for more reliable solutions to social injustice through self help initiatives such as education, temperance and co-operation.

Before the advent of universal elementary education in the 1870s, voluntary bodies offered the best chance the working class had of acquiring basic learning. There had been Sunday Schools in Clitheroe from the 1780s and these gradually extended their classes to weekdays. The Congregational church, for example, opened a day school in the early 1800s, and the catholic church of St. Michael and St. John started one in 1823.[22] The requirement that the 1833 Factory Act placed upon mill owners to give their child-employees some education was often evaded, but there were inexpensive alternatives. They were of varying quality however. Mr Grimshaw ran a respected school for upward of 20 children in Waddington, but another, less well regarded, was held in a Bawdlands' cellar. The largest, and perhaps the most effective, were the Anglican National Society school which was built by public subscription in 1839, and the rival Nonconformist British and Foreign Society school, but both aimed at little more than teaching the Three Rs and only children whose parents could forgo their wages would attend.[23]

In such circumstances it is hardly surprising that mutual aid organisations were active in Clitheroe, providing those with aspiration and energy enough after long hours of labour the chance of improving their prospects. Some of the churches established lending libraries, most notably the United Methodists and St. Mary's, both of which maintained substantial readerships until the end of the century. There had been a public library housed in the Town Hall since 1838, but it was badly managed and little used before 1879 when a new Free Library was opened. Within 20 years it had built up a collection of 7,000 volumes and a large patronage.[24]

No weekly newspapers were published in Clitheroe before 1886 when the *Advertiser* was launched, to be joined by the *Times* two years later, but Reading Rooms which took local and national titles pre-dated them.[25] John O'Neil often walked to Clitheroe to follow the progress of the American Civil War in the Reading Room there, and in 1861 he joined the Low Moor Mechanics' Institute, paying a penny a week for access to its stock of books, papers and magazines.[26]

There was a strand of opinion within nineteenth century dissent which believed that the government could be brought down by abstinence because the Treasury was so heavily dependent on alcohol taxes,[27] but the appeal of the temperance movement was essentially moral, and gained working-class support because it encouraged thrift. The major teetotal organisations were the United Temperance Council and the Independent Order of Rechabites. Both had branches in Clitheroe, the Rechabites also acting as a Friendly Society which offered low cost insurance against sickness and funeral expenses.

Sir Ughtred Kay Shuttleworth, the division's long-serving Liberal MP, was a tireless worker in the cause of temperance, advocating Sunday closing, police inspection of licensed premises, abolition of tied houses, and restrictions on the number of pubs in any locality. There were popular sobriety clubs throughout the constituency, supported not only by the Liberal Party but by socialist groups. The Independent Labour Party promoted teetotalism and was championed locally by Philip Snowden who later became MP for Blackburn and Chancellor of the Exchequer. Clitheroe's first Labour MP, David Shackleton, was a Rechabite, and he stressed the need for temperance legislation in his 1902 campaign speeches. Albert Smith, his Labour successor in the seat, was a long-standing member of Nelson Welcome Lodge, a flourishing, teetotal organisation. Of the emerging political parties of dissent only the Marxist Social Democratic Federation was luke-warm towards temperance, its Padiham branch remaining unconvinced that there was adequate proof that 'teetotalism will cure poverty'.[28]

But the most far reaching working-class expression of self help was co-operation. It took two forms. The first, sanctioned by the Limited Liability Act of 1856, involved worker control of production. In November 1860 John O'Neil attended a public meeting for the purpose of establishing a co-operative mill in Clitheroe, and persuaded of its viability he took a £5 share.[29] The Weavers' Union backed the plan, and by July 1861 450 investors had provided the capital for a site between Primrose lodge and the railway which would house 400 looms and 20,000 spindles. Great optimism attended the project, but it immediately fell victim to the problems of supply caused by the outbreak of war in America. The mill never recovered, and in 1868 it was sold to John Mercer who ran it as an ordinary commercial business.[30]

Unforeseen circumstances denied co-operative textile production a chance of success in Clitheroe, but co-operative retailing thrived. Consumer co-operatives were established in many Lancashire communities in the years following the first successful experiment in this method of trading at Rochdale in 1844. Its central tenet was democracy. All co-operative society members had one vote irrespective of the number of shares they held, and therefore an equal say in who became officers of the society and what its policies should be. But the key aspect of this business model was the distribution of profit in the form of a dividend payment linked to the value of purchases – the more you bought the more you received in dividend. These features secured customer loyalty, avoided the usual capitalist practice of a few wealthy shareholders monopolising profits, and highlighted what was the moral function of co-operation – to help the poor to obtain a greater share of the wealth generated by economic activity. However it was the 'divi' that became the co-operative movement's defining characteristic. It was an egalitarian device which multiplied the getting and spending options of members by augmenting their incomes, and it provided a chance to save for rainy-day needs such as sickness and unemployment.

The Clitheroe Equitable Industrial Co-operative Society was formed in 1861 in response to the north Lancashire cotton strike of that year. Its initial meeting was held at the Commercial Inn and the committee it elected consisted of William Cook, Robert Garner, John Booth, Thomas Atkinson, Matthew Riley, Charles Hutchinson, Thomas Smithies, Thomas Clarkson, John Hall, Thomas Jackson and James Chadwick. This was an organisation for working-class shoppers which opened long hours, from 7 a.m. to 9 p.m., and 10 p.m. on Saturdays, and paid its manager only 16*s* a week. It stocked staples such as second quality flour (3*s* 5*d* per score), butter (11½*d* per lb), sugar (5*d* per lb), candles (6½*d* per lb), common tea (3*d* per oz), cheese (8*d* per lb), and bacon (8½*d* per lb). Salt was not sold, but pepper was (1*d* per oz) and so was vinegar (6*d* per quart) and mustard (1*d* per oz). Among what might be considered luxury lines were best tea (6½*d* per oz), snuff (5*d* per oz) and sweets (1*d* per oz).[31]

Thomas Smithies, one of the strike leaders in 1861, became the first president of the Society, and John Booth its first paid secretary. They and their successors guided the business to prosperity and expansion. In 1863 a branch was opened in Russell Street, and the central shop moved from Lowergate to bigger premises in Moor Lane which could accommodate a drapery as well as a grocery department. (See Figure 20.) Butchery and coal dealing began in the later 1860s, and by 1871 the Society had 430 members

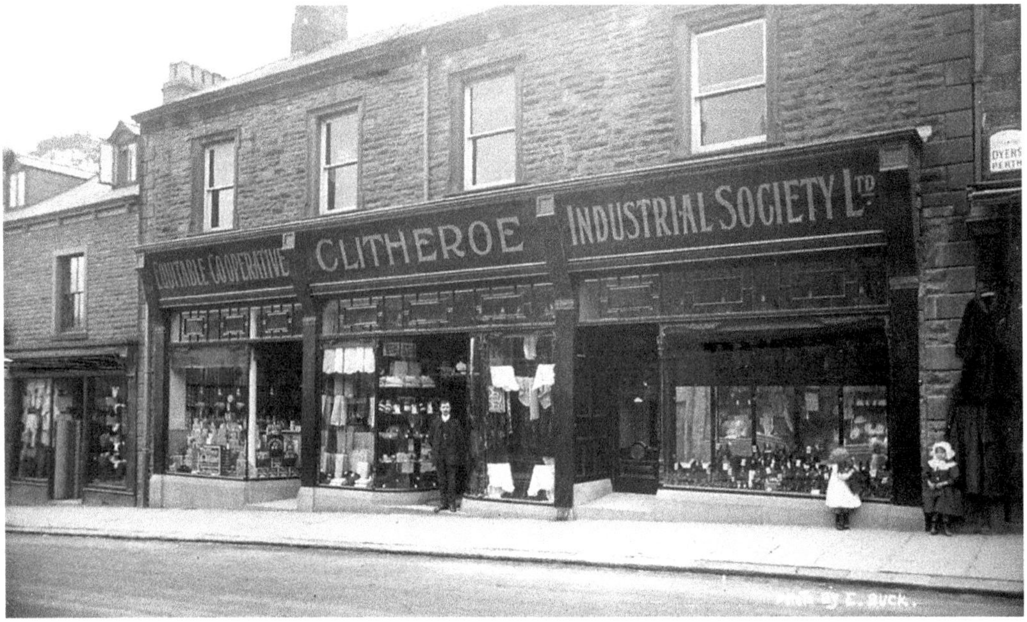

Figure 20 – The Clitheroe Cooperative Society's central store in Moor Lane

Source: Clitheroe public library local studies collection.

who received an average dividend of *2s 3d* in the pound on annual sales of £14,054. The membership increased steadily throughout the nineteenth century, in 1883 for example it had reached 539.[32] Subsequently further shops were opened in Salthill Road (1902), Victoria Street (1905), Peel Street (1906), De Lacy Street (1908), Chatburn (1909), Waddington Road (1915) and Henthorne Road (1929). There was also a bakery attached to the Victoria Street store, butchery departments in Lowergate, Henthorne and Woone Lane, and a hall and warehouse in King Lane.[33]

This was an impressive achievement for textile workers unfamiliar with the requirements of running a business in a town already replete with retail outlets, but Clitheroe's success was not unusual, for the co-operative movement grew rapidly in the late-nineteenth and early-twentieth centuries. Within the constituency's boundaries several other societies were established and did well. Low Moor had two, the first opened in 1859 and thus pre-dated Clitheroe's, the second in 1869. They had 131 members between them in 1893 and made a combined net profit of £816.[34] The Colne Society began trading in 1870 and had 4,830 members by 1909. The Sabden Society, too, was formed in 1870, by employees of the village mills. The population was religiously diverse and provided loyal Roman Catholic, Anglican and

Nonconformist congregations, but the Old Testament Christian names of many society officers – Elijah Birtwell, Hezekiah Wood and Abraham Haworth for example – suggests that local co-operation was run by Baptists and Methodists. However that may be, it has been estimated that four fifths of families used the shop, including those of rival shopkeepers, so economic as well as religious dissent played an important part in life in Sabden.[35]

There were also co-ops with healthy memberships in Padiham, Barrowford, Nelson, and Billington and Whalley, but membership did not necessarily indicate dissent, for many undoubtedly joined for the 'divi' rather than to deal a blow to capitalism. Nevertheless there is evidence of Clitheroe area cooperators becoming involved in the movement's wider aims of promoting thrift, education and political consciousness among the working class. The Sabden Society had a penny bank, made regular contributions to the village library, and organised a series of public lectures,[36] and Mrs Berry spoke on 'Social Problems and Cooperative Development' in Clitheroe.[37] This does not suggest intense activism, and society directors complained about member-apathy when only a handful attended quarterly or annual general meetings, but in Clitheroe as elsewhere cooperation gave the working class the chance to gain organisational experience and to express opinions at the ballot box. The issue then may only have been the composition of the next committee, but a sense of political participation was being nurtured and this would help the development of the working-class political parties then being formed. When this was achieved the issue would be the composition of the next government.

Notes and References

1 D. Bythell, *The Hand-Loom Weavers : A Study of the English Cotton Industry during the Industrial Revolution* (CUP, Cambridge, 1969) pp. 190, 200-201.

2 N. Garnett, *Low Moor, Clitheroe : The History of a Hamlet* (Shireburn, Low Moor, 1930?) pp. 4-5. Clitheroe public library local studies collection, M31.

3 The Manchester dragoons, known as the Queen's Bays, were supplemented by several troops of Lord Ribblesdale's Yeomany Cavalry from Gisburn. See A. Langshaw, *A Child's History of Clitheroe* (Advertiser and Times, Clitheroe, 1938) p. 79.

4 E. Hopwood, *The Lancashire Weavers' Story : A History of the Lancashire Cotton Industry and the Amalgamated Weavers' Association* (Amalgamated Weavers' Association, Manchester, 1969) pp. 37-40. At first unionists met in fields and barns to prevent employers learning of their intentions. In 1905 The Weavers' Institute was opened in Whalley Road by the Clitheroe Labour MP, David Shackleton.

5 *Ibid.*, p. 48. The Clitheroe union affiliated to the East Lancashire Association in 1866 or 1867. For the masters' view of the strike see O. Ashmore, Part 1, *op.cit.*, p. 87. For the workers' view see J. O'Neil, *op.cit.*, p. xix.

6 J. O'Neil, *op.cit.*, pp. xx, 92-121. J. Watts, *The Workman's Bane and Antidote* (Ireland and Co., Manchester, 1861) pp. 31-46.

7 O. Ashmore, Part 1, *op.cit.*, p. 90.

8 The eleven, and the years they started production, were: -

Low Moor	1782	Salford Bridge	late 1820s
Primrose	1788	Waterloo	1858
Upbrooks	1790	Albion	1860
Shaw Bridge Old	1790s	Shaw Bridge New	1860
Pendle	1807	Victoria	1861
Holme	1823		

See M. Rothwell, *Industrial Heritage. A Guide to the Industrial Archaeology of the Ribble Valley* (Bridgestone, Accrington, 1990) pp. 6-17.

9 *Preston Chronicle*, 23 March 1861, p. 6.

10 J. O'Neil, *op.cit.*, pp. xxi–xxiv.

11 O. Ashmore, Part 2, *op.cit.*, p. 111.

12 J. King, ' "We Could Eat The Police!" Popular Violence in the North Lancashire Cotton Strike of 1878', in *Victorian Studies*, (3, 28, 1985), p. 439.

13 The leader of this attack was James Smalley, an Irishman known locally as 'Pat Riley' or 'Seamus O'Malley'. Armed with a cutlass he threatened to kill

Jackson and rape his maidservants. Together with John Watson he was jailed for 15 years for his part in the 1878 strike, four others received sentences of between seven and ten years. See J. King, *op.cit.*, p. 469.

14 See J. King, *op.cit.*, pp. 443-456; S. Clarke, *op.cit.*, pp. 78-89; E. Hopwood, *op.cit.*, pp. 50-51.

15 *Blackburn Standard*, 29 September 1888, p. 3.

16 *Manchester Courier and Lancashire General Advertiser*, 14 February 1885, p. 6.

17 *Burnley Express*, 1 September 1888, pp. 4 and 8; 8 September 1888, p. 5.

18 *Ibid.*, 31 August 1887, p. 3.

19 *Clitheroe Times*, 11 January 1889, a two page special supplement; 15 February 1889, p. 5; 28 June 1889, p. 4; 30 August 1889, p. 5.

20 *Lancashire Evening Post*, 20 May 1891, p. 3; *Manchester Courier and Lancashire General Advertiser*, 13 August 1891, p. 4; *Burnley Express*, 22 August 1891, p. 5.

21 *Blackburn Standard*, 3 September 1898, p. 5.

22 P. Clarke, *op.cit.*, 'Railway Days', pp. 188 and 216.

23 P. Clarke, *op.cit.*, 'Coaching Days', pp. 50-51.

24 P. Clarke, *op.cit.*, 'Railway Days', pp. 123-124, 253-356.

25 A *Monthly Advertiser* was published between 1855 and 1857 and a *Weekly Advertiser* in 1885, but these were lists of local events and advertisements for local businesses, not newspapers. See Clitheroe public library local studies collection, A014.

26 J. O'Neil, *op.cit.*, p. 130.

27 M. O'Brien, *Perish the Privileged Orders : A Social History of the Chartist Movement* (New Clarion Press, Cheltenham, 2009) p. 50.

28 P. Firth, 'Temperance and politics in north east Lancashire, c. 1890 to c. 1910', in *Transactions of the Lancashire and Cheshire Antiquarian Society* (89, 1993) pp. 74-90 *passim.*

29 J. O'Neil, *op.cit.*, p. 108.

30 *Preston Guardian*, 22 June 1861, p. 6, 13 May 1868, p. 6.

31 *Clitheroe Advertiser and Times*, 7 July 1944, p. 5. The details there provided were taken from the Society's minute books, since lost.

32 *Preston Herald*, 3 June 1883, p. 4.

33 *Ibid.* For Thomas Smithies' role in the 1861 strike see *Preston Chronicle*, 16 March 1861, p. 6. The Co-operative Hall in King Lane was opened in 1915 as an exhibition space and social centre for members.

34 *The Times*, 1 July 1893, p. 5. J. Walton, 'The Making of a Mass Movement : The Growth of Co-operative Society Membership in Lancashire 1870-1914',

in B. Lancaster and P. Maguire (eds.), *Towards the Co-operative Commonwealth. Essays in the History of Co-operation* (Co-operative College and History Workshop Trust, Manchester, 1996) p. 24.

35 J. Smith and J. Walton, *op.cit.*, p. 135. *Sabden Industrial Co-operative Society Minute Book*, Lancashire Archives, DDX 7151/1. Birtwell was a committee man in the 1890s, Wood and Haworth presidents in 1903 and 1912 respectively.

36 *Sabden Industrial Co-operative Society Minute Book*, 20 March and 18 September 1900.

37 *Burnley Express*, 24 November 1900, p. 6.

Chapter 4
The Rise Of The Labour Party

The political struggle that culminated in the election of working men to represent the interests of the working class can be traced back to the Chartist Movement. The People's Charter of 1838 had much support in the north west. It demanded political equality and accountability through a programme of reforms embodied in the so-called 'Six Points' – the vote for all adult males; the secret ballot; the creation of electoral districts of equal size; payment of MPs; the abolition of the property qualification for those wishing to stand as MPs; and annual parliaments. Only by such means, the Chartists argued, could oppressive legislation be prevented. They had in mind particularly the Poor Law Amendment Act of 1834 which replaced existing means of poor relief with the workhouse system. Care of the poor was a parish responsibility, and in the nineteenth century those in need in the Clitheroe area received it either in their own homes or in poor houses at Chipping, Aighton and Holden. The financial burden that this arrangement put on ratepayers led to pressure for it to be replaced by a cheaper alternative. It came in the form of union workhouses, purpose built for each group of parishes. In future the poor would only receive relief if they entered them and accepted inferior maintenance and degrading regulations which required, for example, that families be split, women and children being separated from men.

The new workhouses enabled the cost of poor relief to be significantly reduced but they were hated by those who had to use them, and petitions against the Poor Law Amendment Act were submitted to parliament from Bolton-by-Bowland, Bashall Eaves, Chatburn, Downham, Grindleton, Sawley, Rimington, Twiston, Whalley, Slaidburn, Waddington, Trawden and Barrowford, as well as from Clitheroe.[1] The union workhouse for the area between Burnley and Lancaster was built at Coplow on the northern outskirts of Clitheroe, and it was more humanely run than some.[2] Nevertheless the 1834 changes in provision for the poor contributed to the development of the Chartist movement because they highlighted the helplessness of the voteless in the face of callous or indifferent governments.

Chartism galvanised the working class by its strategy of petitioning parliament to accept the Six Points. Between one and six million signatures were collected for the National Petitions of 1839, 1842 and 1848, but all three were rejected by overwhelming majorities, and other tactics were tried, including industrial sabotage and the creation of communities of farmer-Chartists.

Clitheroe was involved with Chartism from the start. A branch of the National Charter Association (NCA) was established in the town with offices in York Street and a membership of over 400 by 1840, a development that so alarmed local magistrates that special constables were sworn in to deal with disturbances which might arise from 'unlawful meetings or other proceedings'.[3] There is no evidence that Clitheroe NCA members were violent, but they signed all the National Petitions and famous Chartist speakers were regularly hosted in the town. In June 1842, for example, a crowd of 1,200 heard Peter McDouall criticise the government for denying working men a say in how the country was run.[4] The venue was on the lower slopes of Pendle, at a location still marked on maps as 'Chartists Well'. The meeting was monitored by the police and infiltrated by government spies who would later give evidence at a trial of Chartists in Lancaster. A few weeks later Feargus O'Connor visited Clitheroe. He was the best known of the Chartist leaders and vast numbers wanted to hear him, but he spoke only from a platform set up in 'a walled bowling green' and to smaller groups in the Swan and Royal Hotel and the Commercial Inn.[5]

O'Connor's visit marked the high point of Chartism in Clitheroe. In the early 1840s local supporters had hoped to see a Chartist candidate contest a parliamentary election in the constituency,[6] but by September 1843 delegates to a meeting of north Lancashire Chartists held in Accrington complained of falling memberships. Blame for this was attributed to the Plug Plot, an attempt during the previous year to force the government to accept the Six Points by removing plugs from factory boilers and halting production. But Clitheroe Chartists preferred constitutional protest, and some of them were amongst the 70,000 who subscribed to the Land Plan, a scheme to provide houses and allotments that would give economic independence and a better standard of living to those who took part. Five such settlements were established, but none nearer than Worcestershire, and it is not known if any of the Clitheroe subscribers who applied for places were successful.[7] Indeed it is difficult to identify any local Chartists from surviving sources, although Henry Ainsworth of Woone Lane and Robert Birtwell of Whalley are named as such in a retrospective article in the *Burnley Express*.[8]

Perhaps the only Chartist associated with the movement's militant wing who had links with Clitheroe was Richard Marsden, the town's representative at the National Convention of 1843.[9] However there may have been others, for contemporary press coverage often frustrates precision by using impersonal references such as 'the Clitheroe delegate who stated that democratic feeling and hatred of injustice and oppression was strong'.[10] Nevertheless it is clear that Clitheroe was an important Chartist centre. Its 400 NCA members outnumbered Colne's by almost two to one, and Blackburn, a town five times the size of Clitheroe in 1841, had a membership of under 300.[11] Too much can be made of these statistics, for most Chartists never joined the Association, but the figure for Clitheroe disturbs the usual characterisation of Chartism as an urban phenomenon. There were NCA branches in Grindleton and Sabden as well, and this rural part of Lancashire was one of only two locations in the north west to be represented on the NCA Executive in 1849.[12]

The Sabden branch was particularly well supported. It had been formed in 1838 at the Black Bull Inn under the chairmanship of Enoch Foster, and Frederick Ainsworth's beerhouse in Step Row became its weekly meeting place. James Howarth was branch treasurer, and John Pollard secretary. He is credited with recruiting up to 300 members and for regular sales of 44 copies of the Chartist newspaper *Northern* Star, remarkable figures for a village with a population of about 1,200.[13] Leaders of the Baptist church were active Sabden Chartists. Its deacon, Henry Wood, chaired the Chartists Well meeting and the Reverend Charles Kirkland, pastor from 1846 to 1851, was a keen branch member and a vigorous campaigner against Church rates.[14]

Those who saw Chartism as the best route to working class influence on government were disappointed, for the movement was over by 1858. Competition from the Anti-Corn Law League partly explains this. It had a branch in Clitheroe, and was strong throughout textile districts because mill workers were persuaded by the League's contention that restricting the import of corn made bread more expensive, and factory owners believed protective tariffs such as the Corn Laws would make selling their cloth abroad harder. The Ten Hours Act of 1847 which improved working conditions in the mills, the use of the army to prevent mass demonstrations, and the movement's divided leadership also contributed to its failure. Some Chartists would have lived to see the extension of the franchise in 1867 and the introduction of the secret ballot in 1872, but it was their successors in the new working-class political parties of the later nineteenth century who adapted and fulfilled the Chartist programme.

*

The Reform Act of 1884 extended the franchise to men in rural districts who met the qualification previously restricted to borough residents, that is to say those who paid rates or rent of more than £10 annually. This still left some adult males, and all females, without the vote, but it increased the working-class electorate everywhere and political parties tried to attract it. The earliest opportunity they had for this was the General Election of 1885, the first to be contested in a redefined Clitheroe division which now included not only more rural voters but urban voters from industrial communities such as Nelson and Colne. Many of them favoured the Liberal Party as the more likely to introduce the social reforms they wanted, and its representative, Sir Ughtred Kay Shuttleworth, easily won the seat. He retained it at subsequent elections until his elevation to the peerage in 1902, but the idea of opposing him with a working-class candidate began ten years earlier.

In the run up to the 1892 General Election most trade unions with branches in the constituency were prepared to support Sir Ughtred again, but the Padiham Weavers and Spinners, and the Nelson Plumbers, preferred to nominate a Blackpool builders' labourer named Burbridge. The plan was dropped for lack of sufficient backing and Kay-Shuttleworth duly defeated his Conservative challenger, receiving 836 more votes than in 1885.[15] He regarded his win 'as a vote of confidence by the working men of this constituency',[16] but in fact it marked the beginning of working-class rejection of the Liberals as the guardians of their interests.

*

North Lancashire has a claim to have been the cradle of British socialism, for the Social Democratic Federation (SDF) was strong in Burnley, the Independent Labour Party (ILP) in Nelson, and the branches of both which were formed in communities throughout the Clitheroe parliamentary constituency helped to secure victory for a Labour candidate in the by-election of 1902. The SDF was founded by Henry Hyndman in 1884. Its philosophy was informed by the ideas of Thomas Carlyle, who indicted capitalism in *Past and Present* (1843), and of Henry George, who blamed social inequality on *laissez-faire* economics in *Progress and Poverty* (1881). In the same year Hyndman's assessment of Marx was published in a cheap edition under the title *England for All*, and became the Federation's most influential text. It persuaded the socialist poet Edward Carpenter to finance

Justice, the weekly paper through which the SDF promoted its programme of collective control of the means of production, distribution and exchange. The Federation has been called 'the most important school for working-class militants and activists, exercising a disproportionately large influence in relation to its size'.[17] Many future Labour Party luminaries such as James Ramsay MacDonald, George Lansbury and Margaret Bondfield were introduced to socialism through the SDF. So was Thomas Duckworth Benson.

Benson was already treasurer of the New Church Socialist Society and editor of its journal *Uses* when he moved to Clitheroe in the early 1890s, but he was also an estate agent and a wealthy man. His two younger sons, Eric and Alfred, were born in the town and their elder brother George, who later

Figure 21 – The Big Lamp, Market Place

Source: The Shaw Collection, Clitheroe public library.

The traditional Clitheroe location for public speaking by visiting politicians, shown here after the redevelopment of the north side of Market Place in the early twentieth century.

became a Labour MP, attended the Royal Grammar School. The Bensons lived at Robey House, half a mile along the Whalley road from Clitheroe. Between 1895 and 1901 it became a powerhouse of the progressive ideas generated not only by T. D. but by his regular visitors Harry Quelch, Tom Mann, James Keir Hardie, James Ramsay MacDonald, Katherine and John Bruce Glasier and Philip Snowden, all of whom tested their views in speeches made to the Clitheroe public from the big lamp in Market Place.[18] (See Figure 21.)

T. D. Benson was one of four socialists who were elected to the Board of Guardians of the union workhouse in the 1890s. The group, which also included Miles Lord, Robert Jones and William Sutcliffe, tried to protect the political rights of inmates, for example by arguing against a majority of the guardians that those who were forced to seek temporary relief through ill health or injury at work should not be disenfranchised.[19] (See p. 149 below.) It was T. D's initiative, too, that led to the formation of a branch of the SDF in the town. Its initial membership was only 12, a number which included four women, but in 1896 premises were acquired in Greenacre Street, by 1897 the membership had grown to 140 and Frederick Alder had been appointed its first secretary. Sought-after SDF orators addressed the Clitheroe branch, locals like Isobel Tiplady and Tom Hurley from Blackburn often, and in 1902 the celebrated Mr Gee of Northampton, whose lecture on 'The History of the Class Struggle' was so well attended that it had to be delivered not in the Greenacre Street room but outside, in Market Place.[20] By that time, however, the focus of Benson's dissent had switched to the Independent Labour Party. At its inaugural conference held in Bradford in 1893 the ILP adopted a reform programme that included the abolition of child labour under the age of 14; a working day of eight hours; state provision for the aged, the sick, the disabled, and for widows and orphans; taxation to extinction of unearned incomes; and the democratisation of government. But there was also an ethical aspect to the ILP's philosophy that appealed to T. D. Benson, and he tried to implement it in his daily life by encouraging a sense of comradeship through cultural and recreational clubs, and by a personal commitment to moral improvement. So he supported the idea of Socialist Sunday Schools such as the one in Nelson because they used alternative 'commandments' like 'love learning which is the food of the mind', 'be a friend to the weak' and 'look forward to the day when all men will be free citizens'.[21]

The reason for Benson's move into the ILP is not clear, but at its 1894 conference an SDF resolution for the amalgamation of the two groups was defeated. This disappointed T. D. who, like many socialists, was open-minded, pragmatic and anxious to forge stronger links with other organisations of the political Left. He welcomed the formation of the Labour Representation Committee (LRC) in 1900 which aimed to establish separate Labour representation more firmly in parliament after the ILP's 29 candidates were all defeated in the 1895 General Election. Both the ILP and SDF affiliated to the LRC, but the SDF withdrew when its call for class war was rejected in 1901. That might also have prompted Benson's withdrawal from the SDF. He was still representing it at political meetings in 1899, but in 1901 he became Treasurer of the ILP, an office he held for the next 20 years.[22] He also became one of the ILP's most persuasive polemicists, the author of numerous pamphlets arguing its cause.

One of his favourite techniques was to compare socialism to a family whose wellbeing is held in trust by the parents for the use of its members in common, an arrangement which mirrored nature and allowed the economy to be run in the service of the community. The implication of this was collective ownership, which would improve mankind by nurturing humanity whilst also providing it with material benefits.[23] Benson supported his case with examples of effective communism such as that practiced by early Christians, and of individuals from the recent past whose behaviour had shown that man is not naturally selfish, Robert Burns, Charles Darwin, Thomas Huxley, William Gladstone and William Morris amongst them.[24] T. D. also argued that the oppression of women, and their exclusion from all but domestic roles, was not only iniquitous but harmful to the national interest because it wasted their talents.[25] His plea for votes for women and a revision of the discriminatory laws governing marriage place Benson in the forefront of male feminists of his time.[26] (See Figure 22.)

*

Nelson's SDF was formed in 1891. It attracted fewer members than its Clitheroe counterpart, but it had a good working relationship with the town's ILP branch, and this made it an effective political force in the 1890s.[27] Both parties had representation on the Nelson Weavers' Association executive during that decade, and were thus able to influence the selection of trade union officials and Trades Council sponsored candidates for municipal government seats. It was a partnership that led to the joint SDF/ILP publishing venture *Socialist Journal*, a four page penny monthly which built up a circulation of about 4,000 between 1893 and 1906, and to the interest shown by leading figures on the political Left in visiting the area. Further instances of united action in a common cause occurred in 1895 when the Nelson Ratepayers Association, which was dominated by SDF

Figure 22 – T. D. Benson

Source: ILP.

Benson promoted the SDF and the ILP in Clitheroe. The meeting place in Greenacre Street was known as the Socialist Clubroom, and hosted visitors from both parties. In 1896, for example, the official opening was attended by James Keir Hardie, John and Katherine Bruce Glasier, and Katherine Conway of the ILP, as well as Isobel Tiplady and Tom Hurley of the SDF. The audience included some who had joined one of these groups, and many who had joined both.

and ILP members, charged the Liberal-run Town Council with corruption, a campaign vindicated when the Borough Treasurer was found guilty of embezzlement, and when the police were shown to have disrupted their open air meetings.[28]

Yet each party had a distinct identity in Nelson. The SDF was Marxist and secular, indeed atheist, for it did not allow practicing Christians to become members. Its leaders were mainly small tradesmen like Walter Parrett and the branch chairman Walter Birtles who were building contractors, and J. W. Horsfall and Ernest Johnson who were managers of local cooperative stores. Little is known of the rank and file, but Miss B. Stacey was a university graduate, and all of the Nelson Cooperative Society committee were SDF members. By contrast the ILP was non-Marxist and Christian, drawing much of its support from the town's many nonconformist congregations, and it was preferred by mill workers who were ethical socialists, temperance practitioners and trade unionists.[29] Accommodating these differences in the 1890s was a notable achievement, but the accord did not long survive the start of the new century. The catalyst for the rupture was the formation of the LRC in 1900. The ILP affiliated immediately but the SDF did not, instead it attacked the LRC candidate for the Clitheroe seat in the 1902 parliamentary by-election as a capitalist sympathiser.

*

By 1900 the concept of separate Labour representation in parliament had stalled. The Trades Union Congress (TUC) had established a Labour Electoral Committee in 1886, but its aim was to promote the return of more working men to parliament, not to create a Labour Party.[30] It worked in conjunction with the Liberal Party in selected, mostly mining constituencies, and successful candidates sat as 'Lib-Lab' members who took the Liberal whip but expressed the views of the TUC on matters of industrial policy and labour relations. Until 1901 the TUC was content to pursue its interests by this means. Consequently the independent Labour presence in the House of Commons was limited to James Keir Hardie, MP for Merthyr Tydfil, and Richard Bell, who represented Derby.[31] In 1901 a legal decision altered this situation. The Taff Vale Railway Company sued the Amalgamated Society of Railway Servants for profits lost during a strike and was awarded £23,000 in compensation, a judgement which exposed all trade unions to similar sanctions and rendered them impotent in future negotiations with their employers. The failure of the Liberal Party to take the Railway Servants' side ended its understanding with the TUC. Separate Labour representation gained from this, for the LRC condemned the Taff Vale decision and henceforth the Labour Party became the natural home of dissident trade unionists.

The first opportunity the LRC had to test shifting voter loyalty was at the Clitheroe by-election necessitated by Sir Ughtred Kay-Shuttleworth's move to the House of Lords. Some unions within the constituency had already responded to the Taff Vale case by declaring that they would no longer put their trust 'in landowners and other members of the capitalist class', but rather send to parliament 'a few able men of our own to take their places'.[32] Their choice in 1902 was David Shackleton, vice-president of the Northern Counties Weavers' Amalgamation, who won the LRC nomination when Philip Snowden of the ILP withdrew. Neither was a local man, but Shackleton was from the nearby Rossendale Valley and Snowden had lived for ten years in Nelson before it became part of the Clitheroe constituency. The records of the Labour Representation Conference held in Colne on 5 July 1902 show that the 81 delegates represented trade union, cooperative society, ILP and SDF branches throughout the division, and that national figures such as James Ramsay MacDonald of the LRC and James Sexton of the TUC were also in attendance.[33] The minutes of the meeting indicate that Shackleton was adopted unanimously (see Figure 23) and the candidate himself claimed such was the case, but contemporary press accounts dispute this, citing a disagreement between the Clitheroe and Nelson SDF branches about Shackleton's suitability.[34] The SDF would certainly have preferred a more avowedly socialist candidate, and the ending of its previously harmonious partnership with the ILP in Nelson three months later may have had its origins in Shackleton's selection, but for the time being differences were suppressed in the interests of unity. The official view followed that of the most influential group at the conference, the weavers' unions:

> 'It is not a Socialist we want…but a Labour man. The textile workers of Clitheroe…feel that they ought to have a representative of their own in Parliament'.[35]

In fact Shackleton's election manifesto was thoroughly socialist. His priorities were topical – overturning the Taff Vale decision and improving the 1897 Workmen's Compensation Act so that more help would be given to those injured in the workplace – but he also demanded pensions for the over 60s, cheap rail travel, Home Rule for Ireland, free secular and technical education, and payment of MPs. It could be argued that a Liberal Party manifesto would have included many of these features, but not adult suffrage, abolition of the House of Lords and 'the nationalisation of Land, Mines, Minerals and Railways'. (See Figure 24.)

The manifesto's socialist content was necessary because the LRC expected to face a Liberal challenge from Philip Stanhope, a former MP for Burnley who was considered to be a friend of labour, but indecision among the Liberal leadership about the advisability of opposing a union candidate who might be persuaded to fit the Lib-Lab mould in due course, caused his withdrawal. (See Figure 25.) As a replacement could not be found, and the Conservative also withdrew, Shackleton had the field to himself, but fearing last minute nominations the LRC drafted in MacDonald, Snowden and other well known Labour figures to campaign on his behalf. Their efforts were unnecessary, for at 12.30 p.m. on 1 August Shackleton's uncontested victory was announced from Clitheroe Town Hall.[36] He had become only the third Member of Parliament to be elected on a ticket of separate working-class representation.

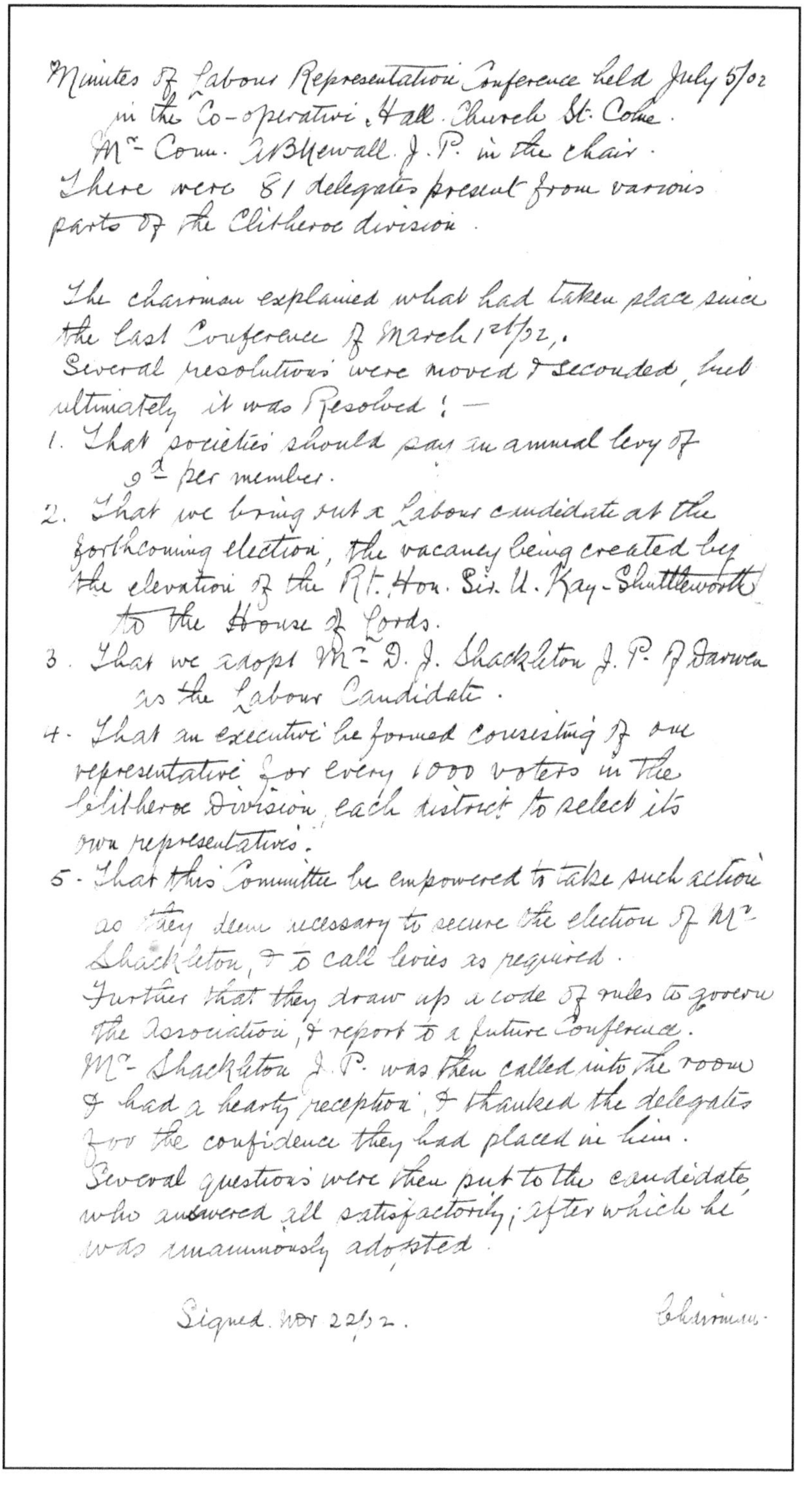

Minutes of Labour Representation Conference held July 5/02 in the Co-operative Hall. Church St. Colne.
Mr Coun. W. B. Newall J.P. in the chair.
There were 81 delegates present from various parts of the Clitheroe division.

The chairman explained what had taken place since the last Conference of March 1st/02.
Several resolutions were moved & seconded, but ultimately it was Resolved: —

1. That societies should pay an annual levy of 9d per member.
2. That we bring out a Labour candidate at the forthcoming election, the vacancy being created by the elevation of the Rt. Hon. Sir U. Kay-Shuttleworth to the House of Lords.
3. That we adopt Mr D. J. Shackleton J.P. of Darwen as the Labour Candidate.
4. That an executive be formed consisting of one representative for every 1000 voters in the Clitheroe Division, each district to select its own representatives.
5. That this Committee be empowered to take such action as they deem necessary to secure the election of Mr Shackleton, & to call levies as required.

Further that they draw up a code of rules to govern the Association, & report to a future Conference.
Mr Shackleton J.P. was then called into the room & had a hearty reception, & thanked the delegates for the confidence they had placed in him.
Several questions were then put to the candidate, who answered all satisfactorily; after which he was unanimously adopted.

Signed. Nov 22/02. Chairman.

Figure 23 – The minutes of the first meeting of the Clitheroe LRC indicating the unanimous adoption of David Shackleton as the constituency's candidate for the parliamentary by-election of 1902.

TO THE ELECTORS

OF THE

CLITHEROE DIVISION OF LANCASHIRE.

GENTLEMEN,

At a Conference of Trade Unionists and other Progressive bodies, held at Colne, on Saturday, July 5th, I was unanimously invited to submit myself as a Candidate at the Parliamentary Bye-Election in your Division, and I have had very great pleasure in accepting that invitation.

In soliciting your votes and support, I can assure you that, if elected, I shall spare no effort to obtain those Legislative Reforms for the Workers and the people of this country which are so much needed.

Many matters directly affecting the interest of labour require the immediate attention of Parliament. The recent decision in the Taff Vale Case, coupled with the decision in the Lyons *v.* Wilkins Case, affect the responsibilities of Trades Unions and the important question of Picketing. They demand serious attention, and I should support reforms of the laws so that workers may have a position equitable with that of their employers.

The Compensation Act of 1897 requires amendment in certain important particulars. Workpeople should be paid from the first day of absence from work through accident, and their compensation based on the wages they earned when in full employment. They should be paid 50 per cent. of the amount of their earnings, and this compensation should be the limit instead of the £1 per week limit allowed under the present Act of Parliament. Young persons injured when following their employment should have compensation assessed on their prospective earnings, that is: a young person permanently disabled when only in the receipt of 2/6 or 3/- per week should have a greater sum allowed than 50 per cent. of that amount. The 30 feet limit should be abolished, and the Act ought to be extended to workers in every trade. In many other respects amendment of the provisions of the Act are urgently required.

The question of the provision of Old Age Pensions requires the early attention of Parliament. I am prepared to support a scheme, universal in application, for the payment of not less than 5/- per week to all persons when they attain the age of 60.

Of supreme importance to the workers in this country is the Housing Question, and I am convinced that it should be compulsory upon public bodies to erect healthy dwellings in their respective districts.

My support would also be given to the movement for placing pressure upon the Board of Trade, to compel Railway Companies to strictly comply with the provisions of the Cheap Trains Act of 1883, by issuing cheap tickets to all classes of working-men, and by increasing the number of trains which may be found necessary to give to work-people the best facilities for travelling to and from their work.

The Miners' Eight Hours Bill has my heartiest support, and I favour the application of the eight hours principle to any trade where the responsible leaders and workers in that particular trade desire it to be introduced.

I am, of course, in full sympathy with the principle of the direct Representation of the Workers in Parliament, and in order to bring this about speedily, should support the payment of Members of Parliament and the payment of official election expenses out of the public funds.

The Registration Laws should be simplified, so that it will be as easy for a man to be on the register of voters as it is for him to be on the rate book—in fact, the rate book in my opinion, should be the register. The responsibility for the name of every person entitled to vote being upon the register should rest with the public bodies or public officials, and not with the agents of political parties.

The question of Adult Suffrage has my sympathy, and I also believe in the principle of one man one vote. Further, I believe there should be immediate amendment of the laws relating to the Franchise, so that women may rank as voters, and be in exactly the same position in all respects as men.

Apart from matters which directly interest and affect trades unionists, I have always allied myself with, and worked for, movements of a progressive character.

I am a Free Trader, and would oppose any proposal that violated its principles.

I am also in favour of the Nationalisation of Land, Mines, Minerals and Railways, believing that we should obtain possession of all monopolies.

I am in favour of Shorter Parliaments, and of the Abolition of the House of Lords, being of opinion that the House as at present constituted, is at variance with the principle of government by the people.

In all International Disputes, I favour Arbitration being tried as a means of settlement.

The Licensing Laws have had close consideration for many years, and the moderate proposals contained in the minority report, signed by Lord Peel, would receive my support, in addition to any other practicable measure brought before Parliament with the object of lessening the evils of intemperance.

In the matter of Education, we ought not in any respect, to be behind any of the other nations with whom we have to compete in industry and commerce. Therefore I should support the free provision of secular and technical education, and give all classes equal opportunity.

I am a supporter of the principle of Home Rule.

For a number of years I have been connected with the Blackburn Chamber of Commerce, and have had opportunities for studying commercial questions from a perfectly independent standpoint. I believe that the knowledge thus obtained will be of great assistance to me when matters relating to trade and commerce are under discussion in the House of Commons.

The particular needs of this Constituency, and the welfare of our Empire, are matters which shall have my constant and close attention, and if you honour me by electing me to be your representative in Parliament, I shall spare no effort to prove to you that your confidence is not misplaced.

I am, Gentlemen, your obedient servant,

The Weavers' Association Office,
Darwen.

David J. Shackleton.

Figure 24 – David Shackleton's manifesto for the 1902 by-election

Source: Clitheroe public library local studies collection.

*

Shackleton's success at Clitheroe provided a great fillip to the Labour movement both locally and nationally. Party and trade union membership increased, a new ILP branch was formed in Brierfield, and seats were won in municipal elections.[37] Shackleton's insistence that he would not be manipulated by Liberals, socialists or trade unions also accelerated the cause of separate Labour representation and helped the LRC to win further by-elections in Woolwich and Barnard Castle in 1903.[38]

The minutes of the Clitheroe branch make it clear that the LRC's aim was to form 'a distinct group in Parliament', not a socialist party, although membership was open to all progressive organisations and individuals whether socialist or not.[39] On this basis Shackleton received his £300 salary as an MP not from the Textile Workers' Association, which was prepared to pay it, but from the LRC.[40] The subject of his first speech to the constituency after the by-election, and of his maiden speech in the House of Commons, was not a union related matter but education, reflecting his position as vice-president of the Northern Education League which opposed the Conservative government's Education Bill. Later Shackleton also used his influence to support female suffrage, temperance reform, the cooperative movement and the Association to Promote the Higher Education of Working Men (better known as the Workers' Educational Association), and he represented the LRC at the 1904 Congress of the Second International which was held in Amsterdam.[41]

It was an auspicious beginning to Shackleton's parliamentary career, gaining him a reputation for assiduous effort on behalf of the LRC and for conscientious attention to the concerns of his constituents.[42] His readoption as the LRC's Clitheroe candidate for the General Election of 1906 was therefore expected, but the size of his victory was stunning, for he polled 12,035 votes in a 77 per cent turnout which gave him a majority of 8,207 over his independent challenger Bernard Belton, a Surrey brewer whose only link with the area was that he was educated at Stoneyhurst, the nearby Roman Catholic public school.[43] 1906 was the year of the Liberals' famous landslide, which enabled them to form a government with a majority of

THE POSITION AT CLITHEROE.

First HOOLIGAN—"You have a go at him."
Second HOOLIGAN—"No; you knock him down and I'll jump on him."

Figure 25 – Press comment on the indecision of the rival parties that allowed Shackleton to win the 1902 Clitheroe by-election unchallenged

Source: *Daily Dispatch*, 14 July 1902.

130 over all other parties. The LRC won 30 seats, changed its name to the Labour Party, and re-elected Keir Hardie chairman, but Shackleton came within one vote of beating him for the position and had clearly established himself as the coming man, a potential future leader. In the new parliament he was credited with persuading Asquith to introduce a Trade Disputes Bill which would give unions effective protection against the sort of legal challenge presented by the Taff Vale case. This further strengthened

Shackleton's standing within the Labour Party, and after fulfilling the role of acting chairman during Keir Hardie's illness in 1907 it was expected that he would soon succeed him.

In fact Shackleton declined to participate in the 1908 leadership election, and it was Arthur Henderson who became the new chairman. It was a development which coincided with Shackleton's greater involvement in a Home Office investigation into the use of artificial humidity in cotton mills, and with his growing influence on the TUC Parliamentary Committee. These moves distanced him from the socialist wing of the Labour Party

Figure 26 – David Shackleton, Member of Parliament for the Clitheroe constituency 1902–10

Source: John Smith.

just as it was celebrating the addition of a new star to its ranks, for the charismatic Victor Grayson had won the Colne Valley by-election in 1907.

Shackleton did not support Grayson's campaign, but for the moment he tried to maintain his often stated position that the Labour Party should be an alliance of socialists and trade unionists, and he made an important intervention in the debate about the Osborne Judgement.[44] This concerned the decision by the House of Lords in 1909 to forbid trade unions the right to use their members' subscriptions 'for political purposes', that is to say in support of the Labour Party. Shackleton's speech did much to unify the Labour movement against the prohibition, although he resisted attempts to involve him in the formation of a non-socialist Labour Party. So when a general election was called in January 1910 he was again adopted as the candidate for the Clitheroe division, and although he faced much stiffer opposition this time, from Tom Smith, a Conservative working man from Burnley who had become a lecturer for the Tariff Reform League, he was returned with a majority of 6,727 in a turnout of 92 per cent.[45] There was a second election in 1910, in December, but by then David Shackleton had resigned his seat and become a civil servant, Senior Labour Advisor to the Home Office. (See Figure 26.)

Notes and References

1 D. Bythell, *op.cit.*, p. 248.

2 The process of change in provision for the poor in the Clitheroe area is complex. In 1838 some consolidation was achieved by closing Chipping workhouse but the resulting savings did not satisfy the Poor Law Board. Aighton and Holden were therefore closed as well, and a union workhouse which conformed to Poor Law Amendment Act requirements was built in Clitheroe, although it was not complete and operational until 1873. See F. Lofthouse, *Keepers of the House – A Workhouse Saga* (Hudson History, Settle, 2001) pp. 16-22.

3 *Blackburn Standard*, 14 August 1839.

4 *Northern Star*, 11 June 1842, p. 16.

5 *Ibid.*, 2 July 1842, p. 8; 9 July 1842, p. 17. The 'walled bowling green' was the Bowling Green Inn.

6 In 1847 W. Roberts stood as a Chartist in Blackburn, a major Chartist centre, and received 68 votes coming bottom of the poll. In the days of restricted franchise dissident candidacies were doomed to failure – of 23 attempts only one was successful, Feargus O'Connor winning Nottingham in 1847. See M. Chase, *The Chartists – Perspectives and Legacies* (Merlin, London, 2015) p. 157.

7 D. Thompson, *The Chartists* (Temple Smith, London, 1984) p. 347. M. Chase, *op.cit.*, p. 53. M. Chase, *Chartism. A New History* (MUP, Manchester, 2007) pp. 259-260.

8 *Burnley Express*, 29 September 1906, p. 6.

9 M. Chase, *Chartism. A New History, op.cit.*, p. 63. D. Bythell, *op.cit.*, p. 224.

10 *Northern Star*, 23 September 1843, p. 1.

11 D. Thompson, *op.cit.*, pp. 343 and 347.

12 M. Chase, *Chartism. A New History, op.cit.*, p. 331.

13 D. Bythell, *op.cit.*, p. 226. J. Smith and J. Walton, 'Property, Employment and the Co-operative Movement : The Social Structure of Co-operation in Sabden, 1923', in *Transactions of the Historic Society of Lancashire and Cheshire* (134, 1984) p. 134.

14 C. Moorhouse, *The Birth of a Lancashire Village*, Clitheroe public library local studies collection, E02 Sabden.

15 *Clitheroe Advertiser*, 20 May 1892, p. 2, 27 May p. 3; 10 June p. 2, 17 June p. 3, 24 June p. 2; 1 July p. 2, 8 July p. 2.

16 *Clitheroe Advertiser*, 15 July 1892, p. 2.

17 M. Crick, *The History of the Social Democratic Federation* (Ryburn, Keele, 1994) pp. 9-10.

18 George Benson represented the Chesterfield constituency as its Labour member from 1929-31 and 1935-1964. Robey House had previously been called Hornshaws and was later renamed Barraclough. Harry Quelch was editor of the SDF newspaper *Justice.* Tom Mann was prominent within the SDF and the trade union movement before joining the ILP and becoming its secretary. James Keir Hardie was the motive force behind the formation of the ILP, its chairman between 1893-1900 and in 1914, MP for West Ham South from 1892-1895 and for Merthyr Tydfil from 1900-1915. James Ramsay McDonald was a leading member of the ILP, Labour prime minister in 1924 and from 1929-1931, and prime minister of the National Government 1931-1935. John Bruce Glasier was on the ethical socialist wing of the ILP and its chairman from 1901-1903. Philip Snowden was chairman of the ILP from 1903-1906, MP for Blackburn from 1906-1918, and Chancellor of the Exchequer in the Labour governments of 1924 and 1929-31.

19 *Clitheroe Times,* 25 November 1898, p. 4.

20 *Clitheroe Advertiser,* 27 September 1895, p. 2; 1 August 1902, p. 7. *Clitheroe Advertiser and Times,* 14 March 1941, p. 4. S. Clarke, 'Railway Days', *op.cit.*, pp. 264-265.

21 R. Frow, 'Educating Socialists', *Working Class Movement Library Bulletin* (Working Class Movement Library, Salford, 2004) pp. 45-51.

22 *Blackburn Standard,* 13 May 1899, p. 6. Benson's switch to the ILP coincided with his move from Clitheroe to St. Annes, near Blackpool, although he may have retained SDF membership as well.

23 T. D. Benson, *Socialism* (ILP, London, 1908) p. 6.

24 *Ibid.*, p. 14. T. D. Benson, *Socialism and Service* (ILP, London, 1908) p. 5.

25 T. D. Benson, *Woman – the Communist* (ILP, London, 1908) pp. 7, 12 and 16.

26 The Council of the ILP attached a disclaimer to the 1908 issue of *Woman – the Communist* (p. 16) to indicate that the views expressed in it were those of the author, and not necessarily those of the ILP.

27 P. Firth, 'Socialism and the Origins of the Labour Party in Nelson and District 1890– 1906', MA, Manchester University, 1975, pp. 1-48. A direct comparison of memberships is difficult, but Nelson SDF had 84 members in 1894, Clitheroe 140 in 1897.

28 *Ibid.*, pp. 24, 41 and 45. Visitors included James Keir Hardie, James Ramsay MacDonald, Ben Tillett, J. R. Clynes, John Bruce Glasier, R. B. Cunninghame Graham, Philip Snowden, H. M. Hyndman, Harry Quelch, Tom Mann, the Countess of Warwick, Robert Blatchford, and Annie Besant.

29 *Ibid.*, pp. 19-20.

30 G. D. H. Cole, *A Short History of the British Working-Class Movement 1789-1947* (George Allen and Unwin, London, 1948) p. 231.

31 Richard Bell was elected in 1900. Derby was a railway town and Bell was an official of the Amalgamated Society of Railway Servants. He behaved in parliament much as the Lib-Lab members had done and was expelled from the Labour Party in 1905. See H. Pelling, *The Origins of the Labour Party 1880-1900* (Macmillan, London, 1954) p. 239.

32 *Nelson Chronicle*, 11 October 1901, p. 4.

33 *Colne and Nelson Times*, 11 July 1902, p. 2. The same issue, p. 5, contains a letter of best wishes for Shackleton's success from Ben Tillett.

34 The minutes, recently discovered by John Smith, will be deposited in the Working Class Movement Library. They are arranged chronologically but the pages are not numbered. See also *Northern Daily Telegraph*, 11 July 1902, pp. 2 and 3.

35 J. Burrows, *A Concise History of the Early Years of Nelson Independent Labour Party* (a private collection taken from the *Nelson Leader*, 29 September 1902). See also R. Martin, *The Lancashire Giant. David Shackleton, Labour Leader and Civil Servant* (Liverpool University Press, Liverpool, 2000) p. 35.

36 *Clitheroe Advertiser*, 1 August 1902, p. 2.

37 J. Burrows, *op.cit. Nelson Chronicle*, 7 November 1902, p. 4.

38 Will Crooks won Woolwich in March and Arthur Henderson won Barnard Castle in July 1903.

39 Clitheroe LRC minutes, 22 November 1902. Individuals had to pay an annual subscription not less than that levied per member on affiliated bodies.

40 The national committee and the Clitheroe branch each contributed £150. See Clitheroe LRC minutes, 24 February 1906.

41 R. Martin, *op.cit.*, pp. 55-56, 64.

42 Clitheroe LRC minutes, 20 February 1904. *Colne and Nelson Times*, 14 April 1905, p. 6. *Souvenir 1904* (Robinson, Nelson, 1904) pp. 28, 29, 33. The *Souvenir* celebrated the tenth anniversary of Salem Church. Three members of the Shackleton family contributed to it, David's being a poem by Robert Burns which includes the lines
'Man's inhumanity to man
Makes countless thousands mourn'.

43 For an account of Belton's campaign see R. Martin *op.cit.*, pp. 66-67.

44 *Ibid.*, pp. 102-104.

45 *Colne and Nelson Times*, 28 January 1910, p. 2.

Chapter 5
The Feminist Revolt

Whatever he might say about being 'a Labour man' who represented the party's broader programme, David Shackleton's background in the Weavers' Association made it inevitable that union affairs would always be a priority with him. The LRC analysis of its Clitheroe division membership in 1906 shows that trade unionists predominated. It was common at that time for political activists to join several of the organisations that championed their aspirations, but only 180 of them chose to identify their affiliation through links with the ILP, whilst 17,771 did so through a union. (See Figure 27.) This may explain why Shackleton continued to receive ringing endorsements from his constituents throughout the period 1902 to 1910, even though his attendance in parliament decreased and his union involvement increased after he was re-elected in 1906. In that year, for example, he became president as well as secretary of the Darwen Weavers' Association, and withdrew from the Standing Orders Committee of the House of Commons. In 1908 he spoke only four times and made only three interventions in parliamentary debates, and ranked 26th out of 32 Labour MPs in terms of regularity of attendance in the chamber. But in the Clitheroe constituency this record attracted little criticism because Shackleton was considered to be well occupied promoting union interests with Board of Trade officials and at the congress of the International Textile Workers which met in Vienna that year.[1] He was indeed censored for accepting a civil service job without consulting his local party,[2] but other comment on his resignation was expressed in a tone of gratitude for past work and good wishes for the future.[3] The sense is that locally Shackleton was popular throughout his tenure because so many of those who voted for him saw no conflict between his concern for union affairs and his responsibilities to his constituents. They were one and the same.

However in one respect Shackleton failed both Clitheroe and the nation. He had made female suffrage a high priority in his 1902 manifesto, perhaps prompted by Emmeline Pankhurst who pointed out that his candidacy was funded by a levy on local unionists, many of whom in a weaving district like Clitheroe were voteless women.[4] Shackleton acknowledged that he would be

Strictly Private and Confidential, and not to be used by the Press.

CLITHEROE DIVISION

Labour Representation Association.

Trade.	Members.	£	s.	d.
Balance in hand January 1st, 1906		30	1	2
Nelson Weavers	6000	300	0	0
,, Overlookers	470	22	14	6
,, Twisters	240	12	0	0
,, Cloggers	20	1	5	0
,, Joiners &c	45	1	2	6
,, Painters	25	1	5	0
,, Co-op. Employees	90	5	7	6
,, Clothlookers	100	5	0	0
,, I. L. Party	120	5	15	0
Colne Weavers ...	3000	150	0	0
,, Twisters, &c.	130	6	10	0
,, Co-op. Employees	29	1	16	0
,, Joiners	25	0	12	6
,, Clothlookers	84	3	14	0
Colne and Nelson Tape Sizers	73	3	13	0
Colne and Nelson Warpdressers	900	46	0	0
Padiham Weavers	3000	150	0	0
,, Clothlookers	56	1	17	0
,, Twisters	90	4	10	0
Clitheroe Weavers	2000	100	0	0
,, Co-op. Employees	11	0	11	0
,, Painters, &c.	30	1	10	0
,, Clothlookers	29	0	14	6
,, Joiners, &c.	20	1	0	0
,, Twisters	42	1	11	6
,, Typographical Association	34	1	14	0
Todmorden Weavers	104	5	4	0
Cornholme Shuttlemakers	20	1	0	0
,, Co-op.	6	0	6	0
Great Harwood Weavers	68	3	8	0
Burnley Weavers' Association	1000	50	0	0
Colne I. L. Party	60	3	0	0
Burnley Twisters	30	1	10	0
Withdrawn from Bank		425	0	0
Received from National L.R.C towards Election expenses		72	6	5
		£1421	18	7

	£	s.	d.
Printing and Pamphlets	3	9	0
General Postage	2	17	4
Executive and Sub-Meetings	33	3	10
Public Meeting Expenses	8	5	5
Organisation, Registration, &c.	28	10	9
Auditing Accounts and Reporting same	1	10	1
Grant to Secretaries	6	6	0
D. J. Shackleton's Wages	150	0	0
Invested in Bank	462	16	6
Grant to Mrs. Tithers	100	0	0
Election Expenses	607	15	9
Balance in hand December 17th, 1906	17	3	11
	£1421	18	7

We have examined the Books, Vouchers, &c., of the above Association, and have found them correct and in good order.

W. HESMONDHALGH, }
R. BROWN, } AUDITORS.

COULTON & Co., Ltd., Printers, &c., "Leader" Office, Nelson.

Figure 27 – Clitheroe LRC membership, 1906

Source: Minutes of the Fourth Clitheroe LRC Annual Conference, 24 February 1906.

in their debt if he won because the contributions of women unionists would make up part of his salary as an MP, and such practical considerations aside, he believed women should have the vote. But once elected he equivocated. In 1907 he criticised a proposal for a limited extension of the franchise to women because it did not go far enough,[5] yet the private members' bill he introduced after the January 1910 election sought only to enfranchise women who already qualified to vote in local elections, that is to say if they were householders or owners of business premises. Nevertheless the bill had cross party support in parliament, the backing of both the National Union of Women's Suffrage Societies (NUWSS) and the Women's Social and Political Union (WSPU), and it received a majority of over a hundred on its second reading. The Lords may have blocked it anyway, but Shackleton resigned before the bill had a chance to reach the upper house and it was shelved.

After the incorporation of more industrial communities within the newly defined constituency in 1885, Nelson became the centre of its dissident activity. It was a rapidly expanding mill town with a population of 22,700 in 1891, over twice that of Clitheroe, and claimed that its ILP was the country's first, pre-dating the national party formed in Bradford in 1893.[6] The Nelson ILP immediately became involved in contesting local elections, operating a lending library, raising money to finance parliamentary candidates, cooperating with the SDF, making socialists through extra-political organisations such as sewing circles and a Glee Club, and by promoting an ethical ethos which embraced temperance and self-improvement. By the end of the century Nelson's ILP membership had surpassed 500, the Labour group won a majority of seats on the Town Council for the first time in 1905, and plans were made to build a socialist institute. Land for this was acquired in Vernon Street. The estimated cost was £3,000, £580 of which was raised at a three day 'Grand International Bazaar' in March 1907. The Institute was opened a year later in the presence of Labour Party notables including Kier Hardie and Bruce Glasier. (See Figure 28.) Amongst its first users were a Young Socialist Citizen Corps and a Socialist Sunday School which aimed to teach Marxism through a study of 'evolutionary history and sociology'.[7]

One of those who laid foundation stones at Vernon Street was Selina Cooper. She had started work as a half-timer in 1876 when she was twelve, became a winder at Tunstill's mill in Brierfield, and was politicised in the 1880s and 1890s when she attended meetings of Nelson's SDF and ILP branches. Subsequently her activism was wide ranging. She worked with the Weavers' Association, the Women's Cooperative Guild, the Labour Party, and anti-war organisations, and as a poor law guardian she criticised

Figure 28 – The Socialist Institute, Vernon Street, Nelson

Source: Jack Aston.

After it opened in 1908 the Institute became a meeting place not only for the ILP but for the radical suffragists and the No-Conscription Fellowship. Although it was attacked by a pro-war crowd on 11 August 1917 the windows were not damaged.[8] One is now in the People's History Museum in Manchester, the other is at Clarion House, Newchurch-in-Pendle. The foundation stone laid by Selina Cooper is bottom left. It commemorates Caroline Martyn and Enid Stacy, pioneer workers for socialism and votes for women.

the workhouse system and those who ran it locally for encouraging paupers to act as blacklegs 'to help defeat those working men and women who resist injustice or seek to better their conditions of employment'.[9] But she is best remembered as a radical suffragist. This is the term used by Jill Liddington and Jill Norris of a ginger group within the North of England Society for Women's Suffrage which campaigned for the vote for all women over the age of 21. The radical suffragists were inspired by women like Esther Roper, Eva Gore Booth, Sarah Reddish and Sarah Dickenson, who rejected the view of the NUWSS (of which the North of England Society was a part) that the vote should be given to women 'as it is, or may be, accorded to men'.[10] The NUWSS demand was thus property based and would have excluded women whose husbands were entitled to vote as heads of households, as well as all women who could not meet the £10 lodger qualification.

The radical suffragists were strong amongst trade unionists in textile areas, and they are closely identified with the Clitheroe parliamentary constituency because of Selina Cooper. She wanted to cooperate with any socialist or feminist organisation in the cause of women's rights, but she thought the NUWSS too restricted in its ambition and the WSPU too militant in its methods. The National Union of Women's Suffrage Societies had been established in 1897 with Millicent Fawcett as its president, and was always the largest of the groups seeking female enfranchisement, but its reluctance to embrace full womanhood suffrage disappointed the radicals. However they were not attracted to the Women's Social and Political Union when it was formed by the Pankhursts in 1903 because it, too, advocated the vote for women only on the same terms as men, and was prepared to use violence to get it.

As opponents of both limited franchise and extra-constitutional tactics, and keen to involve more working-class women, Selina Cooper and the radical suffragists developed an alternative approach. An early example of their work in this respect was the suffrage petition launched in Blackburn on 1 May 1900. Signatures were sought exclusively from women textile workers in a door to door campaign which covered all the communities within the Clitheroe constituency. Almost 30,000 names had been collected before a delegation, which included Selina, presented the petition to parliament in March 1901. Some sections of the NUWSS disapproved of the Lancashire women's initiative, but it was copied by women in textile towns in neighbouring counties and was responsible for votes for women becoming a key issue in the Clitheroe by-election of 1902. The radical suffragists promoted Shackleton's candidacy and urged him to introduce a female suffrage bill if he won. They spoke at open air meetings throughout the division, and Eva Gore Booth was so charmed by Clitheroe that she wrote a poem in its praise that had little to do with the political situation for which it was the backdrop. (See Figure 29.)

Selina Cooper tried to build on the momentum that the 1900 petition and the 1902 by-election victory had created by forming a women's suffrage committee in Nelson. It was based on her socialist and feminist friendship network, and its known members were from the east side of the constituency. They included Harriette and Emily Beanland, and Florence Shuttleworth, all of the Nelson ILP branch, poor law guardian Margaret Aldersley, and local trade unionists Emily Murgatroyd, Nancy Shimbles, and Mary Atkinson who acted as the committee's president. The group was formed in 1904 and had a membership of 29 in 1912, drawn from Padiham,

THE
STREET
CORNER
ORATOR

At Clitheroe from the Market Square
I saw rose-lit the mountain's gleam,
I stood before the people there
And spake as in a dream.

At Oldham of the many mills
The weavers are of gentle mind;
At Haslingden one flouted me;
At Burnley all the folk were kind.

At Ashton Town the rain came down,
The East wind pierced us through and through,
But over little Clitheroe
The sky was bright and blue.

At Clitheroe through the sunset hour
My soul was very far away,
I saw Ben Bulben's rose and fire
Shining afar o'er Sligo Bay.

At Clitheroe round the Market Square
The hills go up, the hills go down,
Just as they used to go about
A mountain-guarded Irish town.

Oh, I have friends in Haslingden
And many a friend in Hyde,
But 'tis at little Clitheroe
That I would fain abide.

Eva Gore-Booth (1870-1926)

Designed, set and painted by hand by William Alderson at the Chandler Press
1 Queen's Gate Villas, Victoria Park Road, Hackney, London E9 7BU

Figure 29 – A radical suffragist falls for Clitheroe

The references to Ben Bulben and Sligo Bay reflect Eva's origins. She had a privileged upbringing at Lissadell, a fine house near Sligo. Her sister was Constance Markievicz, a leading participant in the 1916 Easter Rising and the first woman to be elected as an MP, in 1918. She won the Dublin St. Patrick's constituency for Sinn Féin, but did not recognise the authority of the British parliament in Ireland and refused to take her seat.

Barrowford, Colne and Brierfield, as well as Nelson. Its activities were directed by Selina from her home at 59 St. Mary's Street. She took on the roles of secretary and treasurer, and her accounts for the period 1912 to 1921 have survived.[11] They show that the annual subscription was nominal, for no one paid more than a shilling, most less, and some nothing.

The Nelson and Colne Suffrage Committee intervented in parliamentary elections outside of its home constituency on behalf of feminist candidates. At Wigan in 1906, for example, its help enabled Thorley Smith to poll

Figure 30 – Clitheroe Women's Suffrage Society at Nelson station, 17 June 1911

Source: *Nelson Leader*, 23 June 1911.

Selina and Robert Cooper flank their daughter Mary, who wears the green, white and red sash of the NUWSS. Margaret Aldersley stands at the end of the front row, right.

better than the Liberal in coming second for the LRC, and in January 1910 it backed Arthur Bulley's unsuccessful attempt to win the Rossendale seat on a votes for women agenda.[12]

A major restriction on the effectiveness of the Nelson committee was lack of funds. It was this that persuaded Selina Cooper to become an NUWSS organiser when it began paying its officials in 1907, despite her reservations about its limited aspirations, and she made a great success of the job, becoming one of its most respected representatives. NUWSS work often took her away from Lancashire, but Selina retained her involvement with the group she had founded after it was renamed the Clitheroe Women's Suffrage Society in 1910. Figure 30 shows her the following year with the Clitheroe delegation about to leave Nelson station to take part in a votes for women demonstration in London. Her husband Robert, who had taken over her duties as treasurer of the branch, is holding its furled banner. Unfurled, it can still be seen, part of the Towneley Hall Musuem collection in Burnley. (See Figure 31.)

In 1988 the banner featured in an exhibition entitled 'The Subversive Stitch,' which drew attention to the application of feminine arts in the cause of dissent. The caption that accompanied it offered this advice:

'Seek to be good but aim not to be great

A Woman's noblest station is retreat

Her fairest virtues fly from public sight

Domestic worth still shuns too strong a light.'[13]

These lines seem to encourage women to demand that their position in society be better valued, but to shun recognition for their efforts to do so. It was a position that Ethel Carnie called 'the revolt of the gentle'.[14]

Figure 31 – The Banner of the Clitheroe Women's Suffrage Society

Source: Towneley Hall Museum and Art Gallery, Burnley.

*

The gentle are typified by the Lancashire women Ethel Carnie wrote about in her novels. She lived near Selina Cooper in the 1910s and must have known her, for they shared the same political views, attended the same party meetings, and took part in the same campaigns in favour of reform and against war, but there is no documentary evidence that they ever met.[15] The missing proof hides a connection between neighbours, but this does not mean that the two women coordinated their dissent, for Ethel preferred a propaganda style that isolated her from kindred spirits. Socialist activists used the methods of tackling contemporary problems that best suited their circumstances, and Ethel was a talented writer whose contribution to the feminist revolt was made mainly through her journalism, fiction and poetry.

Ethel Carnie grew up in Great Harwood, which became part of the Clitheroe constituency in 1918. Her experiences as a warper and beamer at the St. Lawrence mill led her to form an uncompromising attitude towards capitalism. In 1909 for example she wrote that:

> 'Factory life has crushed the childhood, youth, maturity of millions of men and women. It has ruined the health of those who would have been comparatively strong but for the unremitted toil and the evil atmosphere.'[16]

She believed that mill owners were not benefactors to be thanked for giving employment to the working class, but its oppressors:

> 'Make cloth profit the master. This is the text taught in the mill. There is no time for laughter, only for toil...Toil is not a curse imposed upon man by God, it ought to be a blessing, and will be recognised as such in the future. Toil is not drudgery but useful service and the worker is a king – but we dress our kings and queens in rags, let them dwell in ugly buildings and wear their souls away fearing for the morrow.'[17]

Anyone who held opinions such as these was likely to gravitate towards dissident political organisations and Ethel Carnie joined both the Burnley SDF and the Blackburn ILP, but much of her formative thinking resulted from the reading she did in the Great Harwood Cooperative Society library. Demand there was high, and she claimed that 'as a half timer I have waited my turn in queues at the top of the newsroom stairs and have often had to be content with four hours sleep.'[18] The Society's records have been lost so it is impossible to know exactly which volumes Ethel borrowed, but she was a voracious reader in the habit of taking books to the mill and reading them secretly, in the traditional manner of textile workers anxious to better themselves. The library stock contained standard works of world literature and the latest texts on socialism, capitalism, trade unions, the constitution, citizenship and political economy, including much of the output of writers such as John Ruskin, Thomas Carlyle, John Stuart Mill, Edward Carpenter, William Morris, Sidney Webb and G. B. Shaw.[19] The library played an important role in Ethel's intellectual development, for it helped to shape the concerns that were to dominate her life subsequently.

By 1906, when she was twenty years old, her poetry was appearing in local newspapers, and it came to the attention of Robert Blatchford who offered her a job writing for *The Woman Worker*, a magazine with a socialist feminist agenda. The fact that he sacked her within a year because her articles transgressed this remit suggests that she was uncomfortable toeing lines, preferring to work from a position on the political Left unencumbered by organisational ties. So she dropped out of the SDF and the ILP, went back to the mill, and devoted what time she could to promoting her beliefs through imaginative composition. Many of her stories were accepted by cooperative movement papers such as *The Wheatsheaf* and *The Millgate Monthly*, and between 1907 and 1931 a dozen novels and three volumes of her verse were published.

In 1890 Blackburn public library modified its acquisitions policy because there was little demand amongst fiction readers for the classics. It started to offer the sensational romances of writers such as Mary Braddon, author of *Lady Audley's Secret* (1862), and within five years loans had more than doubled.[20] Ethel Carnie thought this trend could be exploited to encourage socialist values. Her feeling was that 'it is too easy to give people what they want. The difficult task is to teach them to want something better…to sting them into rebellion against poverty, to fire their hearts with a cause.'[21] Her first such undertaking with fiction was *Miss Nobody* (1913). The story line makes the heroine the victim of a broken marriage and her husband the subject of a murder investigation before a happy ending is contrived, in other words it is the stuff of romance melodrama (see Figure 32), but the author wove an examination of factory conditions into it that won the approval of *The Times Literary Supplement*. Its reviewer thought that 'the chapters on industrial life are wonderfully powerful and vivid, and these alone stamp the book with distinction as a work of art, apart from the value it may have for social students.'[22] This endorsement of her attempt to use the sort of writing popular with working-class women as a way of getting them to take socialist ideas more seriously encouraged Ethel to try again.

When she moved to Nelson in 1914 she wrote *Iron Horses* which was serialised in *The Co-operative News* the following year. The title refers to the power looms used in textile factories. One of them tears off the arm of a weaver whose sweetheart jilts him to avoid being saddled with an invalid,

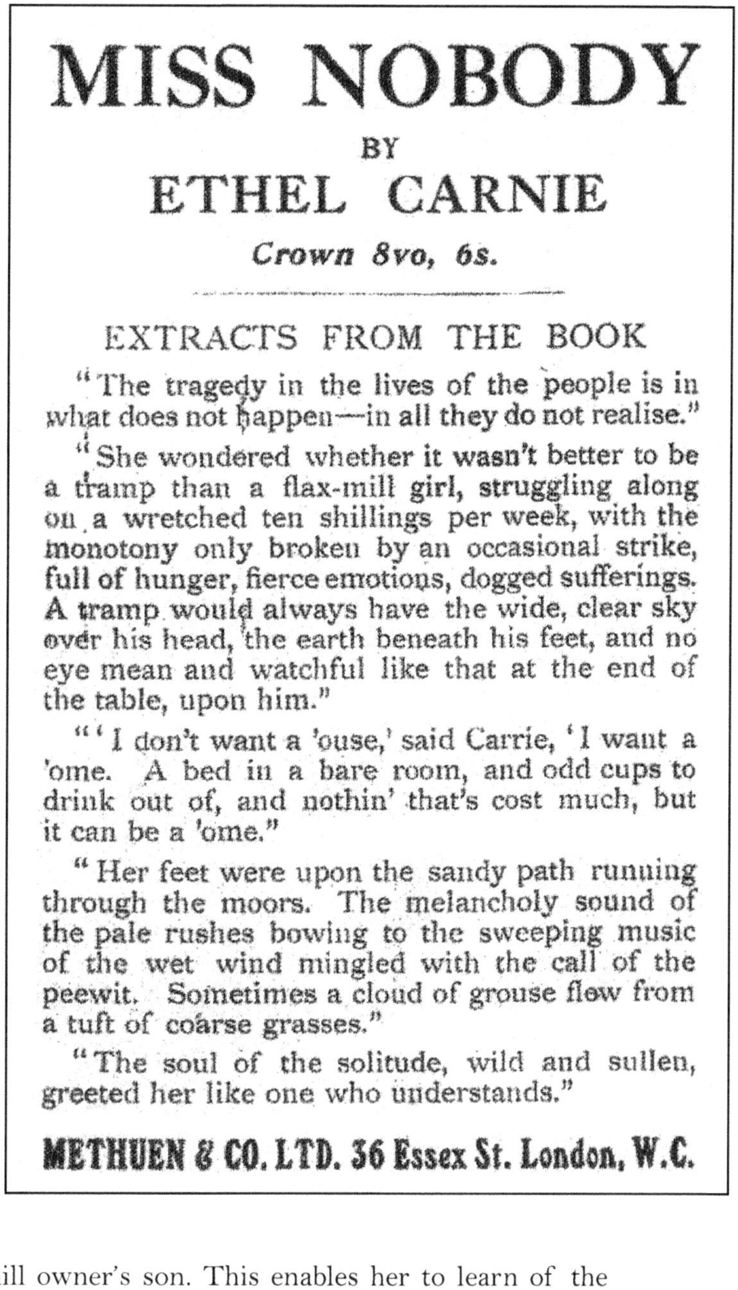

Figure 32 – Advertising *Miss Nobody*

Source: Working Class Movement Library, Salford, PP/Carnie.

A contemporary form of promotion was the use of postcards carrying extracts from the book. This one was sent by Ethel Carnie to Mrs Southworth of Lonsdale Street in Accrington on 23 September 1913.

and then marries the mill owner's son. This enables her to learn of the masters' plan to break a strike and inform the union of it. In the disturbances that follow she is killed. Again the melodrama masks a message – the virus of slavery is in the blood of the workers and it is up to those with the strength to overcome it to fight for freedom for the rest. Ethel called this revolutionary socialism, and claimed that her way of teaching it had more

Figure 33 – The front cover of the Russian language edition of *This Slavery*, published in Moscow in 1926

Source: Chris Lynch.

The title translates as *This Capitalist Slavery*.

impact than conventional Marxist rhetoric.[23] The plot of *Iron Horses* was reworked and used in Ethel's 1925 novel *This Slavery*. By then she was an established writer whose work was being read in Australia, Japan, the USA, Russia and elsewhere. (See Figure 33.) But Ethel achieved her greatest literary success with the publication of *Helen of Four Gates* in 1917, for it became a best seller.

Commenting on women writers of the years between 1914 and 1939 Nicola Beauman poses the question 'why did no one portray, in fiction, the lives led by working-class women?' Her answer is 'for fiction to be believable it demands first-hand knowledge and involvement from the writer…It would have been quite impossible for any of the poor, struggling, coping women… to have won the time or quiet to put pen to paper'.[24] *Helen of Four Gates* suggests that this is too pessimistic a judgement, for it was written in exactly the conditions that Beauman thinks precluded creative endeavour, and it sold very well. Mrs Humphry Ward, one of the most successful writers of the period 1916 to 1919, averaged sales of 35,000, and H. G. Wells at the height of his career only 15,000.[25] By comparison Ethel's new novel had sold over 33,000 copies by 1920.

Helen of Four Gates is set in rural north Lancashire and features real as well as imaginary locations, beginning with a reference to Brungerley in Clitheroe. It is the story of a woman abused by her father and her husband, abandoned by her lover, and vilified by society because of her supposed insanity. The author uses Helen's anguish to examine the position of women in contemporary society and her appraisal is damning. Other writers were highlighting the fact that many women were forced to exchange possession of their persons for the means of existence,[26] but Ethel did so with a new and graphic intensity. Her father only stops short of murder because he wants to prolong Helen's suffering, whilst her husband demands unquestioning obedience and beats her when it is withheld. Indeed the implication is that Helen is the victim of marital rape as she is forced to bear children 'conceived in hatred, born in hatred, suckled in hatred'.[27]

It has been argued that a culture of silence about domestic and sexual violence developed in the early-twentieth century and created a false picture of family harmony,[28] but *Helen of Four Gates* does not give that impression. It is a striking example of the methods used by women trying to break free from the patriarchal code of the time which did not accept that marriage could result from romance. Helen, then, is a feminist icon who asserts her right 'to be the mother of men by the rare and simple virtue of courage', and she confronts 'iron laws, social customs, priests, philosophers and teachers' who would condemn her to an early grave by denying her the basic right to love, because she is a woman.[29]

Helen of Four Gates was primarily an attempt to focus attention on women's human needs, but it also contains lyrical passages that convey a sense of place. Ethel wanted to establish a suitable location for the characterisation of Helen as a witch born of insane stock, and she does so by sustaining an atmosphere of menace and mystery in key scenes set in Pendle Forest, the home of the alleged witches who were hanged at Lancaster in 1612 after a famous trial. The event had remained a strong factor in local folk memory, fostered by Harrison Ainsworth's novel *The Lancashire Witches* (1849), and Ethel had it in mind when she wrote Helen's graveyard incantation:

> 'By the magic of fire, air and water I draw thee to me. By
>
> the seven colours that make earth and heaven, by moon,
>
> sun and stars I draw thee to me'.[30]

MEMORANDUM OF AGREEMENT made this 16th day of HOLDSWORTH May 1915
BETWEEN

ETHEL HOLDSWORTH

(hereinafter termed the Author) of the one part and HERBERT JENKINS LIMITED of 12 Arundel Place Haymarket London (hereinafter termed the Publishers) of the other part. Whereby it is mutually agreed between the parties hereto for themselves and their respective executors administrators and assigns (or successors as the case may be) As follows:-

1. The Publishers shall at their own risk and expense and with due diligence produce and publish the work at present intituled

HELEN O' FOUR GATES

by Ethel Carnie
and use their best endeavours to sell the same subject to Clause 1

4. The Publishers agree to pay the Author the following royalties that is to say:-
(a) A royalty of ten per cent (10%) on the published price of all copies sold (13 being reckoned as 12) of the British Edition up to ~~five~~ two thousand (~~5000~~ 2000) copies and fifteen per cent (15%) upon all subsequent copies sold (13 being reckoned as 12)

Figure 34 – Parts of Ethel Holdsworth's contract with Herbert Jenkins for the publication of *Helen of Four Gates*

Source: Barrie and Jenkins archive, Random House, London.

The preamble and clause 1 indicate that Ethel negotiated this contract soon after her marriage, and that the book's working title was changed before it was published two years later. The hand-written amendments to Clause 4 reduce the standard royalties Jenkins offered, perhaps because Ethel was a first-time author with the firm, but the contract goes on to promise publication of her next six novels.

Figure 35 – Advertising the film *Helen of Four Gates*

Source: Chris Lynch.

She is overheard, and what was a private cry for love from a lonely woman becomes public proof of devilry when her accidental auditor passes the story on, with the comment:

> 'I thowt then for sure she were a witch, an' I took to my heels as if Owd Nick were after me'.[31]

During the First World War there was a sharp increase in the demand for escapist fiction, especially amongst women seeking distraction from the horrors of the conflict. In response the publisher Herbert Jenkins expanded his list and began offering contracts to new authors. He was criticised for putting poor writing into print, but he claimed that he was simply trying to help the distressed 'to forget things occasionally for an hour or so'.[32] He may have been manipulating the popular mood for financial gain as well, but whatever his motive the policy gave Ethel the chance to leave the mill and write for a living, for she made over £1,200 from *Helen of Four Gates* (Figure 34), and an undisclosed sum from the film that was made of it in 1921. (See Figure 35.)

The last of Ethel's books to be published whilst she lived in Nelson was a collection of poems she called *Voices of Womanhood.* They show the influence of Shelley, a hero for many early socialists, and of Wordsworth. 'Civilisation', for example, contains an echo of Wordsworth's 'The world is too much with us':

'Now men worship barren gold,

Tread bloody, worldly ways o'er human hearts

To count their wealth by figures in a book,

And praise a nation for its cluttered marts.

Great God, keep me a pagan; in this night

Of Mammon-worship let me worship light'.[33]

Ethel Carnie was a consistent critic of the church because it taught passive acceptance of capitalism now, in the expectation of eternal salvation. She characterised this as throwing a tombstone at the starving weaver and asking her to wait until she was in heaven for justice. She thought religion reflected the world's selfishness by consigning the unchosen to an unforgiving hell.[34] For her the values claimed by Christianity were more readily to be found in the gentle and unselfish working women whom she grew up amongst and who asked for no recognition. Those

'Who oppose might with right

Though two miles from the threshold of their home

Their name is never heard'.[35]

Ethel had her mother in mind when she wrote these lines. She preferred anonymity for herself too, but her success as a writer prevented it. So did her opposition to the First World War.

Notes and References

1 R. Martin, *op.cit.*, pp. 88-89.

2 Clitheroe LRC minutes, 18 February 1911.

3 *Ibid.*, minutes of a Special Conference, 23 November 1910.

4 *Colne and Nelson Times,* 25 July 1902, p. 2.

5 *Hansard,* 8 March 1907, vol. 170, cols. 1146-48.

6 1891 Census, HMSO, London. In fact the Nelson ILP was formed on 21 January 1893, eight days after the Bradford conference. See F. Brockway, *Socialism Over Sixty Years : The Life of Jowett of Bradford* (Allen and Unwin, London, 1946) pp. 42-43.

7 *Syllabus of Lectures 1913–14* (ILP, Nelson, 1913) p. 35.

8 J. Burrows, *op.cit.*, p. 16.

9 Working Class Movement Library, Salford, 36010038/AG/Election Addresses, Box 11A.

10 J. Liddington and J. Norris, *One Hand Tied Behind Us. The Rise of the Women's Suffrage Movement* (Rivers Oram, London, 2000) p. 5.

11 Lancashire Archives, DDX 1137/1/1.

12 For the detail of this campaign see J. Liddington and J. Norris, *op.cit.*, pp. 254-257.

13 Towneley Hall Museum and Art Gallery, Burnley.

14 See P. Fox, 'Ethel Carnie Holdsworth's "Revolt of the Gentle" : Romance and the Politics of Resistance in Working Class Women's Writing', in A. Ingram and D. Patai (eds.), *Rediscovering Forgotten Radicals, British Women Writers 1889-1939* (University of North Carolina Press, Chapel Hill and London, 1993) pp. 57-74.

15 J. Liddington, *The Life and Times of a Respectable Rebel : Selina Cooper 1864–1946* (Virago, London, 1984). It is based on a mass of personal papers accumulated over a period of 40 years during which Selina lived in the same house. Ethel never lived anywhere for long, and letters or diaries, if they ever existed, were destroyed, lost, or dispersed during her frequent moves.

16 *The Woman Worker,* 3 March 1909, p. 214.

17 *Ibid.*

18 *Women's Outlook*, September 1920, p. 295.

19 Law and Taylor, *Catalogue of the Library* (Co-operative Wholesale Society, Manchester, 1919).

20 A. Duckworth, *Aspects of Blackburn. Discovering Local History* (Wharncliffe, Barnsley, 1999) pp. 103-104.

21 *Women Folk*, 23 May 1910, p. 163.

22 *The Times Literary Supplement*, 11 September 1913, p. 377.

23 E. C. Holdsworth, *Iron Horses* (*The Co-operative News*, Manchester, 1915) p. 1632.

24 N. Beauman, *A Very Great Profession* (Virago, London, 1983) pp. 100-101.

25 P. Keating, *The Haunted Study. A Social History of the English Novel 1875–1914* (Secker and Warburg, London, 1989) p. 424.

26 For example C. Hamilton, *Marriage as a Trade* (1909).

27 E. C. Holdsworth, *Helen of Four Gates* (Herbert Jenkins, London, 1917) p. 215.

28 S. D'Cruze, *Crimes of Outrage : Sex, Violence and Victorian Working Women* (Northern Illinois University Press, DeKalb, 1998) *passim.*

29 E. C. Holdsworth, *Helen of Four Gates, op.cit.*, p. 159.

30 *Ibid.*, p. 17.

31 *Ibid.*, p. 18.

32 J. McAleer, *Popular Reading and Publishing in Britain 1914–1950* (OUP, Oxford, 1992) p. 72.

33 E. Carnie, *Voices of Womanhood* (Headley Brothers, London, 1914), p. 78, lines 37-42. For the comparison mentioned see T. Hutchinson (ed.), *Wordsworth : Poetical Works* (OUP, Oxford, 1978) p. 206.

34 R. Smalley, *Breaking the Bonds of Capitalism : the political vision of a Lancashire mill girl* (Lancaster University, 2014) p. 107.

35 E. Carnie, *Rhymes from the Factory*, (R. Denham, Blackburn, 1908) p. 88, lines 34-36.

Chapter 6
The Anti-War Movement

In 1914 the principal nations of Europe had not fought one another for over 40 years. This sustained period of peace was attributed to a system of international diplomacy designed to balance the interests of the Great Powers, but it was an inherently dangerous arrangement which placed France and Russia on the one hand, and Germany and Austria – Hungary on the other, in obligations of mutual defence that could lead to war if the balance was upset. The assassination of the heir to the throne of Austria – Hungary at Sarajevo in June 1914 caused such a disturbance and drew the members of the two alliances into conflict, but Britain had joined neither of them. There were longstanding rivalries between Britain and the other Powers about colonies, and this was accompanied by an arms race with Germany, but the resulting tensions had been overcome in the past and when the fighting began most people in Britain were able to enjoy the fine bank holiday weather confident that their country would not be involved. However in 1870 Gladstone's government had guaranteed the neutrality of Belgium, and this was violated on 3 August 1914 when German troops passed through Belgian territory on their way to attack France. The following day, therefore, Britain declared war on Germany.

Unlike most countries in Europe, Britain did not compel its citizens to provide military service and Lord Kitchener, the Secretary of State for War, complained that he had no army. In fact the Regulars numbered 250,000 and there were 500,000 more in the Reserves and Territorials, but the armies of the other belligerents were far larger and Kitchener estimated that the war would last three years. He therefore appealed to the nation for a million volunteers, and got them by Christmas.[1] This response reflects the widespread support for the war which followed Britain's unexpected participation, not only from the Liberals and Conservatives but from a majority of the parliamentary Labour Party and the TUC. However the ILP opposed the war and its strength in the Clitheroe constituency explains why Nelson weavers complained about the tactics used by local recruiting agents, and Clitheroe weavers planned a demonstration against increasing government pressure to boost enlistment. The constituency Labour Party was also critical of unspecified 'private armament firms' which supported the war in order to profit from it.[2]

Opponents of Britain's participation were heirs to a tradition of dissent which had been prompted by Victorian imperialism. Radical Liberals such as John Bright and Richard Cobden had argued for free trade on the grounds that commercial interdependence would prevent war. Quakers and Evangelicals stressed the link between peace and Christian principles. Socialists found government policies of colonisation through the use of military force contrary to their belief in the brotherhood of man. Amongst those influenced by the latter group were Ethel Carnie and Alfred Holdsworth. They had met at the Nelson Writers' Circle in 1914, married the following year and set up home in Barrowford. (See Figure 36.) Both were deeply involved in the anti-war movement although an attempt was made to use Ethel's fame in the pro-war cause, for in May 1915 this statement was printed in a local paper:

A DISCLAIMER.

> Sir, – I learn that certain verses, purported to be from my pen, are being used for recruiting purposes. I have never, at any time in my life, been guilty of writing a patriotic poem, but am aware that it is possible that certain verses of mine, detached from their context, and trimmed to suit the occasion, could be abused to serve the ends of the jingo. I am so much concerned on this matter that I would disclaim the authorship of any of my verses if a single line, or even a solitary word of it, were used for the purposes of encouraging recruiting.

Ethel Carnie Holdsworth

76 Garnett Street, Barrowford, Nelson.[3]

The circumstances of the deception have never been established, but they serve to make Ethel's views on the war absolutely clear. However, the way she chose to oppose it was surprising. She could have done so through the ILP, or through the British Socialist Party which had succeeded the SDF as the voice of Marxism in 1911. If she had preferred to work with an independent pressure group there was plenty of choice, for there were north Lancashire branches of the No Conscription Fellowship, the Fellowship of Reconciliation, and the Union of Democratic Control, all of which supported conscientious objection or limitations on the government's war-making powers. Nelson itself had a reputation as an anti-war stronghold because of the activities of Selina Cooper who established a branch of the Women's Peace Crusade there. Wilfred Wellock, who knew the Holdsworths in his capacity as chairman of the Nelson Writers' Circle, also set up the Committee for the Promotion of Pacifism in the town and edited its journal

Figure 36 – Ethel Carnie on her wedding day, 3 April 1915. Alfred Holdsworth inset

Source: Blackburn public library, an unattributed press cutting.

The Pioneer, a Burnley Labour movement newspaper edited by Dan Irving, reported the occasion despite the couple's wish for secrecy. Alfred had started his working life as a weaver, but at some point he acquired secretarial skills and was employed in a Nelson land agent's office when he met Ethel.

The New Crusader. It would have been easy for Ethel to join any of these groups but she did not. Instead she became an organiser for the British Citizen Party (BCP).

The BCP played a significant part in the campaign against conscription in Lancashire in 1915 and 1916. Its leader was Mortimer Holden, who boasted of a long career agitating for 'the absolute nationalisation of everything', and it was supported by Sir Arnold Lupton, who had been the Liberal MP for Sleaford from 1906 to 1910.[4] The BCP promoted adult suffrage, better old age pensions, Isabella Ford's efforts to improve living conditions for working women in Yorkshire, and Margaret McMillan's work to ameliorate child care, but its main aim was to prevent conscription. Ethel Holdsworth condemned compulsory military service as 'a conspiracy of the rich against the workers', and argued that Britain was a participant in the war primarily because it could be used to divert workers from revolution.[5] As an example of the government's fear of dissent she cited the deployment of 'troops' on Lord Derby's extensive properties in Lancashire. In fact they were members of the Colne Volunteer Corps who were simply being given pre-call up training on the Derby estates, however a group of them wrecked a BCP meeting held in Salem School Hall in Nelson on 30 November 1915. (See Figure 37.)

Figure 37 – Salem School Hall, Nelson

Source: Nelson public library, an unattributed press cutting.

Even though the Nelson Socialist Institute had opened in 1908, the BCP hired the Salem School Hall, shown on the left, for 30 November 1915 in anticipation of a big audience. Press reports estimated the attendance at between one and two thousand. The parent body was Salem Chapel, an egalitarian Independent Methodist church which attracted many Nelson socialists. The conscientious objector Wilfred Wellock preached there. When he was conscripted in 1917 Ethel Holdsworth wrote to the local newspaper to chastise the congregation for failing to support him. (See *Nelson Leader*, March 23 1917, p. 6.)

A crowd of over 1,000 attended and Ethel took the chair. When the Volunteer Corps contingent attacked the platform she climbed on to the piano, appealed for calm, and led the singing of 'The Red Flag'.[6] Nevertheless it was an hour before the stewards restored order and the meeting could continue. Even in a town as sympathetic to dissent as Nelson the BCP faced establishment opposition, for it received a bill from the Salem School trustees for the damage caused by the soldiers during the riot, and calls were made to deny it the use of public venues in the town in future. When the matter was raised by Philip Snowden in the House of Commons, the government spokesman, H. J. Tennant, claimed that only four men had been involved in what was a minor disturbance, all of them civilians. In Nelson this was seen as an attempt to hide the seriousness of the incident behind the convenient fact that the Colne volunteers were part of the Home Defence Corps, which was not a uniformed force. But the BCP was intimidated by their behaviour whatever their status, and when a military band prevented some of those trying to get in to its next meeting it cancelled the rest of its schedule.[7]

Conscription was introduced on 2 March 1916, so Ethel Holdsworth's campaign with the BCP failed, as did the efforts of other anti-war organisations. A conscience clause in the legislation allowed for both non-religious and unconditional exemption, but its implementation was in the hands of the often hostile local tribunals which were set up to consider applications. When Alfred Holdsworth applied for exemption he was refused, but, like most conscientious objectors, he was prepared to accept a non-combatant role and was sent to the Western Front in 1917 as a teacher of typing.[8]

Ethel turned her husband's departure into a propaganda opportunity by walking to the railway station with him waving a red flag. The event was witnessed by Bessie Dickinson, a 13-year-old Nelson weaver who was inspired by it to take up political activism,[9] but Alfred's enlistment caused Ethel considerable hardship, for their daughter Margaret had been born in the spring of 1916 and the serviceman's wife's allowance was all she had to live on. Occasionally she was able to supplement it by writing for newspapers and magazines. The *Weekly Dispatch*, for example, commissioned a piece on 'Women and the War', which she used to condemn jingoism and reject the role of patient acceptance recommended by the government. She demanded recognition of the suffering that separation from loved ones caused, and gave vivid examples of it from what she saw around her: women who took on extra work so that they could send food parcels to under-fed soldiers; women who had received no army pay for six weeks despite soaring prices; women who were psychologically damaged by fear of invasion or the taunts of neighbours if their men had not joined up; and women with revolution in their eyes queueing to buy fish tails while duchesses urged them to economise.[10]

This last observation echoes an incident that occurred in Clitheroe and which Ethel may have had in mind. On the outbreak of war a group of women met in the Mayor's parlour to discuss what could be done 'to help our soldiers and the country.' A four point plan was drawn up – economise, give up pleasure, avoid hoarding, and make shirts. It was enthusiastically adopted, the Clitheroe press reported, by women of all classes, but economising was not easy for working women. Mrs Assheton of Downham Hall understood this and told the meeting that her tenants could spare nothing. Mrs Garnett of Low Moor, however, thought that as she was giving up luxuries such as butter, sugar and holidays, the women who worked in her husband's mill should do the same.[11]

The *Weekly Dispatch* article provides an intriguing glimpse into the effects of war and the variety of responses it provoked, but the paper offered Ethel no further work, and her situation became desperate in 1918 when she was informed that her husband had been killed.[12] For over a year she thought that she was a widow, but when the war ended Alfred was discovered alive in a British field hospital, and he was reunited with his family in 1919.[13]

No further details of Alfred's ordeal are available now, but in 1924 Ethel utilised his experiences in her novel *General Belinda.* There she subjects Reggie, Belinda's soldier nephew, to exactly the circumstances that are known about Alfred's military service. Because of this it is possible that other aspects of Alfred's war, about which we would otherwise know nothing, can be inferred from what happens to Reggie, his fictional counterpart. If the conjecture is valid, Alfred was captured in April 1918 during the final German offensive and sent to the notorious prisoner of war camp at Limburg an der Lahn, where rations were barely above starvation level. After the Armistice he was marched to the British lines and discharged from hospital only when he had recovered from shell shock and malnutrition a year later.[14]

The war was a ghastly episode in the lives of both Ethel and Alfred. If *General Belinda* is autobiographical Ethel wept unashamedly on Nelson station not only for her husband but for all the other cold and frightened conscripts gathered there. She did not distinguish soldiers by nationality, 'they're all somebody's lads' Belinda says.[15] Alfred too felt no bitterness towards the Germans he encountered. He believed that conscripts of all countries were victims of a class war which pitted worker against worker for private profit, and he remembered with gratitude the kindness shown towards him by civilians on his march back to the British lines.[16]

*

Alfred Holdsworth was one of at least 70 men from the Clitheroe parliamentary constituency who refused to be conscripted because of their anti-war beliefs.[17] Precise figures are difficult to establish because the government ordered transcripts of tribunal hearings to be destroyed, although a scattering have been located in the papers of tribunal members who kept copies of the proceedings, and some cases were reported in the local press or tracked and documented by organisations such as the Society of Friends and the No Conscription Fellowship. From these sources over 18,000 conscientious objectors have now been identified, and evidence of others continues to come to light.

In the Clitheroe constituency 19 of those who applied for exemption were prepared to serve with the Non-Combatant Corps (NCC), whose members were not required to fight of bear arms. The Home Office set up labour camps throughout the country where NCC manpower was used to quarry stone, build roads or cut timber, and most of the Clitheroe men were sent to the Wakefield camp. Others joined the Friends Ambulance Unit (FAU) or the Friends War Victims Relief Committee (FWVRC) and gave medical aid or repaired battle damage near the front line.[18] However the majority, including those designated 'absolutists' because they refused to engage in any task that could be considered of help to the war effort, faced prison sentences with hard labour. (See Figures 38 and 39.)

Most of Clitheroe's conscientious objectors were working-class men, mainly weavers, but two, Percy Davies and Thomas Foulds, were mill owners. Fifteen gave religious scruples as the reason for their refusal to enlist, several Quakers amongst them, one of whom, Harry Roper, received support from the Society of Friends during his tribunal, yet only Percy Davies was granted exemption. Incomplete documentation makes it impossible to chart the fate of all 70 fully, but what can be said is that most were absorbed by government work schemes at some point during their terms of imprisonment, although 18 served the full two years with hard labour to which they had been sentenced. Daniel Carradice and Peter Allen were brutally treated during their detention, an experience which may have contributed to the death of Allen two weeks after his release from Ipswich jail in November 1918, and two days after the death of his conscientious objector brother Thomas.[19] Albert Pym also suffered maltreatment at the hands of the authorities by being 'stripped and forcibly put in khaki.'[20]

David Wilson's tribunal report has survived. It shows that he was a Bashall Eaves grocer and 49 when he was called up. He pleaded that he was too old to learn how to use a gun which he could never shoot because he believed that killing a foreign solider was as great a wrong as killing a fellow countryman. The tribunal was chaired by William Garnett the Low Moor cotton manufacturer, and the case against Wilson was presented by William King Wilkinson of Slaidburn who had been appointed recruiting officer for the rural area around Clitheroe. Wilson's appeal was refused, as was that of Charles Slinger, a Grindleton labourer who tried to avoid conscription without a genuine conscientious objection. He falsified his occupation in the hope of being placed in the reserved worker category, and when the deception was discovered changed his plea, claiming that membership of the Church of England and of a Friendly Society entitled him to exemption. King Wilkinson noted on Slinger's report that he was 'one of the biggest slackers in existence' who 'would not need a gun to kill Germans, his bad language would do it.'[21]

Figure 38 – The Clitheroe constituency's conscientious objectors, not including the Nelson contingent

Sources: No Conscription Fellowship (NCF) archive, and Cyril Pearce Database of Conscientious Objectors, Working Class Movement Library, Salford.
Nelson Leader.
Clitheroe Advertiser and *Clitheroe Times.*
Lancashire Evening Post.
King Wilkinson papers, Lancashire Archives, Preston.

Name	*Residence*	*Occupation*	*Affiliation*	*Outcome Of Tribunal*
Fred Beardsworth	Padiham	weaver		two years imprisonment with hard labour
Wilfred Bibby	Padiham	weaver	Wesleyan	two years imprisonment with hard labour
Nimrod Bracewell	Colne	weaver	Christadelphian	two years imprisonment with hard labour – Dartmoor
Frank Bradshaw	Padiham	weaver	Wesleyan	18 months imprisonment with hard labour
Cecil Brown	Colne			NCC Preston
James Butterfield	Barrowford		ILP	two years imprisonment with hard labour
Robert Copeland	Clitheroe	forman painter	Socialist	NCC Wakefield – Dartmoor
Percy Davies	West Bradford	manufacturer	ILP UDC NCF Quaker Fabian Society	exempted

Edward Foulds	Colne		Quaker	FWVRC
Robinson Foulds	Colne		Quaker	FAU
Thomas Foulds	Colne	manufacturer	Quaker	exempted
Alban Harrison	Barrow	weaver		NCC Cheshire Regiment Labour Corps
Thomas Haynes	Lanehead	joiner	FOR	prison – NCC Wakefield
James Hindle	Barrowford	watchmaker	ILP NCF	two years imprisonment with hard labour
Moses Holden*	Clitheroe	weaver		prison – NCC Wakefield
Alfred Holdsworth	Barrowford	clerk		NCC Western Front
John Hudson*	Padiham		BSP	two years imprisonment with hard labour – Dartmoor
Ernest Long	Barrowford	weaver	Independent Methodist	two years imprisonment with hard labour
Charles Moorhead	Whalley	flour traveller	Quaker	FAU
James Ormerod	Padiham	librarian	ILP Quaker	FAU
Michael Ormerod	Colne	driver	Wesleyan	112 days imprisonment with hard labour
M. E. Payne	Colne	stone waller		two years imprisonment with hard labour

Herbert Pickles	Colne		NCF	
Albert Pym*	Clitheroe	weaver		NCC – Dartmoor
Arthur Riley	Fence	weaver	Anarchist	two years imprisonment with hard labour
Herbert Robinson	Foulridge	weaver	ILP NCF	two years imprisonment with hard labour ♦
Harry Roper		weaver		NCC Wakefield
Charles Slinger	Grindleton	farm labourer		
Albert Smalley	Chatburn	weaver	Quaker	FAU●
W. Smith	Fence	weaver		imprisonment
John Waterhouse	Colne	cotton warp dresser	NCF	exempted ■
David Wilson	Bashall Eaves	grocer	Quaker?	
William Wood	Whalley	engraver		prison – NCC Wakefield

* absolutists

♦ became a conscientious objector after some military service

● agricultural labour at Elbeck farm, Rimington

■ exemption granted because of reserved occupation, but on condition that he attend a government work camp

Figure 39 – The Nelson contingent of the Clitheroe constituency's conscientious objectors

Sources: NCF archive and Cyril Pearce Database of Conscientious Objectors, Working Class Movement Library, Salford. *Nelson Leader.*

Name	*Affiliation*	*Outcome Of Tribunal*
James Allen	NCF	two years imprisonment with hard labour
Peter Allen	NCF	two years imprisonment with hard labour
Thomas Allen	NCF	two years imprisonment with hard labour
George Allen		NCC Preston
Isaac Anderton	Quaker	FAU
George Bancroft	Wesleyan	two years imprisonment with hard labour
Tom Barnes	ILP	
Karl Birtles	Weavers' Association	two years imprisonment with hard labour
Richard Bland	ILP NCF Quaker	two years imprisonment with hard labour
Harold Buller	ILP NCF	two years imprisonment with hard labour
John Burrows	ILP	nine months imprisonment with hard labour – Dartmoor
Frank Butterfield	ILP	
Daniel Carradice*	ILP NCF	two years imprisonment with hard labour
Harrison Carradice	ILP	one year imprisonment with hard labour
William Cooper		NCC Preston
Henry Disley*	ILP NCF	Imprisonment curtailed on health grounds – NCC
B. W. Driver		
Ernest Heyworth	ILP	
Herbert Higgins	ILP NCF	two years imprisonment with hard labour

Zephaniah Hutchinson	ILP	allowed to continue working as a weaver because of ill health
Alexander Ingham	ILP	NCC Warwick – Dartmoor
John Ingham*	ILP NCF	two years imprisonment with hard labour – NCC Wakefield
William Ingham*	ILP NCF	two years imprisonment with hard labour – NCC Warwick
Charles Jones	ILP	two years imprisonment with hard labour
Hubert Landless		joined South Lancashire regiment
Isaac Laycock	ILP NCF Quaker	one year imprisonment with hard labour
Gilbert Pounder		one year and 112 days imprisonment with hard labour
Robert Roberts	ILP	one year and nine months imprisonment with hard labour
Benjamin Sidwell	ILP Quaker	two years imprisonment
John Sidwell	ILP	NCC, Army Reserve Class Z
S. Sidwell		Imprisonment
Frank Smith	ILP	
Wilson Speak*	Wesleyan NCF	two years imprisonment with hard labour – NCC Wakefield
Herbert Throup	ILP	112 days imprisonment with hard labour
Euclid Thursby	ILP	one year imprisonment with hard labour
Willie Tillotson	ILP	two years imprisonment with hard labour
Harry Watson	ILP Quaker	one year and six months imprisonment with hard labour – NCC Wakefield, Army Reserve Class W
Wilfred Wellock*	ILP NCF FOR	two years imprisonment with hard labour
Ebenezer Williams	Quaker	two years imprisonment with hard labour

* absolutists

The use of conscientious objector data as an indicator of political dissent within the area covered by the Clitheroe constituency is complicated not only by gaps in the record but by the preponderance of cases from Nelson. Between 1885 and 1918 it was the largest town in the constituency with a population according to the 1911 census of 39,478, but even so its 39 conscientious objectors is an unusually high number, equal to that of Westmorland, a constituency of over 65,000 with the reputation of having more conscientious objectors *pro rata* than most comparable areas.[22] The conjunction of effective NCF, ILP and BCP activists in Nelson must explain this statistic, but the number of conscientious objectors in the rest of the constituency was also high. Herefordshire for example, a county of 113,000 had only 23 documented conscientious objectors, whilst there were 33 amongst the 26,000 inhabitants of the Clitheroe constituency outside Nelson.[23] These figures provide an imperfect context, but they represent a significant gesture of dissent. The men who have been identified share a profile unavailable to those anonymous pacifists not threatened by conscription and whose identities cannot therefore be known, but the evidence is sufficient to suggest that the constituency's response to war should not be characterised only by the acceptance and suffering of men who volunteered or submitted to conscription, for it also involved the rejection and persecution of those whose different view of the sanctity of life marked them apart.

*

The war also affected and divided women dissidents. Many NUWSS members accepted Millicent Fawcett's decision that they should support the government by staffing Red Cross hospitals, running canteens for soldiers and filling jobs vacated by volunteers and conscripts. Some radical suffragists, however, rejected the official line and helped to form the Women's International League for Peace and Freedom. It held a Peace Crusade in Nelson in 1917 which was led by Selina Cooper and Gertrude Ingham. At one of the many meetings they organised Deborah Smith, a local weaver, spoke of her conscripted sons, one of whom had been wounded and the other captured and interned in a German prisoner-of-war camp. At another Ethel Snowden condemned the war from the platform of Salem School Hall, although without provoking the violent response that Ethel Holdsworth had met with at the same venue two years earlier. However the central event of the Crusade was the great march of 11 August 1917, when over 2,000 women processed through Nelson and 20,000 gathered to listen to Ethel Holdsworth, Margaret Bondfield and Lilian Anderson address them on the need for peace.[24]

After the war Selena Cooper continued to live in Nelson and work for women's rights. Ethel Holdsworth moved to Heptonstall near Hebden Bridge and started a newspaper, *The Clear Light*, which became the mouthpiece of the National Union for Combating Fascism, the first organisation in Britain to warn of the threat to democracy posed by Mussolini.[25] So after 1918 both women remained deeply committed political activists, although outside the new boundaries which were established for the Clitheroe constituency that year. And just as the record is silent about their interaction when they lived within it, so documentary proof of a later relationship is lacking. Nevertheless the circumstantial evidence is strong, for they were still close geographically and ideologically, and both used Clarion House.

Figure 40 – Clarion House, Newchurch-in-Pendle

Source: Jack Aston.

The first ILP Clarion cafe was opened at Thorneyholme, Roughlee, in 1899. In 1902 it was replaced by one located in Nabs Farm further up Jinny Lane from the present purpose-built structure, which was completed in 1912.

Clarion House has been a meeting place for political dissenters since 1899. It was conceived by the Nelson ILP as part of a network of cafes which Lancashire textile workers could use on Sundays as they enjoyed the countryside and talked of socialist utopias with like-minded regulars. The cafe, which still fulfils its original role, is situated in Jinny Lane near Newchurch-in-Pendle and replaced two predecessors in 1912. (See Figure 40.) It was opened by T. D. Benson who by then had become a member of the ILP National Council, and Andrew Smith the secretary of the Nelson ILP Land Society which had been formed to purchase the site, organise the construction, and supervise the business. After 1916 improvements were carried out by conscientious objectors who also created a sports ground and footpaths in the adjoining area.

The historians of Clarion House claim that its great popular appeal played an important part in promoting socialism in the Clitheroe constituency and beyond because it provided a base for the discussion and dissemination of the principles of dissent, and attracted leading figures in the Labour movement to visit.[26] Many of them are commemorated there, including Keir Hardie, James Maxton and Selina Cooper, but not Ethel Holdsworth, despite the fact that she was one of the earliest users of the cafe when she lived in Nelson and Barrowford, and a member of the support group which met at Clarion House to organise relief for local workers who were involved in the General Strike of 1926.[27]

Clarion House had a residential equivalent in West Bradford – Heys Farm Guest House. It was founded in 1912, the same year the present Clarion cafe opened, and had much the same purpose, although its inspiration was religious rather than secular. Heys Farm looks across Ribblesdale towards Pendle, from the top of which George Fox had the vision that led to the formation of the Society of Friends in the mid-seventeenth century. In 1655 Oliver Cromwell was impressed by Fox when the Quaker told the Lord Protector of his refusal to swear oaths, pay tithes or bear arms. Charles II was less tolerant however, and Fox was frequently imprisoned for his religious and political dissent, on two occasions in the 1660s in Lancaster Castle. But Quakerism had taken root in the north west, and it was a Quaker, the pacifist Percy Davies, who was behind the Heys Farm project. From 1907 he had run an adult school in Blackburn on Quaker principles, favouring a spiritual rather than a materialist attitude to life which valued equality and community. No charge was made for attendance, all were invited to 'come as you are, in your boots or clogs, it doesn't matter'.[28] Heys Farm residents paid a nominal sum for board and lodging, and they accepted its Quaker-inspired philosophy. George Fox had treated women as absolute equals, educating girls in the same way as boys, requiring the same promises from bride and

THE MANCHESTER GUARDIAN TUESDAY MARCH 16 1954

Heys Farm Guest House (top) with below, left, Mr and Mrs J. P. Davies—later Lord and Lady Darwen—with Mahatma Gandhi at the Guest House in 1931, and (right) the interior of the common-room. The house is to be sold by auction on March 24

Figure 41 – Heys Farm, West Bradford, near Clitheroe

The photograph shows the farm after its conversion to a dissident residential centre. Kathleen and Percy Davies pose in front of it with Mahatma Gandhi who stayed there in 1931. Earlier, like Clarion House, it was visited by eminent figures in the Labour movement such as George Lansbury and Philip Snowden.

groom, and supporting the social and political rights of women. Heys Farm continued that tradition by campaigning for contemporary feminist causes, but on the outbreak of war in 1914 the focus shifted to the pursuit of peace. The farm became a refuge for those who opposed the war, and its summer schools were attended by conscripts on leave who were anxious to see an end to the conflict, as well as by conscientious objectors. Participants were not only British. Hans Shindler from Vienna was strengthened in his hope that 'the days of hate and mistrust between people are over' during a visit in 1922, and Mahatma Gandi expressed gratitude for the hospitality he received at the farm in 1931, for it stimulated his thinking on liberty, equality and peace.[29] (See Figure 41.)

In the early-twentieth century Percy Davies was an influential dissident in the Clitheroe area. The values of international peace, community and cooperation which he stood for as a conscientious objector and a christian socialist can still be identified locally, for the Quakers moved their meeting to the centre of Clitheroe in 2017 in order to be more accessible and useful. Davies also agitated for change through political pamphlets printed by his own press at Heys Farm. His publications include *The Politics of a Socialist Employer*, and *Foundations of Peace*, which was co-authored with his wife Kathleen, but his most widely read book was *Glorious Banner*, an attempt as its sub-title put it 'to slay the dragon of want and war'.[30] Its argument is that freedom and happiness will always be prevented by social injustice, and that right-thinking people should oppose it unremittingly. Davies' examples are taken from a wide range of sources, and they remain relevant to the debate about the dangers of the growing gap between rich and poor. His view that entrenched wealth would never willingly give up its powers and privileges was shared by many, Ethel Holdsworth amongst them. They all criticised the waste of human potential imposed by capitalism and the absence of a social conscience on the part of government. Percy Davies' recommendation in *Glorious Banner* is the nationalisation of banks and industry, and the adoption of the ideas of the cooperative and trade union movements. This was standard socialist rhetoric, but Davies also stressed the need to overcome indifference, for he worried that unless more people took an interest in politics they would continue to get the unresponsive government they deserved.[31]

Heys Farm complemented Clarion House well. Between them they helped to create a moral and spiritual awakening in the Clitheroe constituency that played a part in the return of representatives of dissent to parliament from 1902 to 1922. By then the Labour Party was on the threshold of forming its first national administration.

Notes and References

1 D. Boulton, *Objection Overruled* (Dent, London, 2014) p. 73.

2 Clitheroe Labour Party Minutes, 20 February 1915, 19 February 1916, 24 February 1917.

3 *Blackburn Weekly Telegraph*, 21 May 1915, p. 6.

4 *British Citizen*, 25 December 1915, p. 1.

5 *Ibid.*, 11 December 1915, pp. 1 and 4.

6 *Colne and Nelson Times*, 3 December 1915, p. 4.

7 *Ibid.*

8 Alfred Holdsworth archive, Keighley public library, BK63.

9 Ethel Carnie archive, Working Class Movement Library, Salford, PP Carnie.

10 *The Straits Times* (Singapore, 28 September 1917, p. 12) reprinted from *Weekly Dispatch*.

11 *Clitheroe Times*, 14 August 1914, p. 6.

12 Ethel Carnie archive, *op.cit.*

13 Alfred Holdsworth archive, *op.cit.*

14 E. Holdsworth, *General Belinda* (Herbert Jenkins, London, 1924) pp. 301-306.

15 *Ibid.*, p. 251.

16 *Hebden Bridge and Calder Vale Gazette*, 21 December 1923, p. 2, 11 January 1924, p. 7.

17 The documentary evidence regarding H. Butler and H. Fuller is slight enough to suggest it really relates to Harold Buller. Butler and Fuller have, therefore, not been included in the total.

18 Only Edward and Robinson Foulds served in battle zones. Isaac Anderton and Albert Smalley became agricultural labourers, and when he became unfit for farm work Anderton returned to his old job as a weaver.

19 Both Peter and Thomas Allen were recorded as dying from pneumonia contracted during compassionate release from prison to attend the funeral of their sister.

20 Cyril Pearce Database of Conscientious Objectors, Working Class Movement Library, Salford.

21 Lancashire Archives, Preston, DDKW bundles 31/994 and 31/588.

22 *Transactions of the Cumberland and Westmorland Antiquarian and Archaeological Society* (3, 16, 2016) p. 121. The 1921 census put Westmorland's population at 65,746, almost exactly that of the entire Clitheroe constituency.

23 Cyril Pearce Database *op.cit.*

24 A. Ronan (ed.), *The Women's Peace Crusade 1917-1918* (Manchester Metropolitan University, 2017) pp. 60-61. See also *Nelson Leader*, 17 August 1917, p. 2.

25 R. Smalley, *op. cit.*, pp. 96-97.

26 S. Iveson and R. Brown, *Clarion House, a Monument to a Movement* (Lancashire Community Press, Preston, 1987) p. 23.

27 R. Smalley, *op.cit.*, pp. 18-19.

28 *The Manchester Guardian*, 16 March 1954, p. 7.

29 *Ibid.*

30 J. Percival Davies, *Glorious Banner* (Pendle Books, West Bradford, 1945).

31 *Ibid.*, pp. 14-19.

Chapter 7

The Labour Constituency 1910–1922

The high number of conscientious objectors and the activities of groups like the Quakers, the ILP and the BCP, should not obscure the fact that most people in the Clitheroe constituency were prepared to support the war. Although the toll of death and injury left few families unaffected, Lloyd George's Coalition government was able to resist calls for a negotiated peace and carry public opinion along with its resolve to persevere until total victory was achieved. Despite its criticisms of profiteers and enlistment practices the Clitheroe Division Labour Party funded ambulance wagons, and many of its members joined up out of a sense of patriotic duty, repugnant though they judged the conflict to be.

Tom Holland was the first man in Clitheroe to volunteer for Kitchener's Army in August 1914. He had moved to the town from Shropshire, where he had been a miner, looking for work in the cotton mills when the pits in his native county closed, and he became a trade union official and a Labour Party activist. Tom's life was typical of his class and time – factory work punctuated by military service and unemployment. He had joined the East Lancashire Regiment in 1900 when he could not find a civilian job and was posted to South Africa for the duration of the Boer War. The experience he gained there as a private helped to earn him promotion to sergeant in the Great War. (See Figure 42.) He served on the Western Front without complaint until 1919 and returned to his family in Cross Street physically unharmed. For a year he got work as a cloth looker at the Commercial Mill, but lost it during the post war depression and could never find regular employment thereafter. He remained a reliable Labour voter for the rest of his life but gradually withdrew from activism and never tried for public office.[1]

Albert Smith was also a weaver who became involved in local politics, and like Tom Holland he volunteered on the outbreak of war, but at the time he was Clitheroe's Member of Parliament. Smith had gained the nomination as Labour's candidate to replace David Shackleton in the December 1910 General Election against strong competition from Thomas Shaw.[2] Both lived in the constituency, were ILP members, and had backgrounds in local

Figure 42 – Tom Holland with his family

Source: Ruby Holland.

The photograph was taken in Clitheroe to remind the family of Tom during his absence, and to serve as a record in case he did not survive the war.

trade unionism, Smith with the Nelson Overlookers Association, Shaw with the Colne Weavers. Smith was also a Methodist lay preacher, a magistrate, and had served as a councillor and alderman in Nelson.[3]

The December election of 1910 rehearsed the arguments of its January predecessor, for the Labour Party continued to demand the reversal of the Osborne Judgement, Home Rule for Ireland, and Votes for Women, but in the intervening months other matters had also gained in prominence. At the last minute the Tory leader Arthur Balfour proposed a referendum on Tariff Reform, and Clitheroe's Conservative challenger, J. J. Blayney, claimed that this would lead to a reduction in unemployment and an increase in the minimum wage to 30*s* a week. As a Free Trader Smith pooh-

poohed the idea, holding that a tax on land was a better method of raising revenue and a right to work bill a better way of providing jobs. Although there was no candidate standing in Clitheroe for the party of government, Smith criticised the Liberal welfare programme, especially Lloyd George's plan to restrict old age pensions to the over 70s, for 60 was a more realistic retirement age in Labour's view.

But the major issue of the day was the constitutional crisis which had been precipitated by the House of Lords' rejection of the People's Budget, the Chancellor of the Exchequer's instrument for funding government spending through increased taxation, most controversially by the imposition of a 20 per cent duty on unearned income from land. The Liberal government was threatening the upper chamber with the creation of enough new peers to overcome its intransigence, but Albert Smith went further, calling not for reform but for abolition of the House of Lords because the working class was not represented in that assembly.[4] (See Figure 43.) Clitheroe Conservatives were furious and called Smith unpatriotic for attacking cherished British institutions, but he impressed enough of the electorate to win the seat. He thus became one of a group of 42 Labour members in the new parliament, two more than had been returned at the January election. Nationally Labour's share of the vote went down from 7 to 6.4 per cent, but Smith won more of the vote in Clitheroe than Shackleton had done earlier in the year, polling 12,107 to Blaney's 5,783. However the second election of 1910 returned a House of Commons almost identical to that of the first. The Liberals had 272 members, only one more than the Conservatives, although they could rely on the 84 votes of the Irish Party to give them a working majority. Labour's position was therefore not strong enough to have much influence on legislation, and Smith's hopes for the abolition of the House of Lords were not fulfilled. Nevertheless the People's Budget was passed, and the Trade Union Act of 1913 overturned the Osborne Judgement, giving the Labour Party better funding for future contests and the prospect of enhancing its position as the voice of dissent.

Between 1911 and 1914 Albert Smith worked hard to improve the condition of his constituents. The 1902 Education Act had raised the school leaving age to twelve, but in textile districts certificates of exemption which allowed eleven-year-olds to work half time could be obtained. This arrangement suited employers who wanted to cut their wage bills, parents who needed the additional income, and trade unions fearful that rising costs would weaken Lancashire's competitiveness, but Smith, who first entered the mill at the age of eight, thought the half time system iniquitous. He pressed the government to increase funding for education and encouraged local youngsters to enrol in greater numbers for the vocational courses

Who Owns Our Native Land?

Duke of Sutherland owns	1,358,545	acres
,, ,, Buccleuch ,,	469,108	,,
,, ,, Northumberland	186,397	,,
,, ,, Richmond owns	280,409	,,
,, ,, Argyll ,,	175,114	,,
,, ,, Devonshire ,,	198,572	,,
,, ,, Hamilton ,,	157,386	,,
,, ,, Portland ,,	183,199	,,
Marquis of Lansdowne ,,	142,916	,,

Number of Acres owned by members of the House of Lords—**16,411,986,**

RENT ROLL - £13,542,620.

"The House of Lords being an unrepresentative part of the Legislation and, of necessity representative only of interests opposed to the general-well-being, is a hindrance to National progress and ought to be abolished."

Labour Party Amendment, House of Commons, June 26th, 1907,

The Labour Party stands for the ABOLITION of the HOUSE OF LORDS.

VOTE FOR SMITH.

The Land for the People and Ending the House of Lords.

Figure 43 – Albert Smith demands the abolition of the House of Lords

Source: Lancashire Archives, Preston, DDKW/Box 125.

An example of the propaganda used by the Labour candidate in the General Election of December 1910.

relevant to the cotton industry that were becoming more available at the area's technical schools.[5]

Like his predecessor, Smith opposed the use of artificial humidity in textile mills and introduced a private members' bill which aimed to end it. The bill would also have prevented the widespread practice by employers of fining their employees for petty lapses in work standards that, Smith argued, were unavoidable by even the most conscientious operatives because of the oppressive conditions in which they had to work. He estimated that £20,000 was taken from weavers' wages annually in fines to ensure discipline, mainly from children. This lack of humanity appalled him: 'traps and heald smashes do happen' he thundered, 'shuttles will catch and floats do elude the most vigilant of weavers despite their best attention'. With heavy irony, but better to make his point, Smith asked the House if it would consider fining lawyers who lost cases, clergymen who delivered dull sermons, and MPs who paired so that they could miss a session to attend to private business.[6]

Aside from matters of special concern to his constituents, Albert Smith made representations to the Local Government Board in an attempt to amend traffic regulations so that in consideration of pedestrians lorries would be forced to fit mudguards and drive more slowly.[7] He also took a keen interest in the Irish question, criticising the government's Home Rule Bill for offering Ireland no more power than an English county council. He suggested that the autonomy already extended to Australia, Canada and South Africa was being denied Ireland because it was near enough to be cowed by British military might. In Smith's view Home Rule would be 'one of the greatest benefits ever conferred on Irish working people' and would consolidate, not weaken, the Union.[8]

As the threat of war increased, Smith condemned those who clammered for the introduction of conscription and the build up of armaments, for he believed that barracks life was degrading and the arms race based on the greed of weapons manufacturers. He claimed that 12*s* out of every tax pound was spent on the army or the navy, an indefensible proportion at any time, let alone in 1913 when deprivation amongst the working class was so widespread.[9] Nevertheless when Britain became embroiled in the European conflict he asked his constituents to excuse him from parliamentary duties so that he could volunteer for military service, for he felt unable to ask others to do something he was not prepared to do himself. (See Figure 44.) He led recruitment drives in and around Clitheroe thereafter, and favoured the 'Pals' principle, which gave volunteers the guarantee that they would be trained and deployed in groups composed of others from the same trade or area.[10]

On 8 December 1914 Albert Smith was commissioned lieutenant in the 6th Battalion, Royal Lancaster Regiment, a unit he had served with as a private and corporal in his youth. He joined the Mediterranean Expeditionary Force and fought in the Dardanelles campaign, but was invalided home after Gallipoli.[11] The war saddened him, but his commitment to winning it never wavered. This put him at odds with many in the ILP, including Tom Shaw, his friend and rival for the Clitheroe nomination back

HOUSE OF COMMONS.

GENTLEMEN,

As you well know, this country is involved in a deplorable and cruel war which, from all available evidence, is not likely to soon terminate.

The Labour Party has thrown in its lot with the other Parties in the State in order that an early and satisfactory ending may be accomplished. All Parties are appealing for men, including the Parliamentary Committee of the Trades' Union Congress.

That more men are needed at once is an admitted fact, and the more the men which immediately respond the more certain and quicker will be the victory, with the consequent less loss of valuable life and money.

I have, as you are aware, addressed a few meetings in the Constituency with a view to obtaining men which, to me, was not a very congenial task. I therefore asked myself the question, "Have you tried yourself? I could not conscientiously continue to address meetings until I had answered the question by either being accepted or rejected for service myself.

The result has been that I have accepted a Commission (temporary) in a splendid Regiment (for the duration of War only.) I profoundly felt it my duty to use my former experience to aid my country in the hour of peril, and share the hardship of those who have gone before me. I therefore trust you will bear with me during the time I am with the Army. I need not say that my opinions have not changed and my sincere hope is, that when the war is over, the settlement will be such that another war of a like character will be impossible.

Believe me to be,

Yours faithfully,

Nov. 23rd, 1914 **ALBERT SMITH.** M.P.

Figure 44 – Clitheroe's MP enlists

Source: Clitheroe Labour Party Minutes, 23 November 1914.

The 'splendid regiment' was the Royal Lancasters. He was given the rank of lieutenant, and was promoted to captain in 1915. *Burnley News*, 9 December 1914, p. 4.

in 1910. They clashed at the Labour Party Conference held in Manchester in January 1917, a tumultuous event at which both spoke. Shaw supported the ILP motion calling for an immediate end to hostilities and a negotiated peace, Smith opposed it. He assured the meeting that all servicemen desired an early peace, but only on honourable terms, and these Germany was not prepared to countenance. Consequently the only way to safeguard Britain's institutions and freedoms was to persevere until unconditional victory was achieved. It was a principled stand by one of the few delegates with direct experience of the trenches, and when he reminded Ramsay MacDonald, Bruce Glasier, Philip Snowden and other ILP members that the sacrifices of those who were prepared to fight were made for them, they were silent. The integrity with which he spoke impressed the conference, and the motion was overwhelmingly defeated.[12]

Two months later this article appeared in the *Burnley News*:

CAPTAIN ALBERT SMITH, M.P.

> We have always had a sincere admiration for Captain Albert Smith, M.P., the Labour M.P. for Clitheroe, as we regard him as a man of sterling honesty of purpose: no mere office seeker, but a humble, willing worker in the great cause which is represented by men like himself in the House of Commons. We cannot forget that in the earlier stages of the war he displayed his sincerity and consistency by not only asking others to take up active service, but by himself joining the oversea forces and doing his bit to win a victory for the Allies. In view of Mr Smith's health it has been definitely decided that he shall not again go on active service. We hope he will live long to perform the Parliamentary and other work to which he is devoted. We know the United Textile Factory Workers are always glad to see him at their meetings, where he acts as vice-chairman. – Yesterday's "Cotton Times." [13]

Although Albert Smith did not return to active service his reputation remained high, but Nelson, his home town, was the part of the Clitheroe constituency most hostile to war, and when the new division of Nelson and Colne was created in 1918 his candidacy was challenged by local ILP, BSP and Women's Labour League groups, as well by a section of the Nelson Labour Party. Nevertheless he felt honour bound to stand, and the strength of his support amongst the textile unions and the Colne Labour Party ensured his victory.[14]

*

The Labour Party went into the 1918 election with a new constitution. Its principal architect was Arthur Henderson, Labour's representative in the wartime Coalition government, whose aim was to broaden the party's appeal by the creation of branches in every constituency and the enrolment of individuals as well as affiliated groups. The constitution also enshrined socialism as its philosophical basis, in order to 'secure for the producers by hand and brain the full fruits of their industry' through 'the common ownership of the means of production'.[15] However it was Sidney Webb's *Labour and the New Social Order* that guided the policies Labour offered in 1918 – full employment, social reform, nationalisation of industry, progressive taxation, and the redistribution of wealth. The hope and expectation was that post-war voters would return candidates who espoused such values.

The Representation of the People Act enfranchised all the remaining men over 21 who had previously been voteless, and women over the age of 30 if they were ratepayers or the wives of ratepayers. More than two million of them voted Labour in 1918, helping the party to increase its parliamentary representation from 42 to 57, but a new Coalition government was returned with an overwhelming majority, taking 473 seats. The tactic behind this success was 'the coupon'. The prime minister Lloyd George, and the Conservative leader Bonar Law, endorsed candidates who supported the continuance of the wartime Coalition by issuing them with letters of recommendation (coupons) which presented them as patriots whose steadfastness had secured victory. The strategy was remarkably effective. In Blackburn for example the sitting MP Philip Snowden, who had opposed the war, was unseated by Percy Dean, the coupon candidate and recent recipient of the Victoria Cross.

In the Clitheroe constituency, however, Labour won in a three way contest. When Albert Smith decided to stand in the Nelson and Colne division, the Clitheroe Labour Party adopted Alfred Davies as his replacement. He was, like Smith, a long-serving textile union official, but with a spinning rather than a weaving background. He had been a half timer at Arrowscroft mill in Hollingworth and a mule spinner in Hyde, and when he was rejected as too old for military service in 1914 he spent his after-work hours as a military hospital orderly. The committee that selected Davies knew that it would be difficult to retain the seat, not only because he faced coupon candidates from both the Liberals and the Conservatives, but because reorganisation had taken the most reliably socialist districts out of the constituency.[16] Consequently the 1918 campaign was carefully planned and vigorously implemented. Davies' manifesto focused on supporting Woodrow Wilson's peace plan, safeguarding trade union rights, treating demobbed soldiers and their families with consideration, and opposing the vested interests of capitalism. More specifically Davies called for reduced working hours so that an enlarged work force could be absorbed, and for rejection of the proposal to give trading preference to empire countries because it would increase the cost of imports from the rest of the world. He also demanded the provision of more working-class housing, and production for the needs of the poor rather than for the luxuries of the rich. 'If you want to make war impossible abolish poverty' became the local Labour mantra.[17]

Davies won the Clitheroe seat, but with a reduced majority. The count was completed earlier than expected and announced by W. Self Weeks, the deputy returning officer, at St. James' school. The figures were:

A. Davies (Labour)	9,578
E. Hartley (coupon Conservative)	8,419
J. Batty (coupon Liberal)	3,443
Labour majority	1,159[18]

The major new factor in this election was the female vote, calculated to have been particularly high in Clitheroe amongst the 13,282 women who qualified. Their political preferences are not known, but it has been assumed that because many of them were weavers employed in the district's mills, Labour would have been the main gainer. The well-established women's section of the town's ILP certainly campaigned for Davies because of his commitment to the establishment of a League of Nations, but the Labour Party did not set up a women's section until October 1918, only two months before polling day, too late, perhaps, to have much effect on voting intensions. The local press focused on first-time female voter concern with procedure, for some sought assurance from election officials that they had filled in their ballot papers in the way required, and others tried to enter the voting booths with their husbands. None, however, seemed concerned to conceal for whom they had voted.[19]

But if the new electors did, for the most part, support Labour, Davies was handicapped by attacks on his south Lancashire background and jibes in this weaving area that he was 'elected from the mulegate'.[20] Nevertheless his credentials compared well against those of Hartley, a Preston mill owner, and Batty, the director of a London assurance company, and he was one of only four textile trade unionist candidates out of ten who stood, to win his seat. The result therefore confirmed the Clitheroe constituency's reputation as an established centre of working-class opposition, still not prepared to accept the representatives of privilege and monopoly 19 years on from Sir Ughtred Kay-Shuttleworth's incumbency.

The Liberal/ Conservative Coalition failed the working class in the immediate post-war years. Unemployment increased during the recession of 1919–21, accompanied by an outbreak of strike action. The Sankey Commission was tasked with addressing the situation, but when its report on the coal industry recommended nationalisation, the government rejected it in favour of a short term subsidy and cuts in spending on housing, education and health services. But no subsidies were offered to the textile industry and job losses resulted. In the four years after 1918 for example the number of working looms in Blackburn fell from 90,000 to 48,000.[21] Clitheroe operatives were also badly affected, but they accepted their MP's request to trust in Labour Party pressure in parliament, rather than strikes, for an improvement. Until 1921 local branch resolutions dealt with pushing for the release of conscientious objectors, criticism of the government's support for anti-Bolshevik forces in the Russian civil war, and the need to increase female representation on the division's executive. Miss M. Lord was the first to become involved in this way, as Great Harwood's delegate in 1920, and by 1923 Mabel Barker (Great Harwood), Maggie Hargreaves (Clitheroe), and Mrs E. Dewhurst (Padiham) had joined her.[22]

It was not until 1920 that the Clitheroe Labour Party organised a campaign to hold the government to account for failing to honour its pledge to improve employment prospects and provide 'Homes for Heroes'. Similar campaigns throughout the country led to the break up of the Coalition in 1922 and a general election which gave the Conservatives a clear majority over all other parties. Bonar Law was thus able to take office as prime minister supported by 344 Conservative members in the House of Commons. The Liberal vote was split between the followers of Lloyd George and Asquith, but Labour more than doubled its vote, and with 142 MPs was able, for the first time, to fulfil the role of his majesty's loyal opposition. When the new parliament met, many candidates who had lost their seats in 1918 were present again. So were 86 trade union sponsored members, although Alfred Davies was not amongst them. In what the local press headlined as 'A Sensational Victory', he was well beaten by his Conservative rival William Brass:

Captain W. Brass (Conservative)	15,586
A. Davies (Labour)	12,911
Conservative majority	2,675

Why did he lose? He had been re-selected without demur. His campaign focused on just those Coalition weaknesses that won many seats for Labour – its failure to provide adequate care for afflicted soldiers, or decent housing and pensions for the working class. In common with successful Labour candidates elsewhere he criticised the Treaty of Versailles because the restrictions it placed on Germany made it impossible for that country to pay the indemnity the Allies had imposed upon it. He gained praise locally for his efforts to force wealthy landlords to release unused land for cultivation by ex-soldiers who would otherwise have had to emigrate, and he was therefore popular with many servicemen who had not voted in 1918 but who did so in 1922.[23]

Nevertheless Davies' defeat can be explained. In the election of 1918 the anti-Labour vote was split between the Conservative and Liberal candidates, whereas in 1922 not only did the Liberals not stand, they campaigned for Brass. Consequently the new additions to the constituency in the west, the Hurst Green and Chipping areas in which there had been considerable Liberal support in 1918, were lost to the Conservatives in 1922. Captain Brass was a personable candidate to whom the electorate warmed, especially after he disassociated himself from the unpopular protectionist policies of his own party. This undoubtedly attracted some free traders who had voted for Davies in 1918. And the Conservative agents, well organised by Tom Demain and the local chairman William Garnett, were far more effective in getting out the vote by deploying resources unavailable to their Labour counterparts – a fleet of cars to ferry supporters to polling stations, and volunteers from the Women's Unionist Association and Junior Conservatives to deliver propaganda and argue the case for Brass on the doorstep.

Alfred Davies himself attributed defeat to his advocacy of the capital levy, a device for promoting social reforms by reducing the war debt through a tax only on incomes over £6,000, but which, he claimed, voters mistakenly thought was a call for much wider tax increases.[24] The constituency Labour party accepted this analysis, and Davies was again adopted as its candidate in 1923. Ill health had forced Bonar Law to resign in May of that year. He was replaced as prime minister by Stanley Baldwin, who felt obliged to put his belief in protection as a solution to unemployment to the voters because it contravened the Conservatives' 1922 promise not to introduce tariffs. William Brass had ignored that pledge previously and he did so again in 1923, an ambiguous position Davies tried to exploit by arguing that there were benefits in Free Trade that neither Baldwin nor Brass understood, in particular the promotion of peace between nations that was stimulated by commercial cooperation.[25]

Davies was optimistic about his chances of retaking the Clitheroe seat. The capital levy came up again, crudely characterised by the Conservatives as a Labour grab of household goods, but this time Davies was confident

Mr. Davies's Question to Captain Brass.

"WOULD YOU OPPOSE MR. BALDWIN'S TARIFF PROPOSALS?"

LABOUR SUPPORTS FREE-TRADE AS PEACE AGENCY

EFFECT OF REDUCED WAGES ON HOME MARKET

CAPITAL LEVY AND OTHER LABOUR SCHEMES JUSTIFIED

Figure 45 – Alfred Davies and the 1923 General Election campaign

Source: *Clitheroe Advertiser and Times*, 23 November 1923, p. 13.

that he was communicating his idea effectively, and when he ridiculed the Tory claims he was well received.[26] He was also buoyed by the participation in his campaign of Katherine Bruce Glasier who was venerated as one of the founders of the Labour movement. She had been an associate of SDF and trade union leaders, a lecturer for the Fabian Society, a delegate to the first ILP conference at Bradford in 1893 and the only woman elected to its administrative council. She edited *Labour Leader* between 1916 and

1921, and was living in Earby, within a mile of the Clitheroe constituency boundary, at the time of the 1923 General Election.[27]

Together with her husband John, Katherine Bruce Glasier had helped David Shackleton in the 1902 by-election, but her contribution on behalf of Alfred Davies was less effective, for whilst she criticised post-war governments for their failure to introduce social reforms, her emphasis on the dislocation of Europe's economy following the occupation of the Rhur by France had little resonance with Clitheroe voters.[28] Davies pinned his hopes on attacking Tory policies on wages and pensions, both of which he wanted to raise and extend, and on emigration, which he thought should be discouraged. (See Figure 45.) In the event he reduced the Conservative majority but he did not win the seat. The outcome was affected, perhaps decisively, by the Liberal candidate who attracted votes that might otherwise have gone to Davies:

Captain W. Brass (Conservative)	12,998
A. Davies (Labour)	11,469
H. Derbyshire (Liberal)	5,810
Conservative majority	1,529

Nationally the Liberals, now reunited under Asquith's leadership, gained 153 seats, and Labour added 49 to its 1922 tally. Its total of 191 MPs was still fewer than the Conservatives' 258, but enough for it to form a minority government. The Clitheroe Labour Party took comfort from that, and expected that its nominee would join the parliamentary contingent in due course.[29] But Alfred Davies never again contested the division, indeed Labour's only further success in Clitheroe came in 1945, when Harry Randall won the seat as part of the Atlee landslide. Nevertheless 1923 was a landmark in the history of dissent, for though the first Labour government lacked a majority and was short lived, it had altered the political landscape and made the use of legislative power on behalf of the oppressed a practical possibility.

Notes and References

1 Oral testimony of Tom's daughter, Ruby Holland, to R. Smalley, 2001.

2 Clitheroe Labour Party Minutes, 23 November 1910. Shaw received 29 votes to Smith's 32. Shaw went on to represent Preston between 1918 and 1931, and was a member of both interwar Labour governments. See A. Fowler, *Lancashire Cotton Operatives and Work, 1900–1950* (Ashgate, Aldershot, 2003) p. 119.

3 P. Firth, 'Powerloom overlookers: labour aristocracy in north east Lancashire cotton weaving 1890–1920', *Transactions of the Lancashire and Cheshire Antiquarian Society* (99, 2003) pp. 183–184. Smith became secretary of the Nelson Overlookers Association in 1898 and president of the General Union of Loom Overlookers in 1902.

4 *Clitheroe Times*, 9 December 1910, p. 3.

5 *Burnley Gazette*, 20 October 1912, p. 5; *Burnley Express*, 28 September 1912, p. 5, 27 September 1913, p. 6. The 1918 Education Act raised the school leaving age to 14, but 13 year-olds could still obtain exemption until the half time system was abolished in 1920.

6 *Burnley Express*, 22 November 1913, p. 16.

7 *Ibid.*, 4 May 1912, p. 5.

8 *Ibid.*, 17 December 1913, p. 8.

9 *Burnley News*, 6 December 1913, p. 11.

10 *Ibid.*, 9 December 1914, p. 4.

11 *Ibid.*, 4 August 1915, p. 5; *Coventry Evening Telegraph*, 6 August 1915, p. 3.

12 *Burnley Express*, 27 January 1917, p. 10. Smith was the only Labour MP to hold a commission in the armed forces during the Great War.

13 *Burnley News*, 25 August 1917, p. 5.

14 Nelson and Colne Labour Party Minutes, 3 February 1918.

15 M. Worley, *Labour Inside the Gate. A History of the British Labour Party Between the Wars* (I. B. Tauris, London, 2005) p. 12.

16 Clitheroe Labour Party Minutes, 16 March 1918. Davies had two challengers for the nomination, Henry Lees who received two votes and Edgar Bootham who received nine. As the meeting had given Davies 58 votes his adoption was declared unanimous.

17 *Clitheroe Times*, 15 November 1918, p. 3.

18 *Clitheroe Times*, 3 January 1919, p. 3.

19 *Lancashire Evening Post*, 16 December 1918, p. 5. *Clitheroe Advertiser and Times*, 12 July 1918, p. 3; 18 October 1918, p. 1.

20 A. Fowler, *op.cit.*, pp. 124-125.

21 D. Beattie, *op.cit.*, p. 146.

22 Clitheroe Labour Party Minutes, 5 July 1919, 14 August 1920, 24 September 1921, 7 July 1923.

23 *Burnley News*, 21 October 1922, p. 5. *Clitheroe Advertiser and Times*, 27 October 1922, p. 10.

24 *Clitheroe Advertiser and Times*, 17 November 1922, p. 9.

25 *Ibid.*, 23 November 1923, p. 13.

26 *Ibid.*

27 H. Pelling, *op.cit.*, pp. 118, 123-124. N. and J. Mackenzie, *op.cit.*, pp. 185 and 196. Katherine Bruce Glasier lived at Glen Cottage in Earby from 1922 to her death in 1950.

28 *Clitheroe Advertiser and Times*, 23 November 1923, p. 13.

29 *Ibid.*, 7 December 1923, p. 7.

Chapter 8
The Development Of Local Government

Anglo Saxon ealdormen and Norman lords exercised absolute power over the people of the areas their kings had assigned to them. Little is known of how Wada used his authority as ealdorman of the lands that included Clitheroe, but his rebellion against the Northumbrian royal house he was supposed to serve led to his defeat and death at the Battle of Billington in 798.[1] Norman arrangements for local government are better understood, for a charter of 1283 which still survives refers to a lost predecessor issued by Henry de Lacy over a hundred years earlier which transferred the liberties and customs he controlled to Clitheroe's free burgesses. Their new privileges included land grants and common rights such as turbary (cutting peat for fuel) and pasturage (grazing for animals and geese).[2] Those who profited were few in number for only 12 free burgesses held land from the lord, in exchange for which they made payments or gave services of various kinds. It was from these obligations that the de Lacy charters released them, although the borough was still required to pay an annual rent of ten marks (*£*6 13*s* 4*d*) to the lord and each burgess 16*d* rent to his bailiffs. Nevertheless the concessions represented the first stage in the democratisation of local government and the emergence of new power holders. Their entitlements were jealously guarded by the erection of boundary stones to indicate the territory over which the town now had jurisdiction and from which more free burgesses could be drawn.[3]

The conduct of borough business moved from the castle, where it had previously been supervised by the absentee lord's steward, to the Moot Hall, although the castle and its precincts remained an independent administrative unit until the nineteenth century.[4] In practice early local government regulated behaviour through its courts. The most important of these was the Court of Inquiry which audited the borough accounts, adjudicated in cases of claims to burgess or freeman status, and managed corporate property. It was in the Court of Common Pleas, or Court Leet, that personal disputes between residents of the borough were tried. This court had the power to arrest and imprison those accused of crimes such as debt, fraud or affray, although misdemeanours of this sort committed at

Clitheroe markets were dealt with separately, at the Court of Pie Powder. A regional court covered matters relating to land drainage and sewage disposal in Ribblesdale.[5]

Pre-nineteenth century local government varied widely from place to place, but in Clitheroe the principal executive officers were two bailiffs who represented the two groups of burgesses, those who lived within the town's limits and those who lived outside but owned burgess property inside. Bailiffs were elected annually and rarely served consecutive terms.[6] They acted as Justices of the Peace and coroners at Quarter Sessions, but took advice from legal professionals – the Town Clerk and the Recorder – whom they and the burgesses were empowered to appoint. The Sergeant at Mace, appointed solely by the bailiffs, was more than a ceremonial official, for he had to summon juries and execute the decisions of the Court of Common Pleas, and because of that was frequently also the town's gaoler. Another important officer was the Constable, responsible not only for keeping order but for the maintenance of bridges, poor relief, and the burial of anyone who died within the borough's boundaries. In Clitheroe the owners of certain houses were liable for unpaid constabulary service or for supplying someone to take on the job, but with its onerous duties it was not coveted and often badly discharged.[7] Efficient local government needed minor officials to support this elite group – checkers of weights and measures, collectors of tolls and market stall rents, superintendents of common rights such as wood wardens to ensure the legitimate use of timber, pindars to care for stay animals, and scavengers who had an unspecified role but which perhaps involved the gathering and disposal of refuse.

Between them these men governed Clitheroe until 1835. They administered the law, assessed and collected taxes, imposed local rates, supervised elections to parliament and organised local elections. Call Books, that is lists of electors, show that the number of free burgesses fluctuated between 60 and 90 during the eighteenth century, but the Norman notion of a privileged 12 was perpetuated. In 1620 they were being referred to as 'The Bretheren', an inner circle that in the nineteenth century would become the aldermen and councillors of the Victorian municipality.

Although local government was not standardised in the period before 1835, everywhere it provided opportunities for abuse through patronage that was ridiculed by Fielding and Smollett, Hogarth and Cruickshank, and presented in their work as corrupt or indolent officials. Improprieties of the sort depicted by these writers and artists undoubtedly occurred in Clitheroe, although dissent amongst the victims is hard to find. In 1740 however two men, one from Downham and the other from Standen, brought an action against the bailiffs on behalf of the people of the area affected claiming that their rights had been infringed by the enclosure of the common at Goosebutts, thus reducing the amount of grazing available to them. An ambiguous judgement was given which acknowledged the plaintiffs' common rights but failed to require an adjustment to the boundaries of the enclosure. This omission encouraged the Corporation to apply for general enclosure of commons within the borough by Act of Parliament, to widespread annoyance, for when the Clitheroe Enclosure Act was passed in 1786 local government powers of interference were extended to an extra 350 acres.[8] Dissatisfaction also surfaced in the 1830s, for the parliamentary commissioners who were preparing the Municipal Corporations Bill reported that Clitheroe cotton manufacturers complained of difficulty finding labour. The reason was assumed to be the reluctance of potential employees to move to a town where there was a Court of Common Pleas, because this made the recovery of small debts expensive and incurred the possibility of imprisonment. At the time it was a major issue for local mill owners who felt pressure on their profits not only from a scarcity of workers but from neighbouring markets, and they expected the borough fathers to do something about it.[9]

*

This frustration had another cause. By the 1830s the cotton industry was well established in Clitheroe and vital to the local economy, yet the proprietors of the factories upon which the town's new prosperity depended were excluded from political influence because few of them were burgesses. However the situation was transformed in 1835 by the Municipal Corporations Act which restructured town government and replaced the burgess vote with a ratepayer franchise. The effect was to create what has been called a 'bourgeois revolution', for it gave a voice to Whig and Nonconformist industrialists at the expense of Tory squires who were masters of many acres. Clitheroe provides a classic example of the change, for the bailiffs of 1828, Robert Curzon and Peregrine Cust, represented the Anglican landed aristocracy, whereas their 1835 substitutes were the Primrose and Low Moor mill owners James Thomson and Jeremiah Garnett.[10]

In some respects the new Act narrowed rather than widened participation amongst borough residents, for it deprived those women of the vote who had been given it in 1739 for parish and poor law elections if they were property owning widows or spinsters. It also confined the electorate to men who had paid rates for three years, two more than the eligibility qualification required for voting in general elections. Clitheroe was one of 178 boroughs subject to the new arrangements, few of which were disadvantaged by them. In future the Corporation was to consist of 12 ratepayer elected councillors who would serve for three years, a third of whom would retire or seek re-election annually. From amongst their number the councillors could elect four aldermen who would hold office for six years. Only 26 English boroughs, including Clitheroe, still invested chief executive power in two bailiffs prior to 1835. Now they had to conform to the mayoral model and make do with one legal officer, the Town Clerk, for the position of Recorder was abolished.[11] The Act did not specify the responsibilities of these men beyond the formation of a police force, but in practice they exercised local control of matters relating to hospitals, dispensaries, public utilities, summary justice, the enforcement of paternity obligations, and vagrancy laws. Health, education and highways, although devolved responsibilities, continued to be administered by separate bodies, and the Poor Law never came within the Corporation's ambit.

The first municipal election to be held in Clitheroe under the provisions of the 1835 Act dealt a crushing blow to the old order for all 12 successful candidates represented the reform interest, however the transitional team included a rump of members from the previous authority. (See Figure 46.) The *Blackburn Gazette* heralded the result as an end to waste and corruption and the start of government for 'the comfort and welfare of the inhabitants'. The men who were expected to provide it met for their inauguration at the Town Hall on 1 January 1836, presided over by Clitheroe's first mayor, William Horsfall, who had recently sold his share in Low Moor mill to his partner Jeremiah Garnett, one of the new aldermen.[12]

But the *Gazette's* hopes were initially disappointed, for the changes did not lead to the more purposeful activity it predicted. The new Council met only five or six times a year, no committees were appointed to oversee its work, and as a result borough business remained sluggish until 1848. In that year much interest was aroused by the Public Health Act which gave local authorities the power to introduce street cleansing, refuse collection, a water supply and a sewerage system, however the legislation was not mandatory and Clitheroe did not adopt it. Indeed after a cholera outbreak in the town in 1850 a proposed water supply scheme was defeated by rate payers led by mill owners on the grounds of cost. In 1852 further pressure to conform to the Local Government Board's wishes was overcome by the simple expedient of reducing the salary of the surveyor charged with implementing the plan to 25*s* per annum, thus forcing him to resign, and it was only in 1854, when a local board of health was established, that the Clitheroe Waterworks Act was passed.[13]

Reformers

Thomson	J.	Primrose	215	Ald.
Garnett	J.	Roefield	214	Ald.
Horsfall	W.	Waddow	214	
Howarth	J.	Brewer	214	
Hodgson	J.		213	
Cockshutt	W.		213	
Hornby	R.		213	
Stewart	J.		213	
Robinson	H.		212	
Haworth	J.	Grocer	200	
Whalley	H.		183	

Tories

Oddie	W.L.		7
Baldwin	L.		4
Bowman	T.		3
Watson	J.		3
Kay	R.		1
Henderson	J.		1
Nowell	J.		1
Arkwright	W.		1
Garforth	J.		1
Thompson	J.	Hatter	1
Dewhurst	W.B.		1

The Council to consist of 4 Aldermen (Ald)
12 Councillors (Cnr)

Carried over from the previous Authority

Oddie	W.L.	Ald.
Garstang	J.	Ald.
Kay	R.	Cnr.
Mercer	J.	Cnr.
Braithwaite		Cnr.

The Councillors appoint that Ald. Oddie and Ald. Garstang shall be the Aldermen to go out of Office in the year 1838

The Council declares that:-
Cnr. Robinson, Cnr. Whalley, Cnr. Stewart, Cnr. Haworth, grocer, having been selected by the smallest number of votes shall go out of Office in Nov. 1836

And that Cnr. Hornby, Cnr. Cockshutt, Cnr. Braithwaite, Cnr. Hodgson having been elected by the next smallest number of votes shall go out of Office in Nov. 1837.

Figure 46 – The first Clitheroe Municipal Election Results, 1835

Source: C. Ainsworth, *Clitheroe Municipal Elections 1835–1972*, collated from Council Minutes. Clitheroe public library local studies collection. P21, p. 1.

The structure of municipal government which is detailed in Figure 47 suggests that by the mid-1850s the Town Council was more active and better organised than it had been in the immediate post-1835 period, nevertheless it had some problems discharging its functions. Finding a mayor was not always easy for example. In 1850 the office was declared vacant because the incumbent, Robert Stewart, had been absent from the borough for more than two months, and in 1862 no councillor was prepared to take on the role. The situation was resolved only when James Garnett, the Low Moor mill owner who was a newly elected first time member of the Council, agreed to accept the job. Furthermore, when a fire brigade was formed in 1840 and a superintendent of it appointed once housing for the engine had been found, his salary was fixed at £75, and for that he had to carry out the duties of Borough Surveyor, Collector of Rates, and Inspector of Nuisances and Common Lodging Houses as well. The post was always hard to fill.[14]

Implementing local government according to the model imposed in 1835 was clearly difficult in Clitheroe and dissent was an inevitable consequence, but now it was frequently driven by those who had previously been its target – the Tories. In 1870 they accused Low Moor Radicals of intimidating Conservative voters at the polling station by following them into the voting booths or pulling their coat tails to prevent them from doing so. A repetition was avoided in 1871 although only one vote was registered for Brown, the Conservative candidate, against the 130 cast for Johnson, the Liberal, which perhaps indicates residual fear of mistreatment in a reform stronghold, for Tory supporters there were more numerous than these figures suggest.[15]

By the 1880s however local politics had acquired the appearance of permanence and respectability commonly associated with municipal councils in late Victorian Britain. Committees had been set up to deal with finance, school attendance, the cattle market, lighting, highways, nuisance, the free library, the fire brigade, gas and waterworks. In addition the Watch Committee supervised the police force, and the General Purposes Committee oversaw all matters relating to the work of the Council. The borough rate in 1884 was 1¼*d*, which gave the town £1,050 12*s* 6*d* with which to operate. Bickering over its allocation of course occurred, notably the purchase of 380 books to supplement the stock of the library, to which some councillors took exception because of the town's other pressing needs, but the risk of collapse which looked possible in the century's middle years seemed to have been overcome.[16]

Figure 47 – The Structure of Clitheroe's Government in 1855

Source: Clitheroe public library local studies collection. E02 CLI. 103.

The list of townships in the Clitheroe Union refers to those communities whose poor had to apply to the workhouse at Coplow for relief. After the 1894 Local Government Act was passed the Lancashire townships were administered by the Clitheroe Rural District Council. The administration of the Poor Law however remained the responsibility of the Guardians of the Clitheroe Union for both the Yorkshire and Lancashire townships within its boundaries.

CLITHEROE. 1854/5.

Mayor....John Mercer, Esq.
Aldermen .... Jeremiah Garnett, Esq., Robert Clark, Esq., Jude Hargreaves, Esq., John Mercer, Esq.
Councillors....Richard Johnson, Robert Dewhurst, Robert Hargreaves Archibald William Dewhurst, Richard Smith, William Redmayne Henry Hall, Richard Ellison, George Braithwaite, Ambrose Bulcock, Thomas Squires and Edward Hodgson.
Town Clerk....Robert Trappes, Esq., Stanley House, Clitheroe.
Assessors....James Dean and Richard Varley.
Auditors....John Watson and William Bolton Dewhurst.
Recorder....John Addison, Esq., Preston.
Coroner....John Hargreaves, Esq., solicitor, Blackburn.
Sergeant-at-Mace....Thomas Hothersall, innkeeper.
County Magistrates for the district....J. T. W. Aspinall, Esq., Standen Hall, near Clitheroe; William Assheton, Esq., Downham Hall, near Clitheroe; Jeremiah Garnett, Esq.; Theophilus Hastings Ingham, Esq.; John Addison, Esq; W. Winstanley, Esq., Chaigley Manor House; T. G. Parker, Esq., Browsholme; Jonathan Peel, Esq., Hodder Bank; Ralph Assheton, Esq., Downham Hall.
Chairman of Petty Sessions....J. T. W. Aspinall, Esq.
Petty Sessions....Held every alternate Thursday, at the Police Court Church-street.
First meeting of Petty Sessions....January 11, 1855.
Clerk to Magistrates....Henry Hall, Esq., Duck-street; and Dixon R binson, Esq., Clitheroe Castle,
Superintendent of Police....R. Carswell, Burnley.
Inspector of Police....James Clegg.
Police Office....Church-street.
Inspector of Weights and Measures....Christopher Lancaster, Shaw Bridge.
County Court....[See list of County Courts.]
Townships comprised in the Clitheroe Union....Lancashire townships Aighton, Bailey, and Chaigley, Bowland Little, Chatburn, Chipping Clitheroe, Downham, Leagrim, Mearley, Mitton Little, otherwise Mitton, Henthorn, and Coldcoats, Pendleton, Thornley-with-Wheatley Twiston, Whalley, Wiswell, Worston.—Yorkshire townships: Bashall otherwise Bashall-Eaves, Bolton-by-Bowland, Higher Division o Bowland, Lower Division of Bowland, West Bradford, Easington, Gisburn, Gisburn Forest, Grindleton, Horton, Middop, Great Mitton Newsholme, Newton, Paythorne, Rimmington, Sawley, Slaidburn Waddington.
Clerk to the Local Board of Health....Mr. John Eastham.
Surveyor to the Local Board of Health....Mr. William Hargreaves Russell-street.
Board of Guardians meet every Tuesday, at eleven a.m., at their Office in Moor-lane.
Clerk to the Board....Samuel Wood
Superintendent Registrar....Samuel Wood.
Registrar of Births, Deaths, and Marriages....John Harling Bailey, York-street.
Overseers' Office....Railway View.
Collector of Assessed Taxes....Thomas Bourne, Railway View.
Assessor of ditto and Income Tax....Thomas Bourne, Railway View.
Collector of Income Tax....Thomas Bourne, Railway View.
Excise Office....Swan Inn
Stamp Office....William Whewell, Castle-street.
Post Office....Castle-street; postmaster, Henry Whalley.
Bank....Messrs. Alcocks, Birkbecks, and Co., Church street.
Clerk to the Commissioners of Land and Assessed Taxes....Messrs. Trappes and Eastham, Lowergate.

Local government based on a wider franchise than that available for national elections enabled a 'radical' or 'reform' faction not only to contest, but sometimes to win control. Low Moor's overwhelmingly working-class population habitually voted Liberal, though with diminishing enthusiasm because their elected representatives were inconsistent in promoting their interests. This led directly to the emergence of a socialist group within the Council chamber. The catalyst was the defection of James Garnett to the Conservatives, an easy move for a paternalist who expected his employees to vote the way he told them even when he was a Liberal. By the 1880s James, together with his brother William and his son Thomas, were prominent Conservative councillors whose views many considered inimical to working-class aspirations.[17]

The first socialists to try for council seats were Henry Speak, Matthias Mitchell and Miles Lord in 1894, but it was not until 1905 that James Windle, standing for Labour, was successful, elected with the second highest of the four qualifying votes, and well ahead of the Liberal candidates. (See Appendix III.) In that year, however, Labour caused a sensation by gaining control of local government in Nelson.

*

Nelson did not exist at the time of the 1835 Municipal Corporations Act, but further local government legislation in 1858 had enabled it to be created out of the parishes of Great and Little Marsden, and when the population reached 20,000 in 1890 Nelson applied for, and was granted, borough status. A Trades Council was formed the same year, an SDF branch in 1891, and an ILP branch in 1893, so the development of political dissent in the town closely matched both its infancy as a municipality and its inclusion within the Clitheroe parliamentary constituency. The working class seized the opportunity and established a presence on the new Borough Council from the start, for William Ward, president of the Nelson Weavers' Association, and Lawrence Tattersall, a local newsagent, were elected as 'Labour' councillors in 1890, the year the town received its charter. They were re-elected subsequently until Tattersall retired in 1895 and Ward was defeated in 1899, however the first SDF candidate, John Smith, a clogger, lost in Bradley Ward in 1892, and all further SDF attempts to gain council seats between 1893 and 1902 failed, causing it to abandon municipal representation as an aim. The ILP fared little better, and after failures every year between 1893 and 1896 presented only one more candidate, James Aspen in 1899. He also lost, and costs estimated at £14 per attempt put the party out of the reckoning until LRC support became available in 1901. William Rickard's breakthrough that year was followed by victories for Smith and Pickles in 1902, and the growing confidence of the ILP was reflected in the production of detailed manifestos. These promised a public library, abattoir, dispensary and allotments in 1903, and better health provision, inspection of foodstuffs, non-sectarian education, and full implementation of the Unemployed Workmen Act in 1905.[18] That year the LRC won in all five wards with an average of 54.3 per cent of the vote, a result which forced the Liberals to concede that the electorate had finally rejected their leadership and now wanted a Labour administration.[19] (See Appendix IV.)

The Nelson branches of the SDF and ILP have been dismissed as nothing more than propaganda organisations, the SDF too 'exotic' and 'irreconcilable' to be effective and the ILP 'content to act as a left wing pressure group'.[20] This is a harsh judgement, for the influence the Labour Party was able to exert on that part of the Clitheroe constituency between 1905 and 1918 was clearly based on the preparatory work of their predecessors in moving working-class sentiment away from Liberalism and towards a more inclusive political vision which embraced precisely the sort of dissent the Nelson Labour Party represented.

*

Nineteenth century legislation that aimed at improving the way municipal corporations were run had simplified and extended urban local government, but anomalies remained. In Clitheroe the most glaring example was the status of the castle. The Lords of the Honour of Clitheroe had no intention of subjecting themselves to the jurisdiction their charters had granted to the borough, and they deliberately excluded the castle from it. Castle residents therefore paid no rates, and buried their dead outside Clitheroe or in the castle chapel of St. Michael. Neither did they contribute to the cost of poor relief or the maintenance of the borough's roads, bridges and water supply, although they used them like anyone else in the town. The Local Government Act of 1894 ended these privileges by abolishing the parish of Clitheroe Castle and incorporating it into the municipality.[21]

Another anomaly concerned Clitheroe's rural hinterland, for the 1885 boundary changes which had brought more industrial communities into the constituency also embraced rural areas mainly to the north and west of Clitheroe. Administration here was reorganised by the Local Government Acts of 1888 and 1894. In the medieval period county sheriffs had executed royal writs, collected taxes, mustered military levies, presided over courts and organised parliamentary elections outside the incorporated boroughs, and ecclesiastical courts dealt with tithe disputes, matrimonial suits and charges of sexual impropriety. From the mid-fifteenth century Lords Lieutenant gradually replaced sheriffs and the focus of county government switched to training troops and tracking down religious deviants, most famously the so-called 'Pendle Witches' in 1612. Paid officials such as provost marshalls and overseers of the poor were appointed to deal with rogues, vagabonds and paupers, but they were not professional administrators and rural local government was frequently inefficient or corrupt. The Act of 1888 aimed to remedy the situation by creating 50 County Councils in England, and that of 1894 by sub-dividing them into Rural District Councils.[22]

Hitherto day to day business at county level had been conducted by the Court of Quarter Sessions, a wholly unrepresentative body whose members, the Justices of the Peace, were appointed by the Lord Lieutenant. The new County Councils were to be elected by ratepayers and have responsibility for police, bridges, roads, animal health, food and drugs, asylums, reformatories and industrial schools.[23] Lord Salisbury's Conservative government expected the County Councils to provide improved administrative efficiency, but not greater democratic accountability, for women were excluded from the ratepayer franchise and the time demands on councillors restricted men who could consider becoming candidates to the gentry and the newly rich industrialists. The first Lancashire County Council therefore contained 49 Conservatives (mainly country gentlemen from the north), 46 Liberals (mainly manufacturers from the south), 7 Liberal Unionists and 3 Independents. This sort of balance was maintained until 1919 and the major parties tried to govern by consensus. It was an arrangement Labour was unable to challenge before 1910, when Albert Smith, who became Clitheroe's MP later that year, was their one success, but by 1919 there were 13 Labour candidates, 11 of whom were elected.[24] However no Clitheroe County Councillor was a representative of the Labour Party until 1952. (See p. 158 below.)

The Rural District Councils created by the 1894 Act had more limited powers, and they were confined to the civil parishes within their boundaries. In the case of the Clitheroe Rural District Council (CRDC) these were Aighton, Bailey and Chaigley, Little Bowland, Leagram, Chatburn, Chipping, Downham, Clitheroe Castle, Little Mitton, Henthorne and Coldcoates, Mearley, Pendleton, Thornton-with-Wheatley, Twiston, Whalley, Wiswell and Worston. Rural District councillors were elected for three years to represent these parishes either separately or in groups, although Clitheroe Castle was excepted because it contained only one inhabited house and became part of the Borough of Clitheroe in 1895. The ten members of the first CRDC invited Ralph Assheton to be their chairman, appointed John Eastham to be their clerk, and adopted an appropriate coat of arms and motto.[25] (See Figures 48 and 49.)

In theory the ratepayer franchise should have facilitated dissent at this level of local government, but in practice both Rural District and County councillors preferred to avoid confrontation, and voter apathy discouraged the development of faction. This was generally the case with CRDC where Ralph Assheton typified the leisured, educated, deeply conservative country gentlemen who had always been rural political leaders, and whose sense of duty was admired and often kept them in office for years. Ralph Assheton served on CRDC until 1949 and was a Lancashire County Councillor as well, doing trojan work with respect to rural schools and agricultural matters such as cattle plague in particular.[26]

Figure 48 – The Membership of the first Clitheroe Rural District Council, 1894–98

Source: T. Rushton, *Clitheroe Rural District Council Jubilee Year Celebrations Souvenir 1954*. Clitheroe public library local studies collection. P24.

Ralph Cockayne Assheton, Esq., J.P. (elected first Chairman of the Council from outside Council)

The Rev. James Pinnington, S.J., Aighton, Bailey and Chaigley

James Bamber, Little Bowland and Leagram

William Hanson, Chatburn

John Kenyon, Chipping

James Worswick, Downham and Twiston

Robert Hindle, Pendleton

Thomas Kenyon, Thornley-with-Wheatley

Thomas Longworth, Whalley

Arthur Longworth, Wiswell and Little Mitton, Henthorn and Coldcoates

John Porter, Worston and Mearley

Figure 49 – The Coat of Arms of the Clitheroe Rural District Council, created in 1894

Source: T. Rushton, *Clitheroe Rural District Council Diamond Jubilee Year Celebrations Souvenir 1954*. Clitheroe public library local studies collection. P24.

The shield design represents the rivers Ribble, Hodder, Calder and Loud in silver against a green background. The whales with abbots' croziers are a punning reference to Whalley Abbey, linked by red roses of the House of Lancaster.

The crest includes the battlements of Clitheroe castle, the tincture of the de Lacys, the lion of the Sherburnes, the Stonyhurst ermine, the coronet of the Stanleys, and the mullet of the Asshetons.

The latin motto means 'Our task is to look after the needs of the countryside.'

*

The 1894 Local Government Act also created Urban District Councils (UDCs). There were four of these in the eastern part of the Clitheroe constituency, at Padiham, Brierfield, Barrowford and Trawden. The first meeting of Barrowford UDC took place on 3 December 1894 in the Cooperative Society Reading Room, when nine councillors who had retained office from the outgoing administration known as the 'Local Board' were joined by three newly elected members.[27] This group dealt with devolved local government matters through three committees – building and sanitary, highway lighting, and finance and general purposes – and their work was typical of all UDCs in the late-nineteenth and early-twentieth centuries. Concern was expressed when cases of typhoid could not be attributed to the drains;[28] Dr Sim of Gisburn Road was granted permission to install a private telephone line to help him deal with a scarlet fever epidemic;[29] lists of residents excused payment of rates because of poverty (28 of them in June 1896) were regularly updated;[30] application was made to the Local

Government Board for the purchase of a 'steam road roller' at a cost of £355;[31] and consideration was given to the construction of a new light railway.[32]

In the 1890s Padiham UDC, a larger local authority than Barrowford with extra committees dedicated, for example, to technical instruction and school attendance, was also concerned about transport. Indeed in 1898 it formed an alliance with Brierfield UDC to oppose Burnley Coporation's tramways plans. The dispute dragged on until 1901 when the Padiham UDC agreed to levy a rate of 4*s* in the pound to cover the cost of buying track from Burnley for £3,193.[33] But in general the administrative changes initiated by the Acts of 1888 and 1894 led to more efficient local government, although they disappointed political radicals because they did not allow women to become councillors and the Poor Law was not brought under Council control. Both would become contentious issues within the Clitheroe constituency.

Notes and References

1 The battle is mentioned in the Anglo Saxon Chronicle and included in A. Langshaw's *Clitheroe's Thousand Years, op.cit.*, p. 92. See also R. Smith, *Blackburnshire : A Study in Early Lancashire History* (Leicester University Press, 1961) p. 31. Wada had conspired to kill Ethelred, King of Northumbria in its declining years. King Eardulf, Ethelred's successor, avenged the murder at this battle.

2 W. Self Weeks, *Clitheroe in the Seventeenth Century* (Advertiser and Times, Clitheroe, 1927) p. 10. Initially Bashall Moor was designated as the place where peat could be cut. This site was replaced by one on Pendle in another grant of Henry de Lacy, dated 1307.

3 C. Ainsworth, *Clitheroe from Burgage Plots to Boundary Stones* (Ainsworth Research Trust, Darwen, 2003) pp. 2-3.

4 The original location of the Moot Hall is unknown, but in 1608 it was in Church Street and was demolished in 1822 to make way for a new Town Hall which today forms part of the public library.

5 C. Ainsworth, *op.cit.*, p. 18.

6 For a full list of bailiffs from 1694 to 1835 see C. Ainsworth, *op.cit.*, pp. 44-46.

7 W. Self Weeks, *op.cit.*, p. 63. Women who owned qualifying houses were under the same obligations as men.

8 C. Ainsworth, *op.cit.*, p. 111. The areas affected were High Moor and Shay, Low Moor, Little Moor, Salthill Moor, Higher and Lower Back Commons, Church Moor Ing, Lidgeat Green, Devil Upon Dunn Green, Up Brooks, Pimlico Green, and 'Waste at top of Fairy Banks'. See *A Handlist of Enclosure Acts and Awards* (Record Publication No. 1, Lancashire C. C. Preston, 1946) p. 12.

9 W. Self Weeks, *The Surrender of the Charters of the Borough of Clitheroe* (Rawson and Co., Manchester, 1931) pp. 54-55.

10 B. Hilton, *A Mad, Bad and Dangerous People? England 1783–1846* (OUP, Oxford, 2006) p. 163. *Borough Record*, 28 October 1955, p. 3.

11 W. Self Weeks, *The Surrender of the Charters, op.cit.*, p. 285.

12 *Blackburn Gazette*, 30 December 1835, 6 January 1836.

13 J. Eastham, secretary to Robert Trappes, Town Clerk, a manuscript memoir published in part in *Clitheroe Times*, 28 April 1905. Clitheroe public library local studies collection. E02. See also R. Lewis, *Edwin Chadwick and the Public Health Movement 1832–1854* (Longman, London, 1952) pp. 305-306.

14 The Clitheroe Borough Minutes, manuscript extracts, Clitheroe public library local studies collection. E02 CLI.

15 Unidentified press cutting, Clitheroe public library local studies collection. P21.

16 *Ibid.*

17 William, brother of James, was a Council member for 30 years, three times mayor, and a JP. He was made a freeman of the borough in 1905. Thomas, son of James, was a councillor for 20 years, always refusing to become an alderman. Nevertheless he took office as mayor on five occasions and served as a JP for both the borough and the county. He called himself an 'Independent Conservative' and supported some Liberal policies such as their opposition to Tariff Reform.

18 P. Firth, 'Socialism and the Origins of the Labour Party in Nelson and District 1890–1906', MA, Manchester University, 1975, pp. 24-25.

19 *Nelson Leader*, 3 November 1905, p. 5.

20 P. Firth, *op.cit*,. p. 101.

21 W. Self Weeks, *Clitheroe in the Seventeenth Century*, *op.cit.*, pp. 131-132.

22 The long established ecclesiastical parishes had different boundaries and no secular legislative powers.

23 Policing, uniquely, was administered by a Standing Joint Committee of councillors and county JPs.

24 In the 1910 Lancashire County Council election Albert Smith was the Old Trafford candidate.

25 At the time John Eastham was also Town Clerk of Clitheroe.

26 J. Marshall, (ed.), *The History of Lancashire County Council 1889 to 1974* (Robertson, London, 1977) pp. 79-80.

27 Those who had retained office were messrs Wiseman, Nutter, England, Baldwin, Bracewell, Dugdale, Faraday, Hartley and Emmott. The new councillors were messrs Duckworth, Hargreaves and Atkinson. See Barrowford UDC Minutes, 20 August 1892. Lancashire Archives Preston, UDBA 1/1. Council meetings were moved to the offices of the Albert Mills as soon as a seven year lease was negotiated.

28 Barrwford UDC Minutes, *op.cit.*, 5 April 1894.

29 *Ibid.*, 2 May 1895.

30 *Ibid.*, 4 June 1896.

31 *Ibid.*, 3 August 1899.

32 *Ibid.*, 20 December 1900.

33 Padiham UDC Minutes, 19 May 1898 and 21 March 1901. Lancashire Archives Preston, UDPA 8/2.

Chapter 9

Dissent In Local Government

Although the Labour Party did not win a seat on Clitheroe Town Council until 1905, the influence of the Left on local government had been felt from the 1890s. The Poor Law Amendment Act of 1834 had placed governance of workhouses not with municipal authorities but with Boards of Guardians separately elected on a wider ratepayer franchise which included women. The Clitheroe Union guardians were slow to implement the 1834 arrangements for poor relief and the new accommodation at Coplow was not ready until 1873. Its construction and management became a major issue of dissent, especially amongst guardians from outlying communities within the boundaries of the Clitheroe Union, and when the Poor Law Board was replaced by the Local Government Board in 1871, they demanded stronger representation. Their argument was that the poor rate in country areas would rise when the new workhouse opened, as would the workload on guardians. In response the Local Government Board added to the allocation of seats for remote districts, but only by two, far fewer than the country guardians expected. Despite protests the number was not augmented further, indeed it has been claimed that the Local Government Board granted the increase only to secure acceptance of their planning proposals. These had estimated that £6,000 would be needed to build the new workhouse, a figure that guardians from within the borough of Clitheroe considered far too low. They put the cost at £15,000, and claimed that the Board used the offer of extra seats for areas beyond Clitheroe as a bribe to overcome the borough guardians' objections.[1] In the event the initial grandiose scheme had to be modified, the intended imposing central cupola was dropped and the generous window spacing reduced in order to save money. (See Figure 50.)

When Coplow opened in 1873 disputes amongst the guardians continued, now focused on the facilities offered to pauper applicants. Robert Dewhurst, chairman of the Building Committee, thought that a suggestion to purchase dining tables of the sort used at Haslingden workhouse would make inmates feel like prisoners because they would have to sit back-to-back at meal times. He wanted them to be able to face each other and talk, just as domestic servants and agricultural labourers did in the big houses and farms where they worked. However Canon Wilson, rector of Bolton-by-Bowland, argued that 'you cannot consider that paupers should have the same comforts as ratepayers'.[2] He and a majority of guardians favoured limiting the consolations of workhouse dining to Christmas, a common convention at the time. Contemporary accounts indicate that the seasonal fare at Coplow was good, plentiful and appreciated, but in return the poor were expected to be content with meagre rations eaten in silence during the rest of the year.[3]

There was also disagreement about the salary that should be offered to the medical officer. The parsimonious faction wanted to set it at £20, though Thomas Parker of Browsholme, chairman of the guardians, successfully pressed for an increase because the doctor concerned was expected to supply the drugs he prescribed out of it.[4] But thus far differences were above party. It was not until the 1890s that they became political, when

Figure 50 – Plans for Clitheroe Union Workhouse at Coplow

Source: F. Lofthouse, *Keepers of the House* (Hudson History, Settle, 2001) p. 77.

The final version dispensed with the cupola and retained the window reduction.

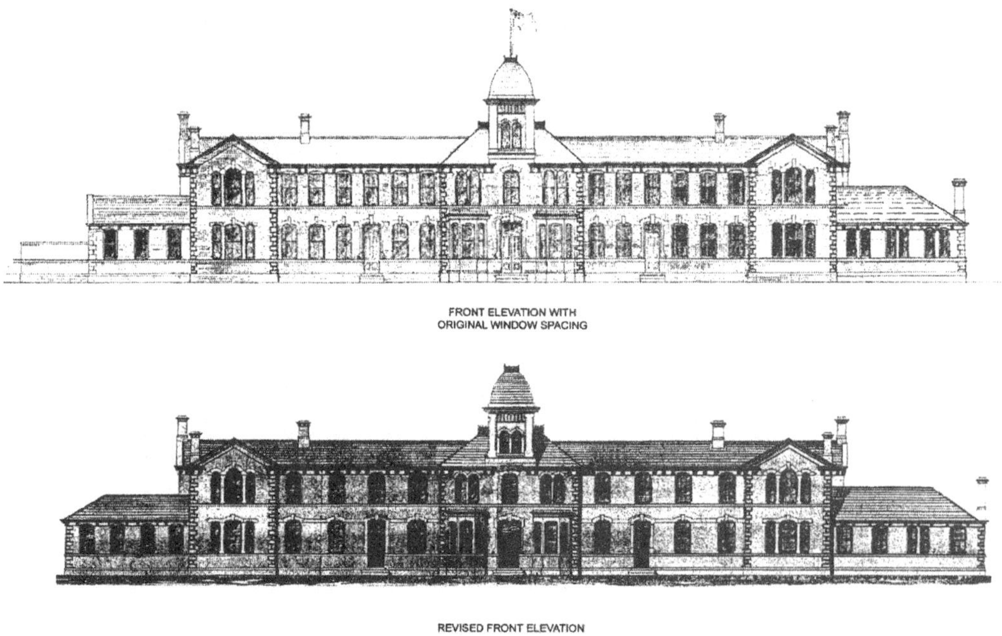

the matter of visiting committees split the guardians on sectarian lines. The spark for this development was a case of birching. The regulations forbade corporal punishment for boys under 14, but in 1898 the Master, Mr Martin, broke a rod whilst administering six strokes to a nine year old, Joseph Westall, for 'disobedience and running off'. His father was in prison, but his mother, also a Coplow inmate, complained and was put on short rations for doing so. The Conservative group, led by Canon Wilson, Thomas Wolfenden, William Dewhurst and James Norcross supported the Master, and when John Clarke, a socialist, intervened on behalf of the Westalls he was accused of undermining discipline simply to gain votes in an imminent election for which he was a candidate.[5] The *Clitheroe Times* sided with Clarke and promoted the idea of visiting committees to monitor the management of the workhouse in future, a measure which the Local Government Board had permitted since 1893.[6] Sam Green, Miles Lord and Thomas Benson, all socialist guardians, called for a Ladies' Visiting Committee, believing it would be of special comfort to workhouse women. The Conservative guardians ridiculed the idea, and Ralph Assheton referred to such a move as tantamount to licencing a team of female spies.[7] However another Conservative, William Self Weeks, pointed out that the proposers' socialism was irrelevant to what would be a beneficial innovation, and the motion to create a Ladies' Committee was approved, though only by one vote, 13 to 12.

The socialist guardians went on to develop the role of champions of more humane treatment for paupers. Robert Jones suggested that the practice of issuing bread by weight be replaced by putting bread on the tables and allowing inmates to help themselves.[8] Thomas Benson asked why a place for early arrivals to wait in until the Relieving Officer came on duty at 5 p.m. could not be provided, and argued against depriving those who applied for relief of the vote if they were on strike, or if bad weather had caused them to lose their employment. He considered such discrimination to be 'outside the pale of civilisation', and highlighted the case of a Dunsop Bridge quarryman, a good worker but 60 years old and slow, who was only able to earn 8*s* a week and therefore had to enter the workhouse. Just then the guardians were planning to increase the amount of stone able-bodied paupers were required to break each day from 13 cwt. to a ton, but Benson suggested that a bonus be paid to anyone who broke more than 13 cwt., and that the extra stone would more than compensate for the labour costs as well as demonstrating a compassionate attitude.[9]

None of these proposals was accepted, but in 1899 a socialist demand that the Clitheroe guardians supplement the government allocation of 2*s* 6*d* a week for each local pauper over 65 years of age to the value of

5*s* was approved. It was a measure that anticipated the introduction of a national old age pension by a decade.[10] Furthermore, by the turn of the century a Ladies' Committee had elected a president and a secretary and was ready to start work, although its first recommendation disappointed its socialist sponsors for it approved the old individual bread allowance and recommended that the bread be cut more thinly.[11]

*

After 1905 it became increasingly possible for matters of dissent to be pursued in the Council chamber. James Windle was elected as the Labour Party's first Clitheroe councillor that year, and Robert Parker the second in 1906. But progress was slow. Windle lost his seat in 1908, coming bottom of the poll, and it was not until 1913 that Austin Cottam, William Seedall and George Hargreaves had joined Parker to form a distinct group in local government which was able to intervene on issues affecting the working class. At the time these were the quality and provision of housing, improvements in public health and education, and the need for voting districts to be adjusted so that workers, the majority of the town's population, would be more fairly represented on the Council. (See Figure 51.)

Of the new councillors it was William Seedall who became the most prominent proponent of political dissent in the post-war years. His family lived in Low Moor and were Garnett employees. William's father was killed in an accident at the mill, and William himself worked there between the ages of 13 and 50. In that period he was active with the village Wesleyan school and chapel, he became secretary of the local Mutual Improvement Society, and was elected to the board of management of the Nelson Street Cooperative Society, from which position he negotiated a merger with its Low Moor rival. Subsequently he worked as an insurance clerk for the Weavers' Association, and, as its secretary, gained a reputation as 'an eloquent and forceful speaker, fearless in the advocacy of the workers' cause.'[12]

Following his election in 1912 Seedall argued for Council meetings to be open to the public and held in the evenings, so as to encourage more working-class engagement with municipal affairs. For over 20 years his energetic leadership, especially as chairman of the Health Committee, forced Conservative dominated Councils to confront issues they would rather have avoided, and as a result he gained respect for his commitment to the town's welfare. His efforts were recognised in 1921 when he became a JP for the borough and the county, in 1923 when he succeeded J. Sunderland as president of the Clitheroe Labour Party, and in 1925 when he was elected Clitheroe's first Labour mayor.[13]

The promotional material issued by Labour each October as local elections neared, demanded that the working class be afforded immediate access to what generations of dissidents had called for – education, recreational facilities, child welfare and work, but the overriding concern in the 1920s and 30s was housing. Like their counterparts across the land Labour councillors in Clitheroe wanted Lloyd George to keep his promise of making Britain 'a fit country for heroes to live in',[14] yet they saw little

Figure 51 – Labour's Manifesto for the 1911 Clitheroe Municipal Election

Source: 'Clitheroe Cuttings Book 1909–29'. Clitheroe public library local studies collection. A33.

Robert Jones missed being elected by 49 votes in 1911 and by 24 in 1922, but he won a council seat in 1923. George Hargreaves became mayor in 1937.

MUNICIPAL ELECTION, 1911.

TO THE ELECTORS OF THE BOROUGH OF CLITHEROE.

Ladies and Gentlemen,

Having been invited by the Trades and Labour Council to contest the forthcoming November Election on behalf of organised labour, we have pleasure in accepting the invitation.

If you elect us, we shall endeavour to do our best for the benefit of the town generally. Along with other measures we shall advocate are Recreation and Playgrounds which we think is a very pressing need, for in this modern age, when the motor traffic is so dangerous to children playing in the streets, we see the necessity of the above measure.

We again advocate dividing the town into wards so as to give the workers a more direct representation.

We are of the opinion that the best Laws are useless unless they are put into practice, and if the Laws relating to Housing, Public Health, Education, Unemployed Workmen, Allotments, Shop Hours, Feeding of School Children and similar Acts are to be of real benefit to the people they must be vigorously administered.

We may point out that the Labour Party, locally, have been instrumental in bringing about the abolition of bath charges, and we are of the opinion that it will be an inducement for more baths in working class houses.

We also wish to draw public attention to the fact that the Labour Party always advocated a reduction in the price of gas, believing that it would be the means of increasing the consumption, which this year has been the case to the extent of about 2,000,000 feet.

We are strongly opposed to the proposed Council School being built on the suggested site as being entirely unsuitable for an up-to-date School.

We shall not attempt an organised canvass of the town, but we shall endeavour by Public Meetings to put our views before you.

Finally, we appeal to you to be true to your own interests and your own class, then the issue is certain to be another glorious victory for Labour.

Faithfully yours,

AUSTIN H. COTTAM,
GEO. HARGREAVES,
ROBERT JONES,
WM. H. SEEDALL.

Yours truly, Austin H. Cottam.

Sincerely yours, Robert Jones.

Yours faithfully, Geo. Hargreaves.

Yours obediently, Wm. H. Seedall.

Printed and Published by C. Robinson, Advertiser Office, 27, Castle Street, Clitheroe.

sign of it. In 1923 Robert Parker referred to the number of houses built by the Tory Council since the war as 'a drop in the ocean', pointing out that schemes agreed over ten years previously had still not been completed.[15] He urged not only more building and lower rents but a change of style and method. The Labour remedy was for blocks or rows instead of semi-detached, constructed by direct labour rather than private contract. The result would be warmer and cheaper accommodation, an easing of the town's chronic unemployment problem and a saving for ratepayers, Labour claimed. It was an argument repeated throughout the decade, and with some success (see Figures 52 and 53) but Clitheroe Conservatives continued

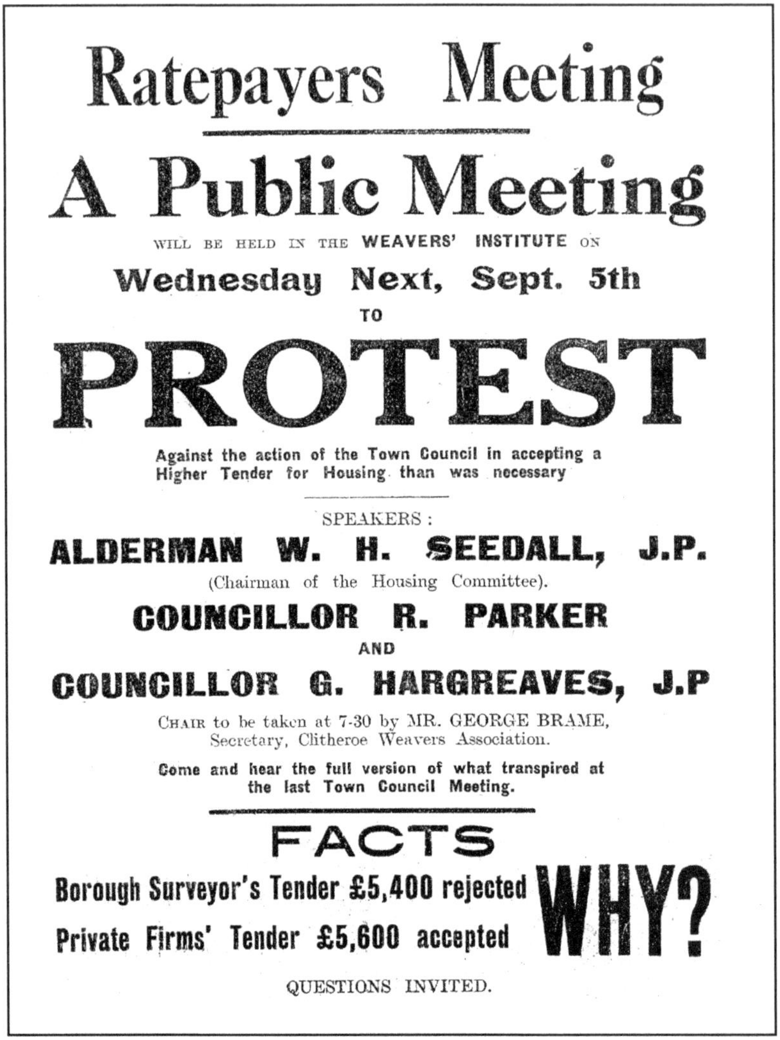

Figure 52 – Part of the Clitheroe Labour Party's campaign for better housing in the 1920s

Source: Clitheroe public library local studies collection. P5.

In 1925 the Conservatives had promised to build more homes for owner occupiers, using private builders. They accused the socialists of wanting to abolish capitalism and kill local enterprise. (*Clitheroe Advertiser and Times*, 30 October 1925, p. 12.)

Municipal Election, Thursday, November 1st, 1928

Look! WHAT IS THIS?

Clitheroe Housing Site as left by the Tories!

Four more houses are now to be built——due entirely to Labour's agitation, which still leaves Eighteen to complete the scheme.

Labour has saved you £200!

Labour agitation has obtained Four more Houses.

Tories have given a contract to a Burnley Firm and they have no guarantee of Local Labour being employed.

Labour's Policy is DIRECT LABOUR and LOCAL LABOUR EMPLOYED. Any saving effected will go to the RELIEF OF THE RATES!

DIRECT LABOUR HAS JUSTIFIED ITS TRIAL! THE TORIES WISH TO SMASH IT! YOU must give your answer on Thursday by

VOTING SOLID FOR LABOUR!

Figure 53 – Labour uses the housing crisis to appeal to the electorate

Source: Ruby Holland.

to prevaricate, preferring to seek votes by posing as champions of liberty against the threat of socialist dictatorship. (See Figure 54.)

This suited the local Labour Party which was pleased to offer pure socialism as the only effective panacea for the national malaise. Dick Trimby, then in his sixth year as party secretary, summarised the position in a report he presented in 1933. It contained much vague hyperbole about the greatness of nations being dependent not of the size of their armies and navies but on their moral integrity and the quality of their culture, but

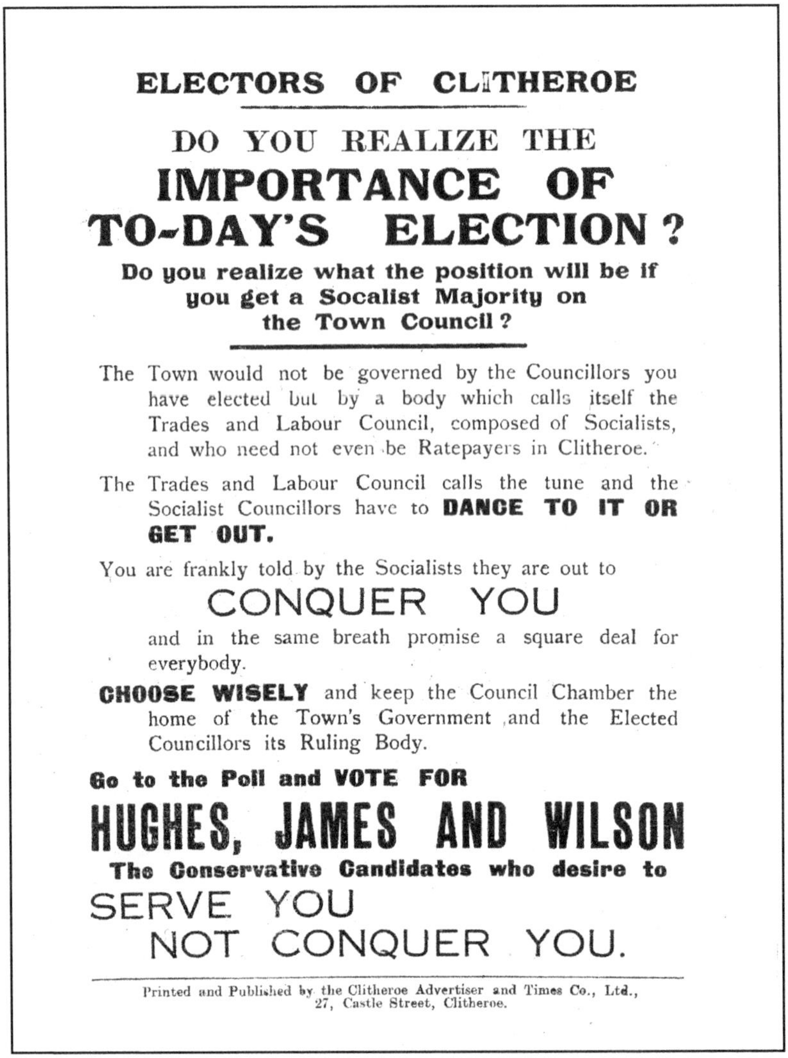

Figure 54 – The Conservative response to Labour's call for more housing

Source: *Clitheroe Advertiser and Times*, 2 November 1925, p. 1.

also a clear message that the needs of the community could only be met by socialism. He condemned capitalism as the cause of poverty and misery, and characterised the current struggle for political power in Marxist terms, as a class war between private interest determined to ignore a democratic mandate and a mass movement acting legally for the common good. Trimby therefore asked the Clitheroe Labour Party to rebrand itself as a socialist organisation and to reject as members any who were not committed to public ownership of essential services. He conceded that this might lead to a drop in enrolment, but he believed it was a price worth paying, for '20 socialists could be more effective than a hundred semi-socialists'. The sort of elite activists he had in mind would have to be content 'sitting around a badly-lighted cottage forming plans for addressing the people at the cold street corners, and perhaps speaking for hours to two or three men'.[16] They were hard, but not impossible to find, and often they were women.

*

Maggie Hargreaves, a founder member of the Clitheroe Labour Party, was elected in November 1929 as the borough's first female representative. She was born in Bolton-by-Bowland and had strong links with Paythorne Methodist Chapel when she lived there, a connection she continued with Clitheroe Wesleyan Methodists following her marriage to George Hargreaves, who was also a Labour councillor. In 1929 Maggie campaigned alongside Louisa Higson, a Clitheroe weaver. They stressed the need for the views of women to be reflected in local government, especially in matters of health, housing, the management of social services and education. (See Figure 55.) Louisa never won municipal office, but she nevertheless became an influential figure in local dissent. In the 1930s she was active on the Labour Party Committee as treasurer and president of the Women's Section, and endorsed its view that Ramsay MacDonald's acceptance of the leadership of a National Government in 1931 was an act of treachery against socialism. She sat on the Borough Bench as a JP from 1930 and, as a member of the Free Library and Education Committees, took a special interest in the development of Pendle Junior and Low Moor schools. She was considered a 'modernist', that is to say a forceful personality able to get things done in the causes of gender equality and the improvement of working-class living standards. The threat to democracy from fascism became a further preoccupation in the later 1930s, and until her death in 1941.[17]

Maggie Hargreaves and Louisa Higson were in the vanguard of Clitheroe feminism in the 1930s, demanding that roles traditionally reserved for men should be opened to women. They were supported by Elizabeth Hargreaves, an ebullient cooperator determined to express her views on taxation. At Cooperative Society meetings she advocated reform of the rating system and the adoption of a direct tax on land values, and carried the argument into the Council chamber after she was co-opted as a member.[18] Miss Hargreaves was scathing in her attack on the Means Test which had been introduced in 1931 and forced those in receipt of unemployment benefits to undergo a stringent examination of their financial circumstances before relief was continued. Income from other family members, savings, and the value of

TO THE BURGESSES
OF THE
BOROUGH OF CLITHEROE

LADIES AND GENTLEMEN,

For the second time, I have pleasure in accepting the invitation of the Labour Party to be a Candidate at the coming election.

I am in favour of houses being built, especially for those people who are now living in unhealthy dwellings.

In my opinion, a " Cottage Hospital " would be a great boon to our Borough, and, as the Council has only limited powers, I should, if elected, propose that a committee be appointed to consider and report on the best method of dealing with the matter.

The presence of women on our Councils is necessary, in view of the growing interest which women are now taking in public affairs, and it is only right that we should take our fair share in the essential work that lies ahead in the sphere of Local Government.

Trusting to receive your support on November 1st.

I am,
Yours faithfully,
MAGGIE HARGREAVES
63, HENTHORN ROAD,

TO THE BURGESSES
OF THE
BOROUGH OF CLITHEROE

LADIES AND GENTLEMEN,

At the request of the Labour Party, I have consented to offer myself again as a Candidate at the forthcoming Municipal election.

It is now well known that on many local councils throughout the country, evidence has been given of the valuable assistance which women are able to render. Especially will this apply now that the work of the Board of Guardians is about to be transferred to the local councils.

My active interest in welfare work and social services has convinced me that a still wider field lies open to women.

I am a member of the Free Library Committee and would support the opening of the Reading Room during the mornings. This would enable those persons who are desirous, particularly the unemployed, to take advantage of a valuable recreation.

I earnestly solicit your support so that I may be able to serve you to the best of my ability.

Yours faithfully,
LOUISA HIGSON
7, MOOR LANE.

Figure 55 – Clitheroe's first two women candidates for municipal office

Source: *Clitheroe Advertiser and Times,* 1 November 1929, p. 5. Mrs Hargreaves was elected and went on to become an alderman and mayor of Clitheroe in 1936 and 1937. Mrs Higson was a candidate in 1928, 1929 and 1931, but was unsuccessful on each occasion.

furniture all threatened the benefit, and within a year it had been withdrawn in over 180,000 cases. The test continued throughout the decade and many in Clitheroe were affected, including Tom Holland, by now unemployed, living in a two up, two down in Cross Street with his wife and children, who was told to make ends meet by selling the family's only table.[19] Dissent against this sort of austerity was common amongst a coalition of Labour Party, Trades Council and Cooperative Society activists. (See Figure 56.) It had little effect before the outbreak of war, however the accumulated resentment it caused was an important factor in Labour's landslide victory at the General Election of 1945.

It was not only within the Labour Party that women made a contribution to local government, for the first female Lancashire county councillor was Katherine Orme, a Conservative, who represented Clitheroe from 1922 to 1925.[20] Her background differed from that of her Labour counterparts, for she lived at Lowfield House and had four servants to manage its 18 rooms. But although her political contribution cannot be described as dissent, she nevertheless had a sense of duty that made her use her privileges on behalf of the community. During the Great War she was a Commandant of the Voluntary Aid Detachment with responsibility for Barraclough, Clitheroe's military hospital, and a tireless fund raiser for that institution until it closed in 1919. The plaudits she earned as its head undoubtedly helped her to win election to the County Council, although her interventions there were few. She was more closely involved in the work of the women's branch of the

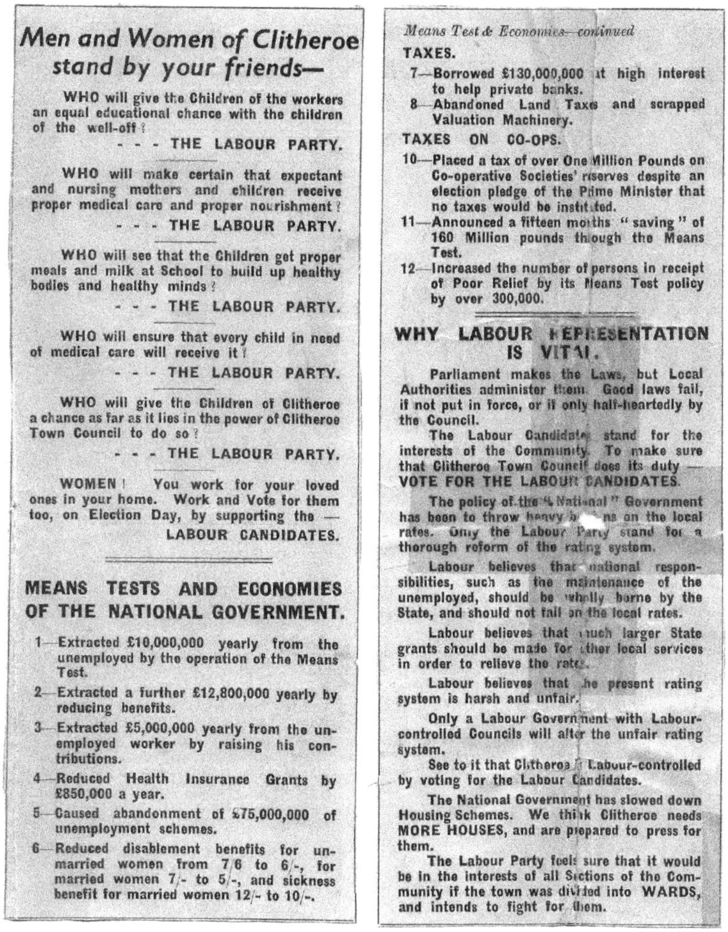

Men and Women of Clitheroe stand by your friends—

WHO will give the Children of the workers an equal educational chance with the children of the well-off?
- - - THE LABOUR PARTY.

WHO will make certain that expectant and nursing mothers and children receive proper medical care and proper nourishment?
- - - THE LABOUR PARTY.

WHO will see that the Children get proper meals and milk at School to build up healthy bodies and healthy minds?
- - - THE LABOUR PARTY.

WHO will ensure that every child in need of medical care will receive it!
- - - THE LABOUR PARTY.

WHO will give the Children of Clitheroe a chance as far as it lies in the power of Clitheroe Town Council to do so?
- - - THE LABOUR PARTY.

WOMEN! You work for your loved ones in your home. Work and Vote for them too, on Election Day, by supporting the — LABOUR CANDIDATES.

MEANS TESTS AND ECONOMIES OF THE NATIONAL GOVERNMENT.

1—Extracted £10,000,000 yearly from the unemployed by the operation of the Means Test.

2—Extracted a further £12,800,000 yearly by reducing benefits.

3—Extracted £5,000,000 yearly from the unemployed worker by raising his contributions.

4—Reduced Health Insurance Grants by £850,000 a year.

5—Caused abandonment of £75,000,000 of unemployment schemes.

6—Reduced disablement benefits for unmarried women from 7/6 to 6/-, for married women 7/- to 5/-, and sickness benefit for married women 12/- to 10/-.

Means Test & Economies—continued

TAXES.

7—Borrowed £130,000,000 at high interest to help private banks.

8—Abandoned Land Taxes and scrapped Valuation Machinery.

TAXES ON CO-OPS.

10—Placed a tax of over One Million Pounds on Co-operative Societies' reserves despite an election pledge of the Prime Minister that no taxes would be instituted.

11—Announced a fifteen months "saving" of 160 Million pounds through the Means Test.

12—Increased the number of persons in receipt of Poor Relief by its Means Test policy by over 300,000.

WHY LABOUR REPRESENTATION IS VITAL.

Parliament makes the Laws, but Local Authorities administer them. Good laws fail, if not put in force, or if only half-heartedly by the Council.

The Labour Candidates stand for the interests of the Community. To make sure that Clitheroe Town Council does its duty — VOTE FOR THE LABOUR CANDIDATES.

The policy of the "National" Government has been to throw heavy b[illegible]ns on the local rates. Only the Labour Party stand for a thorough reform of the rating system.

Labour believes that national responsibilities, such as the maintenance of the unemployed, should be wholly borne by the State, and should not fall on the local rates.

Labour believes that much larger State grants should be made for other local services in order to relieve the rates.

Labour believes that the present rating system is harsh and unfair.

Only a Labour Government with Labour-controlled Councils will alter the unfair rating system.

See to it that Clitheroe is Labour-controlled by voting for the Labour Candidates.

The National Government has slowed down Housing Schemes. We think Clitheroe needs MORE HOUSES, and are prepared to press for them.

The Labour Party feels sure that it would be in the interests of all Sections of the Community if the town was divided into WARDS, and intends to fight for them.

Figure 56 – The issues on which the Clitheroe Labour Party contested the municipal election in 1934

Source: Clitheroe Borough Labour Party and Trades Council, November 1934.

Unionist Association where she was an implacable opponent of a move to allow girls to join its junior section. This suggests that she was reluctant to press the case for a less traditional role for women in society, despite having adopted one herself, and although she took an interest in education equal to that of her Labour contemporaries her constituency activity was mainly supportive, of her husband, Dr Gilbert Orme, who was a Clitheroe borough councillor, and of Captain Brass, the Conservative candidate for the Clitheroe parliamentary division.[21]

Other local Conservative women were successful in County Council elections. Lady Audrey Worsley-Taylor, for example, became Whalley's representative in 1934, and Evelyn Garnett Clitheroe's from 1938 to 1952. Labour played little part in local government at this level, gaining a seat on the County Council for the first time only in 1952 when Harry Pemberton won on a low turnout in an election which saw Labour make big gains across the country.[22]

Figure 57 – Dick Trimby

Source: *Clitheroe Advertiser and Times*, 1 November 1929, p. 5.

Between 1923 and 1963 Trimby was treasurer of the Clitheroe Labour Party for 34 years and secretary for 13. He was co-opted on to the Town Council in 1940 and elected in 1945 and 1952.

It is clear, then, that women made a significant contribution to Clitheroe politics in the inter-war years, but their numbers in positions of power were always small, for this was an era during which women were still seen by most people as more suited to domestic roles. It was not until 1985 for instance, two years after the parliamentary division was abolished, that Christine Curry became the first female chairman of the Clitheroe Labour Party.[23] And in the years immediately preceding the disbandment of the Borough Council in the 1974 reorganisation, the influence of Labour men was also much reduced. The party had only four councillors that year, to the Conservatives' eleven and the Independents' one, indeed in 1970 when long-serving alderman William Sharples was defeated by the Conservative Cecil Buckingham, Labour was without any representation in municipal government at all.[24] Throughout Clitheroe Council's independent history Labour had never been in a position of overall control, and many of its councillors were moderates, but William Seedall's integrity and charisma ensured a receptive following for the arguments of dissent, and the presence of Dick Trimby as a key member of the party executive for 40 years kept a more extreme socialist vision always on its agenda. (See Figure 57.)

Notes and References

1 'The Proposed Division of Clitheroe into Wards', unattributed press cutting, Clitheroe public library local studies collection. P12 54.

2 F. Lofthouse, *op.cit.*, p. 70.

3 *Ibid.*, pp. 107 and 133.

4 *Ibid.*, p. 76.

5 *Ibid.*, pp. 252-256.

6 *Clitheroe Times*, 25 March 1898, p. 4.

7 F. Lofthouse, *op.cit.*, p. 258.

8 *Ibid.*, p. 263.

9 *Ibid.*, p. 265.

10 In 1899 about half the number who applied for relief at Clitheroe workhouse were from within its boundaries, however implementation of the scheme was delayed for eight years. See F. Lofthouse, *op.cit.*, pp. 274-275.

11 *Ibid.*, p. 272.

12 *Clitheroe Advertiser and Times*, 6 November 1925, p. 7.

13 *Ibid.*, 3 November 1925, p. 3; 2 March 1934, p. 9. Clitheroe Labour Party Minutes, 2 August 1924.

14 D. Lloyd George in a speech made at Wolverhampton on 23 November 1918.

15 *Clitheroe Advertiser and Times*, 18 October 1923, p. 6. Parker also pointed out that the promise of public baths for the town had not been honoured.

16 *Ibid.*, 27 January 1933, p. 9, 3 February 1933, p. 4.

17 *Ibid.*, 28 November 1941, p. 4.

18 Elizabeth Hargreaves was co-opted on to the Council in 1941, was elected in 1945 and became an alderman that year.

19 Ruby Holland, in conversation with the author, 2001.

20 J. Marshall (ed.), *op.cit.*, p. 58.

21 *Clitheroe Advertiser*, 6 July 1917, p. 2; 10 December 1918, p. 2; 23 January 1919, p. 4. *Yorkshire Post*, 6 March 1922, p. 10. *Nelson Leader*, 17 March 1922, p. 3. *Burnley News*, 11 November 1922, p. 5. *Burnley Express*, 1 December 1923, p. 3.

22 Pemberton won the seat vacated by Miss Garnett on a poll of 59.59 per cent of the eligible electorate. The Lancashire County Council of 1952 was made up of 65 Labour, 50 Conservative and 6 Liberal members. *Clitheroe Advertiser and Times*, 11 April 1952, p. 3.

23 *Clitheroe Advertiser and Times*, 13 June 1985, p. 1.

24 Of the four returned at the last election to Clitheroe Town Council in 1972, Derrick Akker had been elected only the previous year, and Bertram Jones and Robert Chadwick were first time councillors.

Conclusion

History is distorted if dissent is excluded, for then the past is represented only by the powerful, in Clitheroe's case the kings, queens and nobles who granted its charters, endowed its school, gave it parliamentary representation, and vied to control its political destiny. When the focus is concentrated on the great, dissent becomes a coincidental adjunct to pageant, essential only because of the colour it provides. After the Battle of Hexham in 1463, for example, the Lancastrian king Henry VI sought sanctuary with the Pudsays of Bolton-by-Bowland. They were able to hide him for a year, but when his presence in the area was discovered he was captured as he tried to cross the Ribble hippings into Clitheroe. The incident has dramatic ingredients – loyalty betrayed, a thwarted dash for freedom, the imprisonment of a monarch – and it is for these that it is remembered, not for the fact that the town was the location of high dissent during the Wars of the Roses that led to a change of the ruling dynasty.

In 1536 forces mustered on Clitheroe Moor to challenge Henry VIII's policy of dissolution of the monasteries. They were part of the rebellion known as the Pilgrimage of Grace whose local leaders were abbot Paslew of Whalley, abbot Trafford of Sawley, Nicholas Tempest of Bashall Hall and Sir Stephen Hamerton of Slaidburn. All were executed when the rising failed. Again it is the drama that matters, the debate is focused on whether they died as martyrs, not whether they had lived as dissidents.[1]

Pendle Forest was the home of reputed witches in the seventeenth century. Their activities occupy an important place in local folklore and are perpetuated by commercial interests that exploit public gullibility for the supernatural elements in the story, its fascination with the involvement of the high-born Alice Nutter, and the deadly testimony given against her by the child Elizabeth Device. This is a landmark in the history of the area familiar to all, but few think of it as part of a continuing tradition of dissent which led to a campaign against the government's policy of persecution of witches. It was led by Doctor John Webster who lived in Clitheroe from 1643 until his death in 1682, working first as master of the grammar school and later as vicar of Mitton. During the Civil War he served as a surgeon with the Parliamentary army, but in 1657, during a term as borough bailiff, his great library of 1,650 volumes was seized. It was one of the largest collections in the north of England, built up over many years study of science, metallurgy and medicine. No motive for its appropriation has been established, but conjecture supposes that the authorities disapproved of Webster's opposition to prevailing superstition and his enthusiasm for the new ideas that emerged from the Renaissance and the Reformation.[2]

John Webster has been called 'one of the leading proponents of radical educational, religious and scientific change in seventeenth century England',[3] but his influence was even greater than that, for he encouraged political and economic reform as well, especially of the tithing system. Tithes were taxes on agricultural yields designed to provide for the maintenance of the established church. They were a frequent cause of dispute between religious authorities who had the right to collect them in the form of a tenth of the produce of their parishioners, and those farmers who had to pay them. Doctor Webster had benefitted from tithes as a teacher, for Clitheroe grammar school was endowed with £60 a year from the rectory and tithes of Almondbury, and as the vicar of Mitton he was entitled to a share of the tithes controlled by Richard Sherburne of Stoneyhurst. He had hoped that the republican governments of the 1650s would abolish them, and their failure to do so caused him to complain 'How dare you exact Tythes or pay from poor Labourers by the compulsory power of a Worldly Law?'[4]

Webster's censure went unheeded, and after tithes were abolished in France during the Revolution tithing was portrayed in Britain as a necessary bulwark against the destruction of church and state.[5] So disputes over tithes remained common, and because they supported only the Church of England were resented in north Lancashire where Roman Catholic and Nonconformist sentiment was strong.[6]

A further case of forgotten dissent occurred in the 1680s when Charles II demanded that towns critical of his policies surrender their charters. Clitheroe was one of them, and in 1684 Chief Justice Jeffreys enforced the king's will. The bailiffs, Thomas Braddyl and Robert Sclater, travelled to London later that year to try to obtain a substitute charter on the understanding that it would be remodelled to ensure the borough's obedience, with major offices reserved for royal appointment. However Charles II died before it was ready and the bailiffs' attempt to petition his successor, James II, was ignored. Clitheroe's government continued as if no charter surrender had been made, but the slight was remembered, and when James was deposed in 1688 a Clitheroe Association for the Protection of William III, his adversary and replacement, was formed. It immediately issued a statement of loyalty which was signed by most of the town's burgesses and freemen, and by both its MPs.[7]

*

These examples of thought and action contrary to the official line indicate a willingness to resist authority at frequent points in Clitheroe's pre-nineteenth century past, and they form part of a pattern of protest which later took the form of opposition to industrial exploitation and demands for the political emancipation of women. Britain's first female suffrage society was formed in Blackburn in June 1819 and was soon followed by others.[8] In the early-twentieth century the Clitheroe constituency was in the vanguard of the votes for women movement. Its supporters ranged from national figures like Selina Cooper and Ethel Carnie to the anonymous founder-members of local SDF and ILP branches, and they, it must be supposed, were outnumbered by contemporaries, politicised and active, though totally absent from the record. Amongst them would have been women who went from house to house canvassing signatures for the 1900 suffrage petition for example, but their names are unknown, as is the effect on those involved of the debate about whether the demand should be for limited womanhood or full adult suffrage.

Invisibility is a problem in the search for dissenters. That Nicholas Assheton wrote a journal in the seventeenth century and Lord Ribblesdale a memoir of the nineteenth comes as no surprise.[9] Nor is it remarkable that James Garnett kept a diary. These were men in easy circumstances with the leisure to indulge the fancy in the comfort of book-lined studies. But dissent is a consequence of deprivation, and few ordinary workers could summon the strength to set down their feelings on paper after long factory shifts. So first-hand accounts of dissent are rare, dependent not only on the author's ability to transcend disadvantage, but on chance. Only some parts of John O'Neil's diary were retrieved from a pile of rubbish about to be destroyed, and the surviving fragments contain frustrating gaps. They tell us, for example, that John was not alone on his heroic treks over Pendle to attend union meetings :

> 'We left Clitheroe at a quarter past five. It is 12 miles to Colne and one of the worst roads I ever travelled in my life, over mountain and moor, over bog and mire...We got to Colne by nine o' clock'.[10]

But how many took part, and their identities, have been lost.

A radical interpretation of Clitheroe's history would be hard to argue without such evidence, although better literacy and the emergence of political parties which were dedicated to furthering the interests of the working class stimulated debate about reform, and that left an indelible mark. Clitheroe's working-class MPs and those who voted for them may have written little themselves, but branch meetings were advertised, party minutes kept, election manifestos produced and campaigns reported in the press, and a rich impression of local politics can be gained from them. They show that Enid Stacy's encouragement of the socialist workhouse guardians to try to gain seats on the Town Council changed the course of local government in Clitheroe,[11] for example, just as Ellen Wilkinson and other speakers at the Vernon Street Socialist Institute influenced election results in Nelson,[12] and that the alliance between trade unionists, socialists and cooperators which led to Labour's 1905 triumph in the town, caused emulation throughout the constituency.

*

The Municipal Corporations Act of 1835, and the Local Government Acts of 1888 and 1894, were viewed by some with trepidation because they feared that a ratepayer franchise would place local affairs in the hands of men of low character and revolutionary inclinations, and would therefore put crown, peerage and established church at risk. Others, however, hoped the Acts would promote community welfare and improve law and order. The pessimism of the former was ill-founded, but the optimism of the latter was often unfulfilled. After 1835 the composition of Clitheroe's governing Council was transformed, and by 1905 so was Nelson's. Henceforth dissident elements in both had a stronger voice, in Clitheroe only as a vociferous minority group but in Nelson from a position of control. The work they did has been called 'municipal socialism' and it led to advances in the living standards of the working class in respect of housing, health, the supply of water and gas, and education.[13] On the other hand the minutes of the new Victorian County, Rural and Urban District Councils which were created in the 1880s and 90s typically concern disagreements about such things as the colour of slates to be used for roofing, the regulation of milk sellers, and the repair of drains. These were serious matters for those affected, but they were limited in their impact, for revised arrangements which helped one community were irrelevant to another.

In such commonly encountered circumstances elected representatives were frequently faced with the need to balance the provision of services against demands to keep the rates down without appearing to be self-interested. It was a thankless task and could provoke the sort of protest expressed by the voter who composed the handbill shown in Figure 58. Nevertheless the reforms of the nineteenth century, moderated by such dissent, generally resulted in better management.

Figure 58 – Bitter dissent

Source: Clitheroe public library local studies collection. P12.

The 'Poor Shareholder' went to the trouble and expense of producing this handbill to try to prevent the election of candidates who, in his view, were unsuitable for public office. All four were Liberals, but only Carlisle and Ormerod were successful in 1873.

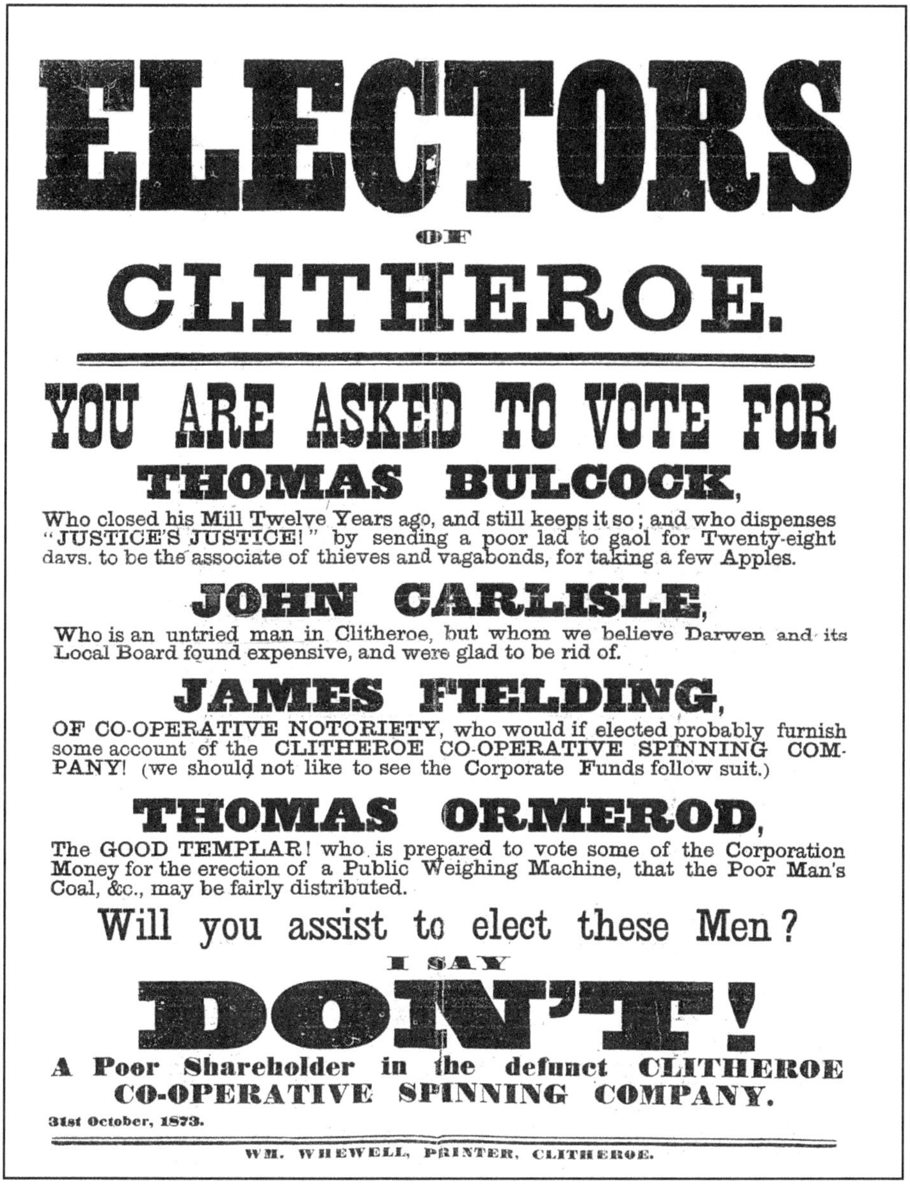

ELECTORS

OF

CLITHEROE.

YOU ARE ASKED TO VOTE FOR

THOMAS BULCOCK,

Who closed his Mill Twelve Years ago, and still keeps it so; and who dispenses "JUSTICE'S JUSTICE!" by sending a poor lad to gaol for Twenty-eight days, to be the associate of thieves and vagabonds, for taking a few Apples.

JOHN CARLISLE,

Who is an untried man in Clitheroe, but whom we believe Darwen and its Local Board found expensive, and were glad to be rid of.

JAMES FIELDING,

OF CO-OPERATIVE NOTORIETY, who would if elected probably furnish some account of the CLITHEROE CO-OPERATIVE SPINNING COMPANY! (we should not like to see the Corporate Funds follow suit.)

THOMAS ORMEROD,

The GOOD TEMPLAR! who is prepared to vote some of the Corporation Money for the erection of a Public Weighing Machine, that the Poor Man's Coal, &c., may be fairly distributed.

Will you assist to elect these Men?

I SAY

DON'T!

A Poor Shareholder in the defunct CLITHEROE CO-OPERATIVE SPINNING COMPANY.

31st October, 1873.

WM. WHEWELL, PRINTER, CLITHEROE.

*

The political identity of a constituency changes over time in response to shifting circumstances, and consequently labels are unhelpful. 'Little Moscow' may have been applicable to Nelson, and 'Labour stronghold' to Clitheroe, in the early years of the twentieth century, but not before or since.[14] Similarly the view that only property holders could provide good government was eventually discredited, for the notion that the working class was not interested in the new political ideas, and lacked the ability to implement them, was patently false.[15] Ultimately T. D. Benson, Louisa Higson and Dick Trimby would get a chance to shape the future, just as Asshetons, Shuttleworths and Garnetts had shaped the past. Nevertheless signs of the old distortion of history against dissent was hard to eradicate. They can be detected for instance in the caption provided for the photograph of Low Moor Reading Room, (see Figure 59.) Its designation as 'The

Figure 59 – The Garnett Memorial

Source: J. Mitcalf (ed.), *The Heritage of Low Moor Mill* (Jenny Press, Clitheroe, 2017) p. 9.

Garnett Memorial' pays appropriate tribute to the builders but ignores the users, for William Seedall, who was one of them, also made a significant contribution to the welfare of local people.[16] So the structure stands as a symbol of paternalism rather than as a monument to working-class self-improvement. It has become a palimpsest which alters reality by promoting personality above function, master above worker. But while the relative worth of these two representatives of orthodoxy and dissent as legislators is a matter of opinion, the centrality of both to the development of the area is not. It establishes the radical element in Clitheroe's history as a matter of fact.

Notes and References

1 A. Swinglehurst, 'The Swinglehursts of Bowland. A Family History', Clitheroe public library local studies collection, G3, p. 11, suggests that Tempest may have been forced to join the Pilgrimage against his will, as does G. Moorhouse, *The Pilgrimage of Grace* (Weidenfeld and Nicholson, London, 2002) p. 296. Moorhouse also, p.279, claims that Thomas Bolton was Sawley's executed last abbot, although that role is firmly assigned to William Trafford by both J. Hovland (ed.), *Historical Account of the Cisterian Abbey of Salley* (Whewell, Clitheroe, 1853) pp. 42 and 48, and J. Lofthouse, *Three Rivers* (Robert Hale, London, 1946) p. 99.

2 W. Self Weeks, *Dr John Webster* (Advertiser and Times, Clitheroe, no date) [1927?] p. 5.

3 P. Elmer, *The Library of Dr John Webster: the Making of a Seventeenth Century Radical* (Welcome Institute, London, 1986) p. 43.

4 W. Self Weeks, *op.cit.*, pp. 7, 12–13.

5 E. Evans, *The Contentious Tithe. The Tithe Problem and English Agriculture, 1750–1850.* (Routledge and Kegan Paul, London, 1976) p. ix.

6 An Act for the Commutation of Tithes, passed in 1836, eased tensions by allowing the parties concerned to negotiate a cash rent equivalent in exchange for the right to tithe, and there are two instances of its use in Chatburn in 1845. John and Mary Hartley agreed to pay a rent of 4*s* in lieu of tithes on 4 acres, 3 rods and 17 perches, and Dixon Robinson £10 7*s* on 207 acres, 1 rod and 14 perches. Clitheroe public library local studies collection, E02 CHA, 19 June 1845.

7 W. Self Weeks, *The Surrender of the Charters of the Borough of Clitheroe* (Rawson and Co., Manchester, 1931) pp. 46-71.

8 M. Bush, 'The Women at Peterloo: The Impact of Female Reform on the Manchester Meeting of 16 August 1819' (*History*, 89, 2004) p. 214.

9 F. R. Raines (ed.), *The Journal of Nicholas Assheton of Downham 1617–1618* (Chetham Society, Manchester, 1848). C. Lister, *Charles Lister: Letters and Recollections, with a Memoir by his father Lord Ribblesdale* (Fisher Unwin, London, 1917).

10 J. O'Neil, *op.cit.*, p. 103.

11 *Clitheroe Times*, 1 April 1898, p. 3, 21 October 1898, p. 7.

12 *Syllabus of Lecturers 1913-14* (ILP, Nelson, 1913) p. 35.

13 R. Morris and R. Rodger (eds.), *The Victorian City 1820–1914* (Longman, London, 1993) ch. 9.

14 S. Macintyre, *A Proletarian Science. Marxism in Britain 1917–1933* (CUP, Cambridge, 1980) p. 1. *Little Moscows. Communism and Working-Class Militancy in Inter-war Britain* (Croom Helm, London, 1980) pp. 19-20.

15 *Clitheroe Times*, 4 January 1889, p. 5; 22 November 1946, p. 3.

16 William Seedall is commemorated by a nearby thoroughfare, Seedall Avenue.

Appendix I

Dissent in Context

The National and International Background		The Clitheroe Constituency	
		1170s	First De Lacy charter grants local government powers to Clitheroe's free burgesses
		1283	Second De Lacy charter confirms these privileges
1314	Battle of Bannockburn		
		1315	Clitheroe castle seized during Banaster Rising
1322	Execution of Thomas Earl of Lancaster		
		1558	Clitheroe constituency created with the right to return two MPs
1642–1648	English Civil Wars		
		1648	Unpaid Parliamentary troops occupy Clitheroe castle
		1650s	Clitheroe's MP excluded from Commonwealth parliaments
1660	Restoration of Charles II	1660	The Honour of Clitheroe granted to George Monk, Duke of Albermarle
1739	Some women given the vote in Poor Law Guardians elections	1716–1780	Lister/ Assheton compact to control Clitheroe elections
		1780	Lister purchases Ribblesdale burgages
		1791	Low Moor mill opens
		1808	Clitheroe food riots

1809	Health and Morals of Apprentices Act		
1811–1812	Luddite Riots		
		1826	Failure of plan to attack Low Moor mill
1832	Great Reform Act	1832	First extension of Clitheroe constituency Representation reduced to one MP Fort/ Irving election violence
1833	Factory Act		
1834	Poor Law Amendment Act		
1835	Municipal Corporations Act	1835	'Bourgeois revolution' – middle class assume power in local government
1838	The People's Charter		
		1839	Clitheroe branch of National Charter Association formed
		1841–1853	Clitheroe General Election results invalidated because of 'bottling' and bribery
		1842	Feargus O'Connor visits Clitheroe Plug Plot
1847	Ten Hours Act		
		1850	Cholera outbreak
		1854	Clitheroe Waterworks Act
		1859	First Low Moor Cooperative Society formed Clitheroe Weavers' Association formed
		1860–1861	North Lancashire cotton strike
1861–1865	American Civil War and the Cotton Famine	1861	Clitheroe Cooperative Society formed
1867	Parliamentary Reform Act		
1872	Ballot Act		

		1873	Coplow workhouse opens
		1878	Strikes and rioting throughout north Lancashire. Riot Act read in Clitheroe
		1879	Clitheroe Free Library opens
1884	SDF formed Parliamentary Reform Act		
1885	Redistribution of Seats Act	1885	Second extension of Clitheroe constituency
		1886	Clitheroe's first newspaper, the *Advertiser*, published
1888	Local Government Act	1888	Grindleton strike
		1890	Nelson incorporated as a borough First Labour councillors elected in Nelson
		1891	Nelson branch of SDF formed. Brooks and Jubilee mills on strike for 25 weeks
1893	ILP formed	1893	Nelson branch of ILP formed
1894	Local Government Act	1894	Clitheroe Rural District Council formed
		1895	Clitheroe castle becomes a part of the borough. Clitheroe branch of SDF formed
		1896	Clitheroe branch of ILP formed
1897	Workmen's Compensation Act NUWSS formed	1897	All 14 Clitheroe mills affected by strikes
		1899	Clarion House opens
1900	LRC formed	1900	Adult Suffrage Petition circulates throughout the constituency
1901	Taff Vale Judgement		
		1902	David Shackleton wins Clitheroe by-election to become the LRC's third MP
1903	LRC wins by-elections in Woolwich and Barnard Castle		

		1904	Nelson and Colne Suffrage Committee formed
		1905	First Labour councillor elected in Clitheroe
1906	General Election. LRC returns 30 MPs in a Liberal landslide	1906	David Shackleton re-elected
1910	General Elections in January and December	1910	January – David Shackleton re-elected but soon resigns December – Albert Smith elected
		1912	Heys Farm Guest House opens
1914–1918	Great War	1913–1917	Ethel Carnie Holdsworth publishes *Miss Nobody* (1913), *Iron Horses* (1914), *Voices of Womanhood* (1914), *Helen of Four Gates* (1917)
		1915	Salem School Hall riot
1916	Conscription introduced		
1918	Representation of the People Act General Election	1918	Albert Smith elected for the new constituency of Nelson and Colne Alfred Davies elected for Clitheroe
		1920	Half-time system abolished
1922	General Election	1922	Alfred Davies defeated Katherine Orme becomes Lancashire's first female county councillor
1923	General Election	1923	Alfred Davies defeated
		1929	Maggie Hargreaves becomes Clitheroe's first female borough councillor
1945	General Election	1945	Harry Randall elected for Clitheroe
		1983	Clitheroe constituency abolished

Appendix II

Members of Parliament for Clitheroe

As a two member constituency 1558–1832

1558	Thomas Greenacres and Walter Hooton
1563	John Newdigate and John Jeffrys (replaced by Thomas Greenacres in 1567)
1571	Richard Greenacres and George Horsey
1572	William Wintorn and Thomas Dockwra
1585	Michael Purefoy and Alexander Fisher
1586	Edward Poley and John Walmsley
1588	Robert Pilkington and John Whitte
1592	William Twissenden and John Chamberlain
1597	William Holt and George Rotherham
1601	John Osbaldeston and Anthony Deering
1603	Sir John Dormer and Martin Lister
1614	William Fanshaw and Clement Coke
1620	Sir Thomas Walmsley and William Fanshaw
1623	William Fanshaw and Ralph Whitfield
1625	Ralph Assheton and William Fanshaw
1625	Ralph Assheton and William Kirke
1628	Thomas Jermyn and William Newell
1640	Richard Shuttleworth and Ralph Assheton
1640	Ralph Assheton and Richard Shuttleworth
1653	No returns, Clitheroe excluded from the parliaments of the Interregnum
1654	
1656	
1658	
1659	
1660	Sir Ralph Assheton and John Heath
1661	Sir Ralph Assheton and John Heath

1678	Sir Thomas Stringer and Sir Ralph Assheton
1681	Henry Marsden and Sir Thomas Stringer
1685	James Stanley and Edmund Assheton
1688	Christopher Wilkinson and Anthony Parker
1690	Roger Kenion and Fitton Gerrard
1695	Christopher Lister and Ambrose Pudsey
1698	Thomas Stringer and Christopher Lister
1701	Ambrose Pudsey and Thomas Stringer
1702	Ambrose Pudsey and Thomas Stringer
1705	Daniel Harvey and Edward Harvey
1708	Christopher Parker and Edward Harvey
1710	Thomas Lister and Edward Harvey
1713	Thomas Lister and Charles Stanley
1714	Thomas Lister and Edward Harvey
1722	Nathaniel Curzon and Thomas Lister
1727	Lord Galway and Thomas Lister
1734	William Curzon and Thomas Lister
1741	William Curzon and Thomas Lister
1747	Sir Nathaniel Curzon and Thomas Lister
1754	Assheton Curzon and Thomas Lister
1761	Assheton Curzon and Nathan Lister
1762	Thomas Lister and Assheton Curzon
1768	Thomas Lister and Assheton Curzon
1768	Thomas Lister
1774	Thomas Lister and Assheton Curzon
1780	Thomas Lister and John Parker
1782	John Lee after Parker resigned
1784	Thomas Lister and John Lee
1790	Penn Assheton Curzon and Sir John Aubrey R. E. D. Grosvenor after Curzon raised to the peerage, 1794
1796	Lord E. C. C. Bentinck and Hon. Robert Curzon
1801	Lord E. C. C. Bentinck and Hon. Robert Curzon
1802	Hon. John Cust and Hon. Robert Curzon
1806	Hon. John Cust and Hon. Robert Curzon
1807	Hon. John Cust and Hon. Robert Curzon
1808	James Gordon in place of Hon. John Cust, who had become a peer

1812	Oct 10, Viscount Castlereagh and Hon. Robert Curzon
	Dec 30, Edward Wilbraham Bootle in place of Castlereagh
1818	Hon. Robert Curzon and Hon. William Cust
1820	Hon. Robert Curzon and Hon. William Cust
1822	Henry Porcher in place of Hon. William Cust
1826	Hon. P. F. Cust and Hon. Robert Curzon
1830	Hon. P. F. Cust and Hon. Robert Curzon
1831	Hon. P. F. Cust and the Hon. R. Curzon junior

As a one member constituency 1832–1983

L = Liberal, C = Conservative, Lab = Labour

1832		John Fort	(L)
1835		John Fort	(L)
1837		John Fort	(L)
1841		Mathew Wilson	(L)
1842		On petition Cardwell (C) seated after Wilson was declared unduly elected	
1847		Mathew Wilson	(L)
1852		Mathew Wilson	(L)
1853	March May Aug	On petition, last election declared void for bribery and treating:– John T. W. Aspinall Aspinall being unseated on petition:– Le Gendre N. Starkie	(C) (C)
1857		John T. Hopwood	(C)
1859		John T. Hopwood	(C)
1865		Richard Fort	(L)
1868	July	Ralph Assheton, after R. Fort deceased	(C)
1868	Nov	Ralph Assheton	(C)

After the Ballot Act 1872

1874		Ralph Assheton	(C)
1880		Richard Fort	(L)

Since the Redistribution of Seats Act 1885

1885		Sir Ughtred Kay-Shuttleworth	(L)

1886		Sir Ughtred Kay-Shuttleworth	(L)
1892		Sir Ughtred Kay-Shuttleworth	(L)
1895		Sir Ughtred Kay-Shuttleworth	(L)
1900		Sir Ughtred Kay-Shuttleworth	(L)
1902		David Shackleton	(Lab)
1906		David Shackleton	(Lab)
1910	Jan	David Shackleton	(Lab)
1910	Dec	Albert Smith	(Lab)
1918		Alfred Davies	(Lab)
1922		William Brass	(C)
1923		William Brass	(C)
1924		William Brass	(C)
1929		William Brass	(C)
1931		Sir William Brass	(C)
1935		Sir William Brass	(C)
1945		Harry Randall	(Lab)
1950		Richard Fort	(C)
1951		Richard Fort	(C)
1955		Richard Fort	(C)
1959		Francis Fenwick Pearson	(C)
1964		Francis Fenwick Pearson	(C)
1966		Francis Fenwick Pearson	(C)
1970		David Walder	(C)
1974		David Walder	(C)

Sources: E. Bains (ed. J. Harland), *The History of the County Palatine and Duchy of Lancaster* (Routledge, London, 1870); W. Pink and A. Beavan, *The Parliamentary Representation of Lancashire (County and Borough) 1258–1885* (Henry Gray, London, 1889); J. Arnold, *A History of Britain's Parliamentary Constituencies : The Ribble Valley Constituency* (P. Arnold, West Malling, 1998).

Appendix III
Municipal Election Results in Clitheroe
1894–1919

The following statistics show the increasing influence of representatives of the working class in local government. Only contests which featured candidates identified as socialist, Trades Council or Labour, terms used interchangeably, are listed.

1894

Thomas Cowman	Conservative	936	elected
Abraham Roberts	Liberal	709	elected
William Whiteside	Conservative	689	elected
Thomas Cowgill	Liberal	655	elected
John Eatough	Conservative	646	
Tempest Seedall	Conservative	520	
John Hitchen	Liberal	421	
Newton Aspden	Liberal	397	
Henry Speak	Socialist	363	
Matthias Mitchell	Socialist	198	
Miles Lord	Socialist	183	

1897

John Sagar	Conservative	1080	elected
Thomas Cowgill	Liberal	1057	elected
John Cowman	Conservative	864	elected
Tempest Seedall	Conservative	658	elected
Hugh Chippendale	Conservative	609	
James Eastwood	Liberal	596	
Abel Bridge	Socialist	460	
William Orr	Socialist	430	
Albert Whittaker	Socialist	416	

Alfred Yates	Socialist	405	
William Gill	Liberal	316	
Richard Lund	Liberal	221	

1898

William Hardacre	Conservative	873	elected
Thomas Garnett	Independent	800	elected
Edmund Crabtree	Conservative	780	elected
William Braithwaite	Conservative	716	elected
James Eastwood	Liberal	636	
Newton Aspden	Liberal	523	
Miles Lord	Socialist	437	
James Walker	Socialist	431	
Stephen Myers	Liberal	426	
William Sutcliffe	Socialist	422	
Albert Whittaker	Socialist	403	

By-election 24 November 1898

James Eastwood	Liberal	873	elected
William Self Weeks	Conservative	805	
John Dawson	Conservative	712	
Albert Whittaker	Socialist	255	
Barker	Socialist	241	

1900

John Sagar	Conservative	1108	elected
John J. Carter	Conservative	957	elected
John Southworth	Conservative	930	elected
Thomas Cowgill	Liberal	928	elected
John Cowman	Conservative	895	
John Smithies	Liberal	772	
John Fullalove	Liberal	706	
William Lang	Liberal	504	
James Walker	Socialist	163	
Spencer Booth	Socialist	137	

1901

Clement T. Mitchell	Liberal	970	elected
Thomas Garnett	Independent	944	elected
John Smithies	Liberal	914	elected
William Hardacre	Conservative	814	elected
W. Lidsay Grime	Liberal	809	
Edmund Crabtree	Conservative	807	
William Braithwaite	Conservative	798	
John Trafford	Socialist	175	
George Taylor	Socialist	160	

1905

Henry Parkinson	Conservative	1134	elected
James Windle	Labour	942	elected
James A. Wade	Liberal	860	elected
W. Lidsay Grime	Liberal	854	elected
James Crabtree	Conservative	853	
Henry Carus	Labour	786	

1906

John T. Whipp	Liberal	1183	elected
John Cowman	Conservative	1104	elected
James Crabtree	Conservative	1089	elected
Robert Parker	Labour	744	elected
William Green	Liberal	738	
James Hargreaves	Labour	703	
Joseph Scott	Liberal	665	
John Clark	Liberal	553	

By-election 30 January 1907

John J. Carter	Conservative	1083	elected
James Hargreaves	Socialist	655	

1907

William Hardacre	Conservative	1209	elected
Thomas Garnett	Independent	1114	elected

Clement T. Mitchell	Liberal	970	elected
William W. Whiteside	Conservative	886	elected
Abel Bridge	Socialist	844	
John W. Carlisle	Liberal	652	

By-election 3 December 1907

Abraham Roberts	Conservative	1085	elected
Abel Bridge	Socialist	797	

1908

Henry Parkinson	Conservative	1167	elected
John Holden	Conservative	966	elected
Henry H. Baldwin	Conservative	927	elected
William Wells	Conservative	927	elected
James A. Wade	Liberal	835	
James Fell	Labour	701	
John Eltoft	Liberal	689	
Abel Bridge	Labour	591	
James H. Seedall	Labour	588	
John Miller	Liberal	580	
James Windle	Labour	577	

1909

John J. Carter	Conservative	1150	elected
Robert Parker	Labour	1035	elected
John Cowman	Conservative	1032	elected
William Braithwaite	Conservative	1013	elected
James Crabtree	Conservative	938	
William Green	Liberal	794	
John W. Dixon	Labour	737	
T. Neilson	Socialist	257	

1910

Thomas Garnett	Independent	1346	elected
James Thornber	Liberal	1090	elected

William Hardacre	Conservative	1014	elected
Abraham Roberts	Conservative	888	elected
Austin H. Cottam	Trades Council	750	
Walter W. Whiteside	Conservative	741	
Samuel Booth	Trades Council	740	
W. Lidsay Grime	Liberal	672	

By-election 24 November 1910

Walter W. Whiteside	Conservative	1068	elected
Austin H. Cottam	Labour	941	
James Robinson	Liberal	896	

1911

William Wells	Conservative	995	elected
Austin H. Cottam	Trades Council	973	elected
Alfred W. Musson	Conservative	819	elected
John H. Ramsbottom	Conservative	778	elected
William H. Seedall	Labour	748	
Robert Jones	Labour	729	
George Hargreaves	Labour	717	
Walter Greenwood	Conservative	684	
William Westhead	Liberal	680	
A. Aitken	Liberal	473	
John Miller	Liberal	459	
Edgar Jackson	Liberal	414	

By-election 24 January 1912

Walter Greenwood	Conservative	758	elected
Richard Blackburn	Liberal	721	
William H. Seedall	Labour	687	

1912

Robert Parker	Labour	1069	elected
John J. Carter	Conservative	1040	elected

William H. Seedall	Labour	952	elected
John Cowman	Conservative	930	elected
William Braithwaite	Conservative	929	
Richard Blackburn	Liberal	894	
William Standring	Conservative	852	
George Hargreaves	Labour	785	
William Birch	Labour	710	
John Jackson	Liberal	610	
Edward Chester	Liberal	441	

By-election 30 April 1913

George Hargreaves	Labour	1047	elected
William Standring	Conservative	1026	

1913

William Garnett	Conservative	1265	elected
Walter W. Whiteside	Conservative	1116	elected
William Standring	Conservative	1092	elected
James Thornber	Liberal	993	elected
William Birch	Labour	962	
Walter Greenwood	Conservative	959	
Robert Fullalove	Labour	949	
Samuel Booth	Labour	881	
Arthur Dixon	Labour	852	
E. Johnson	Liberal	523	

No elections were held during the war years 1914–1918, but the following councillors were re-appointed:

1914

James Boothman	Conservative		
Austin H. Cottam	Labour		
George Hargreaves	Labour		
Alfred W. Musson	Conservative		

1915, 1916 and 1917

John J. Carter	Conservative		
John Cowan	Conservative		

Robert Parker	Labour		
William H. Seedall	Labour		

By-election 15 January 1919

Dr G. E. Orme	Conservative	2232	elected
E. Blacklock	Labour	1497	

1919

William H. Seedall	Labour	2503	elected
Walter Clayton	Conservative	2381	elected
John Carter	Conservative	2064	elected
Thomas Barber	Labour	1871	elected
Henry Parkinson	Conservative	1863	
Thomas Miller	Conservative	1708	
Robert Tingle	Labour	1667	
Albert Hallows	Labour	1665	

By-election 6 December 1919

E. Blacklock	Labour	2345	elected
T. Wrigley	Labour	2225	elected
H. Parkinson	Conservative	2027	
Thomas Miller	Conservative	1876	

Source: C. Ainsworth, 'Clitheroe Municipal Elections 1835–1972', Clitheroe public library local studies collection. P21. The elections were also reported in the Clitheroe press, where the votes received by candidates sometimes differs, although not significantly, for example Ainsworth credits Abel Bridge with 844 votes in 1907 whereas the *Clitheroe Times* gives him 842.

Appendix IV
Municipal Election Results in Nelson
1890–1918

Although election results were published in the press and new councillors listed in the Borough minutes, details were recorded inconsistently. Consequently candidates' full names, the wards they contested and the number of votes cast were sometimes omitted. The following data indicate the fortunes of SDF, ILP, Socialist, LRC and Labour Party representatives in all years they were put up for election.

1890

Lawrence Tattersall	Labour	elected
William Ward	Labour	elected

1892

John Smith	SDF	defeated

1893

Lawrence Tattersall	Labour	elected
William Ward	Labour	elected
John Smith	SDF	defeated
Caley	SDF	defeated
Carr	ILP	defeated
Harrison	ILP	defeated

1894

Johnson	SDF	defeated
John Breese	ILP	defeated
Overton	ILP	defeated

1896

William Ward	Labour	elected
Robert Broughton	ILP	defeated

1899

William Ward	Labour	defeated

Hartley Eastwood	SDF	defeated
James Aspen	ILP	defeated

1901

William Rickard	LRC	elected

1902

John Pickover	SDF	defeated
Albert Smith	LRC	elected
Pickles	LRC	elected

1904

William Rickard	LRC	elected

1905[1]

Albert Smith	LRC	elected
Stephen Lowe	LRC	elected
Thomas Lambert	LRC	elected
William Dinsdale	LRC	elected
Thomas Caffry	LRC	elected

1906

John Breese	Labour	elected
Richard Winterbottom	Labour	elected
Hartley Duerden	Labour	elected

1908[2]

Edgar Bootham	Labour	elected
Thomas Caffry	Labour	elected
William Dinsdale	Labour	elected
Albert Smith	Labour	elected
S. Lowe	Labour	defeated
J. Greenwood	Socialist	defeated

1909

John Rickard	Labour	elected
Richard Winterbottom	Labour	elected

1910

Joseph Husband	Labour	elected
Thomas Lambert	Labour	elected
Fred Constantine	Labour	defeated
Mark Wilson	Labour	defeated
Andrew Smith	Labour	defeated

W. Throup	Socialist	defeated
1911		
Edgar Bootham	Labour	elected
William Dinsdale	Labour	elected
Greenwood	Labour	defeated
1912		
John Rickard	Labour	elected
Richard Winterbottom	Labour	elected
J. Duxbury	Socialist	defeated
1913		
Joseph Husband	Labour	defeated
Andrew Smith	Labour	defeated
McCall	Labour	defeated
1914		
Edgar Bootham	Labour	elected
William Dinsdale	Labour	elected
1915–1918[3]		
No elections held.		

Sources: *Nelson Leader; Borough of Nelson Minutes of Committees.*

[1] After Labour's clean sweep of the five wards into which the municipality was then divided, William Rickard was elected mayor at the Council's first meeting in 1906. See *Borough of Nelson Minutes of Committees, November 1906* (Coulton and Co., Nelson, 1906) p. 3. Rickard, a tea and china dealer, was re-elected mayor in 1907. He was the first Labour Party member to hold the office.

[2] Albert Smith was elected mayor at the first Council meeting in 1909, and re-elected the following year. He stood as Labour's candidate for the Clitheroe constituency in the parliamentary election of December 1910 and withdrew from local government work on his success.

[3] Existing councillors were invited to serve without election. Amongst them was Andrew Smith who became an influential Labour member of the Council after the war. He is first listed in the minutes for 1915 after winning the last pre-war by-election the previous year.

Selected Bibliography

All references to material consulted for this study are given in the end notes to each chapter, but the sources of particular use are listed below.

Primary Sources

The only archive collections concerning individual dissidents are of Selina Cooper in Lancashire Archives, Preston; Ethel Carnie in the Working Class Movement Library, Salford; and Alfred Holdsworth in Keighley public library. However two diaries are available in edited editions, O. Ashmore, 'The Diary of James Garnett of Low Moor, Clitheroe, 1858–65. Part 1, Years of Prosperity 1856–60; Part 2, The American Civil War and the Cotton Famine 1861–65', in *Transactions of the Historic Society of Lancashire and Cheshire*, 121 (1969) pp. 77–98, and 122 (1970) pp. 105–173; and M. Brigg (ed.), *A Lancashire Weaver's Journal 1856–1864, 1872–1875* (Record Society of Lancashire and Cheshire, CXXII, 1982.)

Manuscript extracts from Clitheroe Borough Minutes are held in Clitheroe public library. The printed Minutes of Nelson Town Council are held in Nelson public library. The Minute Book of Sabden Industrial Cooperative Society and those of the Barrowford and Padiham Urban District Councils are in Lancashire Archives, Preston. The Clitheroe LRC and Labour Party Minutes will be deposited in the Working Class Movement Library, Salford.

Documents of varying quality and comprehensiveness relating to elections at all levels are filed in the local studies collection at Clitheroe public library. Both general and municipal elections are covered in depth from the 1880s by the local press, for Clitheroe in *Clitheroe Times*, *Clitheroe Advertiser*, and *Clitheroe Advertiser and Times* after amalgamation in 1920; for Nelson in *Nelson Leader* and *Colne and Nelson Times.* Earlier nineteenth century elections involving the Clitheroe constituency are detailed in Preston newspapers – *Preston Guardian*, *Preston Chronicle* and *Preston Herald* – as well as in *Blackburn Standard.* Microfilm copies are held in the relevant public libraries. These papers also deal with strikes and other cases of industrial and social unrest.

Secondary Sources

For the history of Clitheroe see:

D. Best, *A Short History of Clitheroe in Lancashire* (Carnegie, Preston, 1988.)

S. Clarke, *Clitheroe in its Old Coaching and Railway Days* (Advertiser and Times, Clitheroe, 1929.)

P. Elmer, *The Library of Dr John Webster: the Making of a Seventeenth Century Radical* (Welcome Institute, London, 1986.)

A. Langshaw, *Clitheroe's Thousand Years* (Borough Printing Company, Clitheroe, no date.)

J. McKay, *Pendle Hill in History and Literature* (H. Davies, London, 1888.)

W. Self Weeks, *Clitheroe in the Seventeenth Century* (Advertiser and Times, Clitheroe, 1927.)

W. Self Weeks, *The Surrender of the Charters of the Borough of Clitheroe* (Rawson and Co., Manchester, 1931.)

For the political context of dissent see:

C. Ainsworth, 'Clitheroe: the Parliamentary History of a Rotten Borough' (manuscript, file P12, Clitheroe public library local studies collection.)

H. Forrest, 'Notes on Clitheroe Elections up to c. 1860' (manuscript, file P12, Clitheroe public library local studies collection.)

J. Hill, *Nelson: Politics, Economy, Community* (Keele University Press, Edinburgh, 1997.)

J. Marshall (ed.), *The History of the Lancashire County Council 1889–1974* (Robertson, London, 1977.)

W. Pink and A. Beavan, *The Parliamentary Representation of Lancashire (County and Borough) 1258–1885* (Henry Grey, London, 1888.)

For key families and individuals see:

O. Ashmore, 'Low Moor, Clitheroe: A Nineteenth Century Factory Community,' in *Transactions of the Lancashire and Cheshire Antiquarian Society*, (73–74, 1964–65) pp. 124–152.

N. Garnett, *Low Moor Clitheroe: The History of a Hamlet* (Shireburn, Low Moor, 1930?)

J. Liddington, *The Life and Times of a Respectable Rebel: Selina Cooper 1864–1946* (Virago, London, 1984.)

R. Martin, *The Lancashire Giant. David Shackleton, Labour Leader and Civil Servant* (Liverpool University Press, Liverpool, 2000.)

R. Smalley, *Breaking the Bonds of Capitalism: the political vision of a Lancashire mill girl* (Lancaster University, Lancaster, 2014.)

For key events see:

R. Hall, 'A poor cotton weyver: poverty and the cotton famine in Clitheroe' (Social History, 28, 2, 2003.)

L. Longmate, *The Hungry Mills* (Temple Smith, London, 1972.)

James Thomson of Primrose and Jeremiah Garnett of Roefield, *Narrative of Occurances at Clitheroe on Tuesday 31 July 1832* (J. Burrell, Blackburn, 1832.)

J. Watts, *The Facts of the Cotton Famine* (Simpkin, Marshall, London, 1866.)

For key organisations see:

J. Burrows, *A Concise History of the Early years of the Nelson Independent Labour Party* (collected from the *Nelson Leader.*)

M. Chase, *Chartism. A New History* (MUP, Manchester, 2007.)

M. Crick, *The History of the Social Democratic Federation* (Ryburn, Keele, 1994.)

P. Firth, 'Temperance and politics in north east Lancashire c. 1890 to c. 1910,' in *Transactions of the Lancashire and Cheshire Antiquarian Society* (89, 1993) pp. 74–90.

J. Liddington and J. Norris, *One Hand Tied Behind Us: The Rise of the Women's Suffrage Movement* (Rivers Oram, London, 2000.)

F. Lofthouse, *Keepers of the House. A Workhouse Saga* (Hudson History, Settle, 2001.)

Cyril Pearce Database of Conscientious Objectors, Working Class Movement Library, Salford.

J. Smith and J. Walton, 'Property, Employment and the Co-operative Movement: The Social Structure of Co-operation in Sabden, 1923.' In *Transactions of the Historic Society of Lancashire and Cheshire* (134, 1984.)

J. Walton, 'The Making of a Mass Movement: The Growth of Co-operative Society Membership in Lancashire 1870–1914,' in B. Lancaster and P. Maguire (eds.), *Towards the Co-operative Commonwealth. Essays in the History of Co-operation* (Co-operative College and History Workshop Trust, Manchester, 1996.)

Index